AN INTRODUCTION TO ANTHROPOLOGY

VOLUME ONE

Physical anthropology and archaeology

THE DORSEY SERIES IN ANTHROPOLOGY AND SOCIOLOGY

EDITOR ROBIN M. WILLIAMS, JR. *Cornell University*

AN INTRODUCTION TO ANTHROPOLOGY

VOLUME ONE

Physical anthropology and archaeology

VICTOR BARNOUW
Professor of Anthropology
University of Wisconsin—Milwaukee

1971
THE DORSEY PRESS   Homewood, Illinois   60430
Irwin-Dorsey Limited, Georgetown, Ontario

FIRST PRINTING, March, 1971
SECOND PRINTING, July, 1971
THIRD PRINTING, September, 1971
FOURTH PRINTING, March, 1972

Library of Congress Catalog Card No. 72–146732

Printed in the United States of America

This book is dedicated to my wife
SACHIKO

Preface

This two-volume work was designed as a general introduction to the field of anthropology. Both volumes could be used together in a one-semester introductory course on that subject. Courses in Introduction to Anthropology are also often presented in two semesters, the first usually dealing with physical anthropology and archaeology, the second with ethnology. With this division in mind, Volume One of the present work was prepared to cover the first semester, Volume Two the second. A brief section on linguistics is included in Volume Two. Chapter 1 of Volume Two presents a brief recapitulation of material on physical anthropology and archaeology which may be skipped by those who have read Volume One.

Anthropology today has to do with man at all times and places; it is not limited to the study of early man and "primitive" non-Western cultures, as it was sometimes held to be. This two-volume work ranges from the distant past, before man actually appeared on the scene, down to our troubled present and deals with both the physical and cultural evolution of man.

In general, my approach to this broad field has been eclectic. Where controversies occur I have presented the contending viewpoints, as, for example, in the different interpretations of the relationship between *Australopithecus* and *Paranthropus* in the evolution of the hominids, or in the controversy between substantivists and formalists in economic anthropology.

Let me now acknowledge my gratitude to some people who helped me while I was preparing this work. Elizabeth Thorndike, John C. MacGregor of the University of Illinois, and William M. Bass of the University of Kansas read and commented on the chapters on physical anthropology in Volume One. Creighton Gabel of Boston University read and commented on Chapters 16 through 25 on archaeology and prehistory in Volume One. Three readers read both volumes: Bert Gerow of Stanford University; James Clifton of the University of Wisconsin, Green Bay; and Iwao Ishino of Michigan State University. Thanks are due to them all, for I have benefited from the criticisms of everyone mentioned above. I am also grateful to Robin M. Williams, Jr., an editor of The Dorsey Press, for his comments.

I also owe thanks to Robert E. Ritzenthaler, Curator of Anthropology, and his colleagues in the Department of Anthropology and in the Department of Photography of the Milwaukee Public Museum for their help in my search for illustrations; and to John W. Alley of the Photography Department of the University of Wisconsin—Milwaukee for his photographic work.

Finally, I am especially grateful to my wife Sachiko, to whom this book is dedicated, for all her patience, encouragement, and help while the manuscript was in progress.

February, 1971   Victor Barnouw

Contents

Part ONE

Physical anthropology

I

Historical background

II

Evolution

Part TWO

**Archaeology and
prehistory**

VI
Introduction to archaeology

Selection of a site. Social and cultural inferences. Excavation procedures. Dating techniques: *Dendrochronology. Varve analysis. Radiocarbon dating. Potassium-argon dating. Pollen analysis. Associated fauna. Other methods.*

VII
Early prehistory

Subdivisions of prehistory. Lower Palaeolithic stone technology. The middle Palaeolithic: *Implications of religious beliefs.*

Upper Palaeolithic inventions. Decorative art. Cave paintings. Upper Palaeolithic cultures. The Mesolithic.

Domestication of plants. Domestication of animals. Advantages of village life. Housing. Stonework. Weaving. Pottery. Trade. "World view" of Neolithic farmers. Some early agricultural settlements: *Natufian culture. Jarmo. Jericho. Çatal Hüyük. Khirokitia.*

Westward diffusion of Neolithic traits: *Megalithic cults.* Adaptations to different environments: *Swidden cultivation. Pastoralism.* The Neolithic in southern, eastern, and central Asia: *India. China. The Southeast Asiatic Neolithic. Occupation of the Steppes.*

VIII
Civilization in the Old World

Criteria of civilization. Agricultural productivity: *New farming techniques. Irrigation.* Social control: *Monumental constructions and mass labor. Class stratification: slavery.* Division of labor: *Metallurgy. Pottery. Other specialties. Peasantry. Trade and communication.* Warfare.

IX

Cultural evolution in the New World

Chapter 1

Introduction: the field of anthropology

Anthropology is the study of man (from Greek *anthropos,* man, and *logia,* study). It is mainly concerned with a single species, *Homo sapiens,* rather than with many diverse organisms, as in the case of botany and zoology, although physical anthropologists also study the various primate species related to man. Our objective is to learn all we can about the single organism, man—how he has become what he is, what he has accomplished, and what his potentialities are. One obvious difficulty in such an enterprise is that since we are ourselves human beings, we find it hard to be objective about studying *Homo sapiens.*

Of course, anthropology is not the only field which focuses on man. There are many others, including sociology, psychology, history, law, economics, and political science. We do not need to draw clear-cut boundary lines between these various disciplines. While each field has its own distinctive characteristics and emphases, there are many areas in which they overlap.

Anthropology may be broadly divided into physical anthropology and cultural anthropology. Cultural anthropology may in turn be subdivided into three main branches: linguistics, archaeology, and ethnology.

Physical anthropology

One unique aspect of anthropology which distinguishes it from the other social sciences is that it contains a branch, physical anthropology, which is concerned with man as a physical organism and with man's evolution from simpler forms of life.

Whatever else he may be, man is an animal (not a mineral or a plant); he is a vertebrate, a mammal, and a Primate, the order of mammals which also includes, among others, the apes and monkeys. The animals with which man is most closely related are the chimpanzee and the gorilla, but he also has much in common with the gibbon and orangutan and, more distantly, with the Old World monkeys and other primates. Physical anthropologists are concerned with tracing man's relationships to these related species and with reconstructing the evolutionary branching and differentiation of the Primate order, particularly with respect to man and his closest relatives.

Physical anthropologists have pursued at least four kinds of research: (1) the analysis of primate fossils, with an attempt to place them in a geological, temporal sequence; (2) comparative anatomical study of living primates, including such features as blood chemistry, tooth cusp patterns, and many other features; (3) observation of living primates in the field, with an emphasis on their patterns of social interaction; and (4) laboratory experimentation with apes and monkeys.

In 1961 a chimpanzee named Ham was rocketed into suborbital flight, before any human beings were sent aloft in space capsules. Ham was chosen for this important experiment because chimpanzees resemble human beings in so many ways. Chimpanzees have similar blood types and suffer from some of the same diseases that afflict humans, with similar symptoms. New types of surgical techniques are sometimes tried out on chimpanzees and other nonhuman primates before being attempted on humans. The close resemblances between ourselves and the chimpanzee are not a matter of chance; they reflect relationship, a common ancestry. One focus of physical anthropology, then, is human evolution.

A second focus of physical anthropology is human variation. All human beings on earth today belong to a single species, *Homo sapiens* and, therefore, are capable of breeding with members of other human groups and of producing fertile offspring. Within this single species, however, there is a good deal of variation. Some human populations are more dark skinned or light skinned than others. There are many varieties of hair form, some groups having straight hair, some curly, some wavy, while others have mixed forms. There are differences in nose height, nose breadth, hair color, eye color, and many other features.

On the basis of traits such as these, anthropologists in the past have tried to sort human beings into different races, such as Negroids, Caucasoids, Mongoloids, and others. Some physical anthropologists have recently argued that such classifications are unreal and lack scientific validity. (The pros and cons of this issue are discussed in Chapters 11 and 12). But no one denies the existence of human variations. Anthropologists are trying to determine how variations in pigmentation, hair form, and other features have come about in different populations.

Physical anthropologists not only study the distribution of such observable traits as hair form and skin color but they are also interested in the distribution of blood types such as A, B, AB, O, Rh, M, N, and other biochemical factors. They also study the incidence of ailments determined by heredity, such as sickle-cell anemia and hemophilia, and the relative susceptibility or immunity of different human populations to certain diseases. They have made studies of patterns of human growth and nutrition, climatic adaptation, and body composition.

Some physical anthropologists engage in a form of applied anthropology. By making bodily measurements (anthropometry) of large samples of a population—for example, Air Force pilots—and also through studies of muscular strength and bodily structure (biomechanics), they have often contributed to the planning of design and arrangement of machines which must be worked by human beings—for example, in the arrangement of seats and equipment used in the cockpits of airplanes.

The field of physical anthropology has expanded greatly in the past 20 years. Physical anthropologists were formerly concerned mainly with body measurements and the classification of human types. Their training is now more diversified and exhaustive, with an emphasis on genetics, blood chemistry, and the acquisition of specialized laboratory techniques. These emphases seem to have brought physical anthropology closer to the other biological sciences than to the cultural branches of anthropology. At the same time, the growing specialization of physical anthropology has made it difficult for cultural anthropologists to keep abreast of new developments in physical anthropology. Despite this specialization, physical and cultural anthropologists generally share a desire to see man as a whole—as a product of both physical and cultural evolution; for ever since man first used tools, his physical evolution has been influenced by his culture, and the cultures of man have always been affected by the nature of his physical structure.

The other main branches of anthropology—linguistics, archaeology, and ethnology—are all concerned with aspects of human culture and may therefore be bracketed under the general heading of cultural anthropology, as distinguished from physical or biological anthropology. **Culture**

Culture is an important key word in the vocabulary of the social sciences. It refers to man's learned behavior, acquired by experience, as opposed to inborn, genetically determined behavior. This usage of the term must be distinguished from older colloquial meanings expressed in phrases like "a man of culture." In the anthropological sense, all men have culture.

Although anthropologists sometimes use the word *culture* in a broad generic sense, they also speak about *a culture*, like Eskimo culture or Hopi culture. Here is a definition of culture in this sense: *A culture is the way of life of a group of people, the configuration of all of the more or less stereotyped patterns of learned behavior which are handed down from one generation to the next through the means of language and imitation.*

The nub of this definition is "the way of life of a group of people." This way of life has some integration and cohesion to it—hence the term *configuration.* It consists of patterns of learned behavior which are transmitted through language and imitation—not through instinct or any direct action of the genes, although the *capacity* for culture is determined by heredity. These patterns are only relatively fixed and are amenable to change; hence they are said to be "more or less stereotyped."

Examples of patterns of learned behavior are: speaking English, Chinese, Bantu, or Hindi; wearing trousers in our society, kilts in Scotland, togas in ancient Rome; sitting on chairs in the Western world or sitting cross-legged on the ground in many societies; eating at set mealtimes—breakfast, lunch, and dinner, or twice a day in some societies, or four times, as when the English add afternoon tea; using knife, fork, and spoon to eat with in the Western world, chopsticks in China and Japan, or the fingers of the right hand in India; believing in the tenets of Jesus Christ, Confucius, Mohammed, or Buddha; consulting the medicine man, the priest, the doctor, or the psychiatrist; making a Navaho sand painting, a Kwakiutl totem pole, or an abstract painting. A person is destined to learn the patterns of behavior prevalent in the society in which he grows up. He does not necessarily learn them all, for there may be cultural differences appropriate to persons of different age, sex, status, and occupation, and there may also be genetically determined differences in learning ability. Moreover, the culture patterns of his society may change with the appearance of new inventions or through contact with other ways of life.

Some knowledge of the diversity of human cultures is a useful antidote to provincialism. Generalizations about human nature should always be checked to see if they are applicable to societies other than our own, for we are often led to assume that some characteristic of our own way of life is true of all mankind.

Linguistics

Linguistics is the study of languages. Although other animals besides man have communication systems, and although the cries of apes and monkeys seem to have communicative functions, no other organism is known to have as elaborate a system of symbolic communication as man. The transmission of culture from generation to generation is made possible by language, which enables man to preserve the traditions of the past and to make provisions for the future.

Not all linguists are anthropologists, but some anthropologists specialize in the study of languages. Ethnologists often learn the language of the people whom they are studying in the field. It is possible to do ethnological fieldwork with bilingual interpreters, but it is much better if the anthropologist understands the local speech. All kinds of subtleties may be lost in translation, for example, in a discussion of religious concepts.

Descriptive or *structural linguistics* deal with the characteristic sound units employed in a language, its phonemic system, and its grammatical system.

A *phoneme* is a minimal sound unit which serves to distinguish one word or syllable from another for the speakers of a particular language. English *p* and *b* are separate phonemes; *pig* and *big* have different meanings. But we cannot assume that *p* and *b* will be separate phonemes in another language, for different languages may make use of different significant sounds. One task of a linguist in learning and analyzing an unfamiliar language is to find out what phonemes it contains. In recording such a language, linguists make use of systems of phonetic transcription such as the alphabet adopted by the International Phonetic Association. This is more accurate than our traditional alphabet and the inconsistent spellings associated with it, for we often spell differently words which sound alike and spell alike words which sound differently. So linguists have devised new symbols or letters which distinguish between such sounds as, for example, the *th* in *then* from the *th* in *thin*.

In addition to phonetics, linguists analyze the grammatical system of a language. Here the basic unit is the *morpheme,* which may be a single syllable or phoneme or may consist of several syllables. *Dogs,* for example, consists of two morphemes, *dog* and *s,* the latter indicating plurality. Linguists also learn the ways in which morphemes are arranged and sentences constructed in the language under consideration, the study of syntax.

Historical linguistics deals with changes in language over time, including sound shifts and the influence of one language on another. Sometimes efforts have been made to reconstruct culture patterns of past times from a study of items of vocabulary, as has been done in the case of the Indo-European languages of the Old World.

The comparative study of languages has shown that they have many different ways of classifying the phenomena of nature. Some linguists are particularly interested in folk taxonomies, the ways in which plants, animals, colors, and other aspects of the environment are classified in particular languages. Some anthropologists have tried to assess the ways in which the language of a particular society structures the perceptions or world view of its speakers.

Linguistics, then, has a bearing on many other fields of research, not only on ethnology but also on fields outside of anthropology, such as psychology and philosophy.

Archaeology

Archaeology is the study of extinct cultures, as distinguished from ethnology, which is the study of living ones. Archaeologists are usually, although not always, concerned with what are called prehistoric cultures, those which existed before the development of written records. Archaeologists willingly make use of written records if they are available, as in Mesopotamia, Egypt, and Guatemala, but often they have nothing to work with but such relics and remains of bygone peoples as potsherds, arrowheads, clay figurines, and tools of bone, stone, or other durable material. History begins with the appearance of written records; prehistory is the domain of the archaeologist. Both the historian and the archaeologist want to uncover the story of man's development through time. The historian is concerned with only a brief segment of man's existence on earth, for writing originated only about 5,000 years ago, while potassium-argon dates have shown that man's ancestors used stone tools about 2 million years ago. Prehistory therefore comprises an immense stretch of time. We depend upon the archaeologist, working with the palaeontologist, geologist, physical anthropologist, and other specialists, to reconstruct what happened during these hundreds of thousands of years. In many parts of the world—Australia, Melanesia, Polynesia, most of the New World and Africa—writing was not known until its relatively recent introduction by Europeans. Here again the archaeologist works to uncover the past.

Because much of man's life is intangible and perishable, leaving no permanent imprint behind, the reconstruction of prehistory will never be complete. There are many gaps in the archaeological record. There were many hunting-gathering peoples who left few durable artifacts behind them. Time, weather, and destruction by human beings and other animals, have wiped out much of the evidence. Even so, archaeologists have been able to learn a great deal about the distribution and ways of life of the hunters of the Old Stone Age. They have also learned where agricultural settlements first appeared in the Old World and the New, where metal tools were first employed, and where writing and city life first developed. Through a combination of archaeology and ethnology, we can determine much about the evolution and spread of man's cultures.

Ethnology

Ethnology is the study of contemporary cultures. An ethnologist goes to a particular society, let us say an Eskimo group; he gets to know the people, learns something of their language, and keeps a record of his observations and interviews. Ethnologists have varied interests and objectives, but all of them try to delineate some of the characteristic culture patterns of the group they study. An ethnologist may, for example, be particularly interested in how kinship is reckoned in an Eskimo community, what religious beliefs the people have, or how the religion is related to other aspects of the culture. He may study techniques of food getting, seal hunting, and the material equipment used in the process: methods of making dogsleds, harpoons, warm clothing. He may be interested in how children are brought up and what personality traits are fostered in the society under study, how people get along with one another, how men acquire their wives, and how many they may have.

An ethnologist usually studies a particular society, or at least one at a time. But it should be pointed out that ethnological works are not limited to descriptions of particular cultures or to comparisons of two or three of them. Efforts are also made to generalize on a broad scale about cultures in general, for example, about societies with a hunting-gathering basis of subsistence, peasant societies, matrilineal societies, and so on.

Some of the first American anthropologists, under the influence of Franz Boas, tried to get as complete an inventory of the culture they were studying as possible, including material culture (tools and equipment used), kinship organization, religious beliefs, marriage customs, subsistence techniques, folklore, games, food recipes, and so forth. More recently there has been a tendency to focus on particular problems and to narrow the scope of investigation. We now have some specialized subfields within the general branch of ethnology, such as social anthropology and culture-and-personality.

Social anthropology

Social anthropology is concerned with the social structure of a society, its patterns of social interaction. This field is really no different from sociology, except perhaps that social anthropologists generally study non-Western societies.

Social anthropology is not the same thing as cultural anthropology. It may be seen as a branch of cultural anthropology, which covers a larger field. For his purposes, the social anthropologist ignores many aspects of culture, such as material culture, how traps and snares are made, food recipes, and so on.

Social anthropologists have a particular interest in kinship systems. In every society there is some system of reckoning kin and classifying relatives, but these vary remarkably in different societies. Some trace descent in the male, some in the female line. Some require the marriage of particular cousins, such as the requirement, found in many societies, that a man marry his mother's brother's daughter or his father's sister's daughter. Some societies have clan or caste groupings which have various rules as to who may marry whom.

The structure of the family varies in different societies; there are large extended families and small nuclear ones, polygynous families with plural wives and polyandrous ones with plural husbands. The social anthropologist studies the kinship network and its ramifications. He also analyzes the power structure characteristic of the society and whatever class stratification there may be.

Culture-and-personality

Culture-and-personality is a field which overlaps with psychology, particularly the psychology of personality. Personality may be defined as *a more or less enduring organization of forces within the individual as-*

sociated with a complex of fairly consistent attitudes, values, and modes of perception which account, in part, for the individual's consistency of behavior. Like the definition of culture, this definition is admittedly rather vague. But personality, like culture, seems to be something real, even though it may escape precise definition. We know that our friends differ from one another in certain consistent ways. Some persons are more extroverted or aggressive than others; some have tendencies to depression, hypochondria, or anxiety and others are self-confident and full of the joy of living. The field of culture-and-personality is concerned with the mutual interplay of culture and personality, but especially with the ways in which the culture of a society influences the individuals who grow up within its milieu.

The definition of personality given above refers to attitudes, values, and modes of perception as aspects of personality. Surely, many, if not all, attitudes, values, and modes of perception are culturally derived. The Cheyenne and other tribes of the western plains in the early 19th century exalted military bravery; the ideal type of adult male was a successful fighter and hunter. A contrasting ego ideal may be found in the Buddhist monk or Hindu ascetic. Persons growing up in a particular society are influenced by the ideal types held up for imitation and often model their conduct accordingly, although they may also rebel against the pressures which drive them to approximate the ideal. Ideal types differ in different societies and subgroups: tough fighters, crafty merchants, selfless saints, sophisticated men-about-town, and so forth. An individual is thus influenced by the available models for imitation current in his society.

The Eskimo have usually impressed travelers as being rather sociable and extroverted, while northern Algonkian Indians such as the Chippewa have often been described as more introverted, more cautious and reserved in interpersonal relations. Here a number of questions may be raised. Are these impressions based on accurate observations? Are they just stereotypes, or is there some basis for them? And if the groups do differ in the manner described, what factors can be responsible for the differences? How could we determine which factors are the crucial ones?

Groups such as the Eskimo and Chippewa could differ from one another because of contrasting cultural traditions, differing world views, or differences in methods of child rearing and typical childhood experiences. Some combination of all these factors might be involved. Workers in the field of culture-and-personality study various aspects of culture such as implicit world view, child-training patterns, and child-adult relationships. Such ethnologists often give psychological tests in the course of fieldwork, usually projective tests like the Rorschach (ink blot) and modified Thematic Apperception Tests. For example, in the case of the Eskimo and the Chippewa, Rorschach tests do seem to support the generalizations that the Eskimos are more extroverted and the Chippewa more introverted and guarded in interpersonal relations.

The cross-cultural study of religion

Many volumes have been written about the religions of non-Western peoples, and many colleges and universities offer courses titled "Primitive Religion." The title is misleading insofar as it gives the impression that the religions of hunting-gathering peoples are essentially alike. They are only partially alike. Beliefs in a soul, an afterlife, and magico-religious practices are found in all such societies. There is usually a shaman, or medicine man, who appears to cure the sick and who claims to communicate with spirits. But there are also great differences among primitive religions. Among the Australian aborigines, such as the Arunta, an important religious focus is on the transition of youths from childhood to adult status. Long and elaborate ceremonies concern this rite of passage. Male puberty rites are also found among the Yahgan and Ona of Tierra del Fuego and in many other societies, but they are missing in others, as among the Chippewa and most Eskimo groups.

The concept of possession, the invasion of a person's body by a disincarnate spirit who temporarily dislodges the soul normally connected with it, is an important notion in many parts of the Old World. Possession may be involuntary and struggled against by the "victim"; and ceremonies may be performed to exorcize the invading spirit. On the other hand, possession may be voluntary and sought after, as in the case of some modern spiritualist mediums or Chukchee shamans in Siberia. While phenomena associated with possession are important in the religions of many primitive peoples, they are absent in others. The concept of possession plays a very small role in the aboriginal religions of most North American Indians.

These examples illustrate the point that the religions of "primitive" peoples are varied in content. Anthropologists study religion in relation to social structure or to culture and personality, depending upon the focus of interest. They try to understand the functions of religious systems in different societies, what they do for the individuals involved or for the maintenance of the group.

Folklore, ethnomusicology, and the study of art

Folklore, ethnomusicology, and the study of art are other specialized fields of study within ethnology. Folklorists record the legends, myths, jokes, riddles, and yarns told in the societies they investigate. They are interested in knowing if the oral literature is unique to the area they study or related to other bodies of folklore. Folktales often have a very wide distribution. Some stories told in some American Indian tribes closely resemble Old World legends. The student of music or art may also find local styles of expression characteristic of a particular region or discover musical themes, design forms, or stylistic motifs which are common over a wide area. Such distributions tell us something about past culture contacts and pathways of cultural diffusion. The student of culture-and-personality is interested in seeing if the folklore or art of the society he is studying is characterized by any particular themes, mood, or world view, and what sort of gods, heroes, or ideal types appear in the oral literature.

Cultural evolution

Some anthropologists are more interested in reconstructing a picture of man's general cultural evolution than in dealing with the details of particular cultures. From information about hunting-gathering societies studied in recent times, composite pictures have been drawn of the probable composition and structure of early human groups. Ethnological data about more advanced agricultural societies provide evidence for later stages in cultural evolution. Such reconstructions are risky and have often been criticized, but the attempt seems worth making.

There are cases where parallel cultural developments have taken place in geographically separated and historically unrelated cultures. For example, there are many aspects of culture in the advanced civilizations of Peru and Mexico which have close parallels in the Bronze Age cultures of Egypt and Mesopotamia. This applies not only to aspects of material culture, such as the development of weaving, pottery, and metallurgy, but also to some aspects of social organization, religion, and art. Some of the similarities between advanced Old and New World civilizations may have been due to pre-Columbian trans-Pacific diffusion, but it seems likely that the civilizations of the New World developed mainly without such influence. The occurrence of parallel cultural evolution leads to hypotheses about the dynamic causative factors responsible for such similar developments in different societies.

Applied anthropology

One final subdivision of ethnology may be singled out: applied anthropology. Anthropologists have worked in community development projects in different countries, where a knowledge of local culture patterns may help the authorities to understand why there is resistance to certain programs. Why are members of a highland Peruvian community reluctant to boil their drinking water, despite lectures and explanations to the effect that boiling the water greatly decreases the incidence of dysentery? The value of compost pits is explained to the members of a small town in India; some pits are dug, but they are not maintained. A small, low-priced clinic is established in a Mexican town, but nobody patronizes it. Anthropologists have investigated problems of this sort and tried to suggest ways of surmounting the difficulties involved. The United States Bureau of Indian Affairs has employed anthropologists to work with Indian groups. Applied anthropologists have also studied labor-management problems in industry and worked in various other sensitive areas where analyses of social and cultural factors may help to clarify the issues.

Some anthropologists state that anthropology is a science, while others **Is** make no such claim. It would be hard to make a blanket statement about **anthropology** the field as a whole, since it has so many subdivisions, each with its own **a science?** special objectives and methods. What are the requirements of a science? A science is an organized body of empirically derived information and theory which shows the operation of general principles or laws. We tend to associate science with controlled experiments designed to test hypotheses, but not all sciences rely on such procedures. Astronomy, for example, depends upon observation; we cannot make experiments with the stars. Geology also relies heavily upon naturalistic observation. This is true of ethnology as well. Ethnologists sometimes do engage in controlled experiments, but observation and interviews are their main sources of information. In contrast, psychology has much greater resort to controlled experiment.

In physical anthropology and archaeology, much work depends upon chance finds—a fossil skull or cave site, for example. There is no question of performing controlled experiments here. What is required is a careful examination of the find *in situ* and dating of the find by various means, such as associated fauna, stratigraphy, and radioactive carbon. The specimen must be related to others of the same or similar type and placed in a temporal sequence, if possible. Whether we call this "science" or not, the work of the archaeologist leads to an increase in knowledge.

A good ethnological account always contains generalizations based upon a large number of observations. Consider, for example, the kinship structure of a society. It may take a good deal of interviewing, questioning, and behavioral observation before an ethnologist learns to understand the kinship system of the society he is studying. Once it is formulated in his mind, however, he can describe it so that others who read his work will understand it too. In other words, he has discovered some general principles which work for that particular society, if not for mankind as a whole, and which help to account for some of the behavior of individuals in that society. A person who has read an account of Hopi kinship organization can expect to find certain types of behavior in evidence if he visits a Hopi community. He will, in fact, encounter such behavior if he stays there long enough. It is as if the Hopi were living out their lives in accordance with the anthropologist's descriptions of them. Of course, cultures change over time. The Hopi in 1972 may not be living as they were described in 1927; the ethnological description may need to be revised. Still, there will not be a complete change, for the present has been influenced by the past.

We can understand and to some extent predict much of the behavior of human beings in different cultural contexts of the present day if we have the relevant ethnological data. Without the work of ethnologists, much of the traditional behavior of peoples in Africa, India, and other parts of the world would be quite incomprehensible to Europeans and Americans. However, an understanding of non-Western cultures is not the only contribution of ethnology. By learning more about other ways of life, we gain more perspective on our own. Any aspect of human behavior is better understood when seen in cross-cultural perspective.

Whether or not it be decided that archaeology and ethnology are sciences, there is no doubt that archaeologists and ethnologists have added greatly to our understanding of man's past and current behavior in different parts of the world. The significance of anthropology's contribution may be gauged by trying to imagine what the state of our knowledge would be like without it. Without the work of physical anthropologists and archaeologists, we would have little understanding of man's place in nature and of the long process of human evolution. This will be made clear by a consideration of the historical background of physical anthropology, to which the next chapter is devoted.

Suggestions for further reading

Since this volume deals with physical anthropology and archaeology, no books on these topics need be recommended at this point; many suggested titles are given at the ends of the chapters that follow.

Since linguistics and ethnology are not dealt with in this volume, the following books are recommended for those who may wish to investigate these subjects further. Broad, general works are emphasized in this list.

The field of linguistics is presented in Charles F. Hockett, *A Course in Modern Linguistics* (New York: The Macmillan Company, 1958). Three good collections of readings are available: Dell Hymes (ed.), *Language in Culture and Society: A Reader in Linguistics and Anthropology* (New York: Harper and Row, 1964); Eric H. Lenneberg (ed.), *New Directions in the Study of Language* (Cambridge: The M.I.T. Press, 1966); Stephen A. Tyler (ed.), *Cognitive Anthropology* (New York: Holt, Rinehart and Winston, Inc., 1969).

The best history of ethnological theory is Marvin Harris, *The Rise of Anthropological Theory: A History of Theories of Culture* (New York: Thomas Y. Crowell Co., 1968). A recent general text on cultural anthropology is Philip K. Bock, *Modern Cultural Anthropology: An Introduction* (New York: Alfred A. Knopf, 1969). For economic aspects see Edward E. LeClair, Jr. and Harold K. Schneider (eds.), *Economic Anthropology: Readings in Theory and Analysis* (New York: Holt, Rinehart and Winston, 1968).

On the field of kinship: Robin Fox, *Kinship and Marriage: An Anthropological Perspective* (Baltimore: Penguin Books, 1967). On legal institutions: E. Adamson Hoebel, *The Law of Primitive Man: A Study in Comparative Legal Dynamics* (Cambridge: Harvard University Press, 1954). A good reader on the cross-cultural study of religion is William A. Lessa and Evon Z. Vogt (eds.), *Reader in Comparative Religion: An Anthropological Approach* (2d. ed., New York: Harper and Row, 1958). For an introduction to the field of culture-and-personality see Victor Barnouw, *Culture and Personality* (Homewood, Illinois: The Dorsey Press, 1963).

On cultural evolution see Leslie A. White, *The Evolution of Culture* (New York: McGraw-Hill Book Company, 1959) and Julian H. Steward, *Theory of Culture Change: The Methodology of Multilinear Evolution* (Urbana, Illinois: University of Illinois Press, 1955). On applied anthropology see George M. Foster, *Applied Anthropology* (Boston: Little, Brown and Company, 1969).

Physical anthropology

Part **ONE**

Historical background I

Chapter 2

The historical background of
physical anthropology

Two principal topics in the following chapters on physical anthropology are human evolution and human variation. The first concerns the stages of development in the evolutionary course that led to modern man and the problem of how these changes were brought about; the second concerns differences in physical type in modern man, including groups which have been referred to as "races." This chapter will deal with ideas which were held about these subjects in the days before the development of physical anthropology. This will help us to see what has been accomplished since then and to understand how some of our views about man have undergone changes in the past hundred years.

The concept of evolution   The idea of evolution occurred to some of the ancient Greeks and Romans. Archelaus of Miletus in the sixth century B.C. suggested that man had evolved from a fish which came ashore and developed on land. The Roman philosopher Lucretius (99–55 B.C.) in his long poem *De Rerum Natura* ("On the Nature of Things") set forth a scheme of both biological evolution and the cultural evolution of human institutions. Life, he argued, developed from a chance arrangement of atoms. Man was once a brutish, naked creature who lived in caves and did not even know the use of fire.

Speculations of this sort were discouraged in the Christian era, particularly after the junction of church and state under Constantine, when heresy became linked with sedition. The orthodox view, as set forth by St. Augustine (A.D. 354–430), was that all human beings were descended from Adam and Eve, who had been created by God about 6,000 years before. This was a monogenetic (single-origin) conception of man's creation as opposed to a polygenetic (multiple-origin) view. Belief in the story of creation told in the book of Genesis was hardly challenged until the 18th century.[1]

When the lands of the New World and their Indian inhabitants were discovered, the question was raised: Were the American Indians human beings? Were they descended from Adam and Eve? This was an important question, for it involved a decision as to whether or not the Indians had souls; if not, they could be slaughtered at will, as some of the conquistadores proceeded to do in Mexico and Peru. In 1512 the papacy announced that the American Indians were, after all, descended from Adam and Eve. This raised the question: Then how did they get there? Many solutions were suggested, including the notion that the American Indians were descended from the ten lost tribes of Israel.

Sir Paul Rycaut, who translated Garcilaso de la Vega's 17th–century account of the Inca civilization, suggested that the ancestors of the American Indians must have migrated over a land bridge connecting Siberia with the northwestern American mainland, a view still held today by most anthropologists.

Europeans at the beginning of the Middle Ages believed that the creation of the world and of man had taken place only a few thousand years in the past. The timing was made more specific by Archbishop Ussher (1581–1656) whose dating of biblical events was widely accepted. By calculating the ages of the generations after Adam recorded in the Bible, Ussher arrived at a date of 4004 B.C. This was made still more specific by Dr. Lightfoot, vice-chancellor of the University of Cambridge, who stated that man had been created by the Trinity at 9. A.M. on October 23rd, 4004 B.C.

Such a chronology could be passively accepted by Europeans, even in

---

[1] Apparently the Islamic religion was more tolerant of evolutionary speculation in medieval times. At any rate, the following passage by the North African Muslim scholar Ibn Khaldun (1332–1406) gives that impression: "[the world of creation] started out from the minerals and progressed, in an ingenious, gradual manner, to plants and animals. The last stage of minerals is connected with the first stage of plants, such as herbs and seedless plants. The last stage of plants, such as palms and vines, is connected with the first stage of animals, such as snails and shellfish which have only the power of touch. The word 'connection' with regard to these created things means that the last stage of each group is fully prepared to become the first stage of the next group.

"The animal world then widens, its species become numerous, and, in a gradual process of creation, it finally leads to man, who is able to think and reflect. The higher stage of man is reached from the world of monkeys, in which both sagacity and perception are found, but which has not reached the stage of actual reflection and thinking. At this point we come to the first stage of man" (Ibn Khaldun, *The Muqaddimah: An Introduction to History*. Bollingen Series XLIII (copyright © 1967 by Bollingen Foundation), Princeton University Press, 1967, translated from the Arabic by Franz Rosenthal and abridged and edited by N. J. Dawood, p. 75).

the 17th century, because they had little knowledge of geology. They knew that fossils existed, and some scholars, notably Robert Hooke and Nicolaus Steno, thought that these were the remains of former plants and animals. But this view was not universally accepted, and neither of these men believed that the earth was more than about 6,000 years old. It was then the fashion to account for geological anomalies in terms of the biblical flood. More was learned about geology and paleontology in the 18th century, as we shall see.

Meanwhile, with the increasing exploration of the globe, new species of plants and animals were encountered, which led to an interest in the classification and comparison of organisms.

In 1699 a British anatomist, Edward Tyson, wrote a book in which he compared the anatomy of a "pygmy" with that of a monkey, an ape, and a man and concluded that the "pygmy" was intermediate in form between ape and man. It has since been discovered that what Tyson called a pygmy was in fact a young chimpanzee. His work was important, nevertheless, as an early comparative anatomical study of different primates.

The classification of Primates, grouping man with the apes, was first made by the Swedish botanist Linnaeus (Karl von Linné) (1707–78) in the 10th edition of his system of classification, *Systema naturae,* or *System of Nature.* It was Linnaeus, the father of taxonomy, who designed the binomial system whereby each plant and animal is assigned a genus name and a species name. By grouping man with the apes, Linnaeus showed his awareness of the close physical similarity between them, but this did not lead him to speculate about their common ancestry or evolution. The very process of labeling species may have tended to freeze them into separate compartments, so to speak, so that the species currently known were assumed to have been the same as those brought into being by the Creator at the beginning of time.

The French naturalist Buffon (1707–88) did have ideas about evolution and envisioned a larger span of geological time than that generally held, but he was forced by the Sorbonne in 1751 to publicly recant some of his speculations and to declare that he did not mean to contradict the text of the Bible, in which he most firmly believed.

James Hutton (1726–97), a Scottish geologist, argued that the earth was much older than a few thousand years. He believed that the earth had been shaped by certain regular agencies; strata were formed by gradual deposition in the oceans and were affected by subterranean heat and pressures, while the surface of the earth was continually being eroded by wind, water, and organic decay. The idea that the earth had been shaped and was still being shaped by natural forces operating over long periods of time with considerable uniformity came to be known as *uniformitarianism,* a doctrine which later received its classic expression in Sir Charles Lyell's *Principles of Geology* (1834), a work which had a great influence on Charles Darwin.

In the early 19th century, the viewpoint of uniformitarianism was opposed by a rival doctrine known as *catastrophism,* which held that the earth had periodically undergone violent cataclysms or upheavals such as floods and volcanic eruptions. These disasters, which were sometimes held to have been worldwide or nearly so, were believed to have extinguished previous organic forms, so that new ones came to replace them. Catastrophism represented a compromise between the growing knowledge of geology and paleontology, which was lengthening the age of the earth, and the conservative biblical point of view. The outstanding exponent of catastrophism was the great French zoologist, founder of comparative anatomy and vertebrate paleontology, Georges Cuvier (1769–1832). Cuvier rejected theories of continuous evolution and believed that the last great cataclysm was the biblical deluge; hence human remains would not be apt to be found in the prediluvian strata of the earth. Despite his conservatism, Cuvier greatly advanced knowledge of the past; it was he who reconstructed and named the Pterodactyls, flying reptiles of the Mesozoic.

During the 18th century, many fossil remains of strange extinct animals were found in Europe. In some cases, they seemed to be associated with human remains. In 1715 the skeleton of an elephantlike creature was reported to have been recovered from gravel deposits near London, and next to it was a worked flint tool. In 1771 human bones were found in association with extinct cave bear remains in a site in Germany. In 1797 John Frere found hand axes along with the remains of extinct animals at Hoxne, England.

A Frenchman, Boucher de Perthes (1788–1868) found hand axes in such deep geological strata that he declared them to be tools made by "antediluvian man," or man before the flood. This claim met with much skepticism but led others to search in similar deposits, where similar finds were sometimes made.

Gradually, more was being learned about geology and paleontology. William Smith (1769–1839) announced that geological strata could be identified by the fossils they contained and that lower strata were generally older than those above them. This "law of superposition" is a principle which we take for granted nowadays, but someone had to discover and state it first. Knowledge of geology advanced in England as the Industrial Revolution led to the cutting of canals, construction of railways, and the digging of coal and iron mines. Smith was an engineer involved in such processes. Both England and France had much geological diversity, and the new sciences of geology and paleontology made progress in both areas during the first half of the 19th century.

With the growing awareness of the age of the earth and living things, it is not surprising that evolutionary theories were being proposed, despite theological disapproval. Among others, Erasmus Darwin (1731–1802), grandfather of Charles Darwin (1809–82), and the French naturalist

Chart showing
appearance of
different forms of
life on earth at
different periods.

ERA	SYSTEM AND PERIOD	SERIES AND EPOCH	YEARS BEFORE PRESENT
CENOZOIC	Quaternary	Recent	11 thousand
		Pleistocene	.5 to 3 million
	Tertiary	Pliocene	13 ± 1 million
		Miocene	25 ± 1 million
		Oligocene	36 ± 2 million
		Eocene	58 ± 2 million
		Paleocene	63 ± 2 million
MESOZOIC	Cretaceous		
	Jurassic		135 ± 5 million
	Triassic		180 ± 5 million
PALEOZOIC	Permian		230 ± 10 million
	Carbon-iferous	Pennsylvanian	280 ± 10 million
		Mississippian	310 ± 10 million
	Devonian		345 ± 10 million
	Silurian		405 ± 10 million
	Ordovician		425 ± 10 million
	Cambrian		500 ± 10 million
			600 ± 50 million
	Precambrian		

Lamarck (1744–1829) were forerunners who boldly presented evolutionary concepts. But it was not until the publication of Charles Darwin's *On the Origin of Species by Means of Natural Selection* (1859) that a turning point was reached; for Darwin not only presented a very careful and detailed argument that evolution had in fact occurred but he also presented a concept, that of natural selection, to help account for evolutionary change. His arguments will be presented in the following chapter, along with some of the theories of Lamarck.

Origin of Species was about evolution in general, not just human evolution, a topic to which Darwin turned in a later work, *The Descent of Man* (1871). Darwin's arguments about human evolution did not rest on fossil forms of early man, which were then beginning to be found in Europe, but on comparative anatomical data.

When a primitive-looking human skull was found at Gibraltar in 1848, no one knew what it was. The skull was sent to England, where it was briefly discussed at some meetings in 1864. In 1856 a strange-looking skull cap was found in the Neander valley in Germany, which gave the name Neandertal (see footnote 1, Chapter 10) to a form of early man. It was not until several such finds had been made that it was realized that these were not aberrant pathological skulls but remains of a former widespread population. These and later discovered finds of early man will be discussed in Chapters 8 to 10.

The fossil evidence for the evolution of living things has increased greatly since Darwin's time. It has been further clarified by the development of dating techniques which show that some forms of life appeared on our planet earlier than others; moreover, these techniques make it possible to indicate approximately when the various forms appeared. Traces of one-celled creatures, such as algae or bacteria found in South Africa, have been estimated to be at least 3.2 billion years old and may be 3.5 billion years old. The crust of the earth is judged to have been formed about 4.5 billion years ago, so the appearance of living forms came with relative suddenness. We also know that invertebrates preceded vertebrate forms by more than 240 million years. Vertebrates first appeared about 480 million years ago. The evolution of the vertebrates through different stages, from fish through amphibian to reptilian and then mammalian forms will be briefly traced in Chapter 4.

During their period of expansion and exploration, Europeans encountered human beings of different physical types. Europeans seem, from the beginning, to have believed in their superiority over these other human beings. Superior armament enabled the Europeans to dominate these peoples. The Europeans' feelings of superiority were further enhanced by their conviction that Christianity was the only true religion, while these other people were regarded as heathens. In the Americas, Euro-

Early notions about race

peans generally encountered Indians with cultures less advanced than their own, but even when they entered regions of high civilization, they could generally find other reasons for looking down on the natives. The buildings of Tenochtitlán awed the Spaniards, but they were disgusted by the large-scale Aztec practice of human sacrifice. Believing their white skin to be essentially better than dark skin, Europeans particularly looked down on Negroes. According to Winthrop D. Jordan, the shock effect of encountering black-skinned peoples was especially marked among the English, whose contact with Africans was sudden, in contrast to the Spaniards and Portuguese who had been in contact with North Africa for centuries. British attitudes of prejudice toward Negroes antedated the development of the English slave trade; perhaps, without such prejudice, the slave trade would never have been allowed to expand. Jordan traces this prejudice partly to deep-seated associations of blackness with dirt, evil, and death, while white was associated with purity, virginity, and virtue. In addition, Africans were non-Christians. It happened that Africa was also the home of apes, the chimpanzees, and Europeans professed to see similarities between Negroes and apes in their blackness and alleged lustfulness.[2]

Confronted with varieties of human physical type, scholars tried to draw up classifications of types. Linnaeus, who first classed man as a primate, made some subdivisions, of which four were based on geographical areas—American, European, African, and Asiatic—while others were more fanciful, such as an alleged *Homo monstrosus,* and *Homo ferus* or wild man, suggested by speechless wild children who had sometimes been found wandering in the woods of Europe. A later taxonomist, Johann Friedrich Blumenbach (1752–1840), rejected the latter two categories and added a fifth geographical variant, Malayan. These were the first leading racial classifications; many more were to be drawn up in succeeding generations.

Racial variations were often interpreted as degenerations from a primordial type. Both Blumenbach and Buffon believed that Adam and Eve were white, and Oliver Goldsmith argued that white was the original, natural color of man. Goldsmith thought that proof of this lay in the fact that the babies of other races were born light skinned. In the late 18th century, Samuel Stanhope Smith asserted that man had originated, fully civilized and white, somewhere in Asia, but some offshoots had developed dark skin due to the effects of heat. A contemporary, John Hunter, claimed that savage living conditions generally led to dark complexion.[3] On the other hand, James Cowles Prichard, in 1813, asserted that Adam

---

[2] Winthrop D. Jordan, *White Over Black: American Attitudes Toward the Negro, 1550–1812* (Chapel Hill: University of North Carolina Press, 1968), pp. 6–8, 30.
[3] *Ibid.,* p. 514.

had been a Negro and that, in the process of civilization, man had been slowly turning white. Although these theories differed from one another, a common thread which ran through them all was the conviction of white superiority held by the white theorists.

As evidence for a whitening tendency among Negroes, some "white Negroes"—who were not mulattos—were reported and even publicly displayed. Although the condition of albinism was then known to Europeans, these cases were not recognized as such. Dr. Benjamin Rush (1745–1813), an ardent antislavery advocate, argued that the dark pigmentation of Negroes was due to leprosy, which also accounted for some other attributes such as thick lips, flat nose, woolly hair, and an alleged insensitivity to pain. There was no basis for this view, but it raised the hope that a "cure" would bring about an eventual whitening of Negro skin.

Although there were various prophets of such a tendency, skepticism increased as time went on and no such lightening—apart from the results of interbreeding—could be observed.

Those who followed the monogenetic tradition of descent from Adam and Eve had to account for the racial diversity which had developed since. Not all thinkers accepted this view, however. Some 18th-century writers believed that different races were the products of separate acts of creation. Voltaire, who held polygenetic views, thought that Negroes were not capable of achieving an advanced civilization. Some American defenders of slavery held that blacks and whites were separate species. An obvious weakness of this notion was that the two races could interbreed and produce fertile offspring. Nevertheless, there were several proponents of what came to be known in Europe as the "American school," founded by a physician and anatomist, Samuel George Morton. Between 1830 and 1851, Morton acquired a collection of 968 skulls from different parts of the world. He developed certain standard measuring practices involving about a dozen separate measurements, including that of the cranial capacity. Skull measurements of this sort became standard procedure in the physical anthropology of the rest of the 19th century and the early decades of the 20th. Racist claims about the superiority or inferiority of particular races were often based upon comparative measurements, as will be seen in Chapter 13. Members of the "American school" thought that Negroes and whites belonged to separate species and that Negroes were inferior to whites. But despite their implicit support for slavery, polygenetic views did not prevail in the South, since they challenged biblical authority. Fundamentalists could find support for the inferior position of blacks in Noah's curse of his third son, Ham, whose descendants were destined to be the servants of servants. This was believed to refer to the Negro race.

After the publication of Darwin's *Origin of Species*, there was less concern among scholars to find biblical justification for their views. The term *anthropology* became increasingly used for a separate field of inquiry. The Anthropological Society of London was founded in the 1860's. Its members were opposed to slavery and tended to believe in the perfectibility of man. There was a rival group of British "anthropologists" who were skeptical of perfectibility, favored polygenetic views, and were supporters of the American South and of slavery. They started a journal in 1862 called the *Anthropological Review*. The two factions made up their differences toward the end of the decade and formed the Royal Anthropological Institute of Great Britain and Ireland, which is still flourishing today.

In the 19th century, racist views continued to be expressed in England and the United States and by German writers such as Gustav Klemm and Frenchmen like Count de Gobineau. Perhaps the greatest bulwark against racist ideology appeared in the person of Franz Boas (1858–1942), who was both a physical anthropologist and an ethnologist. Boas was the teacher of the first generation of American anthropologists, including, to name only a few, A. L. Kroeber, Robert Lowie, Edward Sapir, Melville Herskovits, Ruth Benedict, Margaret Mead, and Ashley Montagu. Most of these persons were active in combating racist assumptions. Only the last mentioned, however, was a physical anthropologist. Indeed, physical anthropology was rather slow in developing as a separate discipline. The *American Journal of Physical Anthropology* was started in 1918, and it was not until 1930 that the Society of Physical Anthropologists was formed. Despite this late start and the fact that relatively few persons have specialized in this field, physical anthropology has perhaps been the most rapidly advancing branch of anthropology. The nature of research has greatly changed. No longer is skull measurement the chief activity of physical anthropologists; it now occupies a minor place, having given way to the study of physiology, biochemistry, and genetics.[4]

Despite the influence of the Boas school and their successors in the United States, racist views continue to be expressed in some scholarly circles today. We shall return to this subject in Chapter 13.

Suggestions for further reading

The history of evolutionary theory is well presented in Loren Eiseley, *Darwin's Century: Evolution and the Men Who Discovered It* (New York: Doubleday & Co., 1958) and John C. Greene, *The Death of Adam. Evolution and Its Impact on Western Thought* (Ames: Iowa State University Press, 1959).

For a work on the development of early speculation about man, see Stanley Casson, *The Discovery of Man: The Story of the Inquiry into Human Origins* (New York: Harper & Bros., 1939). A selection of texts on anthropological subjects dating from the 14th to the 18th centuries is available in J. S. Slotkin (ed.), *Readings in Early Anthropology* (Viking Fund Publications in Anthropology,

---

[4] See Stanley M. Garn, "The Newer Physical Anthropology," *American Anthropologist,* Vol. 64 (1962), pp. 917–18.

No. 40 [Chicago: Aldine Publishing Co., 1965]). For British and white American attitudes toward the Negro, see Winthrop D. Jordan, *White over Black: American Attitudes toward the Negro, 1550–1812* (Chapel Hill: University of North Carolina Press, 1968), and William Stanton, *The Leopard's Spots: Scientific Attitudes toward Race in America, 1815–59* (Chicago: University of Chicago Press, 1960). See also Chapter 4, "Rise of Racial Determinism," in Marvin Harris, *The Rise of Anthropological Theory: A History of Theories of Culture* (New York: Thomas Y. Crowell Co., 1968), pp. 80–107.

Evolution

Chapter 3

Mechanisms of evolutionary change

Evolutionary changes are such remarkable developments that they are hard to believe. That a single-celled animal should give rise to a multi-celled one, that an invertebrate should evolve into a creature with a backbone, that fishes should start to live on land—all these seem like miraculous transformations. And how can we explain the formation of such a wonderful organ as the human eye or the human brain? These and many other aspects of evolution seem almost incredible, as one thinks about them.

Some writers, who may be characterized as vitalists, finalists, or tele-finalists, have argued that evolution is directed by a mystical life force or by God, perhaps leading, as Tennyson put it, in the last two lines of *In Memoriam,* to "one far-off divine event/ To which the whole creation moves."

These views may be right, but they have not, so far, shed much light on evolutionary processes. As George Gaylord Simpson has written, "The most successful scientific investigation has generally involved treating phenomena *as if* they were purely materialistic, rejecting any metaphysical or transcendental hypothesis as long as a natural hypothesis seems possible."[1] To follow such an approach does not necessarily mean to commit oneself to a mechanistic or materialistic view of life. It is through such an approach that scientists have discovered much about the mechanisms which operate in evolutionary change. These discoveries do not lessen the mystery inherent in evolution, for as we learn more, more mysteries appear.

An early naturalistic theory about evolutionary change, which is not

---

[1] George Gaylord Simpson, *The Meaning of Evolution* (New Haven, Conn.: Yale University Press, 1967), p. 128. Italics as in the original.

generally accepted today, developed from the suggestion of Lamarck (1744–1829), the French naturalist, that organs are strengthened through use and come to atrophy through disuse. Lamarck interpreted the long neck and long forelegs of giraffes as due to their stretching up to browse in the upper leaves of trees over long periods of time. Blind cave fishes have been found in both Europe and America; Lamarck would explain their blindness as being caused by the atrophy of organs which have ceased to be used in the dark.

The difficulty with these views is that they assume the inheritance of characteristics acquired in the lifetime of an organism. Most scientists today do not accept the notion that such acquired characteristics are inherited, although that was, until not long ago, a dogma in Soviet biological science.

Another evolutionary theory, that of *orthogenesis*, held that there is a constant direction in the evolution of organisms, leading seals, for example, to become increasingly streamlined or giraffes to develop progressively longer necks. No special mechanism was posited for such tendencies, merely a vague directive influence. The idea of orthogenesis is therefore similar to vitalistic and finalistic interpretations of evolution. Such views have not helped to clarify the processes of evolutionary change.

Our present understanding of the mechanisms involved in evolution has been largely derived from the work of two men: Charles Darwin (1809–82) and Gregor Mendel (1822–84). Darwin provided the concept of natural selection and synthesized data bearing on the theories of evolution; Mendel founded the science of genetics.

Natural selection

Darwin's *Origin of Species* (1859) opens with a discussion of variation among cultivated plants and animals. Darwin drew attention to the great changes which breeders have been able to develop in domesticated species through artificial selection. But changes also take place in nature through the operation of natural selection. Everywhere in nature there is a struggle for survival—for resources of food, sunlight, and the other needs of life. Plants and animals reproduce many more of their kind than can survive, and most of them perish.

The principle of natural selection is stated as follows:

Owing to this struggle, variations, however slight and from whatever cause proceeding, if they be in any degree profitable to the individuals of a species, in their infinitely complex relations to other organic beings and to the physical conditions of life, will tend to the preservation of such individuals, and will generally be inherited by the offspring.[2]

---

[2] Charles Darwin, *The Origin of Species by Means of Natural Selection or the Preservation of Favored Races in the Struggle for Life* (New York: Modern Library, n.d.), pp. 51–52.

Charles Darwin
(left) and
Gregor Mendel

Darwin pointed out that organisms, if unchecked, tend to increase in geometrical ratio. The elephant is the slowest-breeding animal known, but Darwin calculated that if an elephant pair were to give birth to six young in a lifetime of 100 years, and if this rate continued, there would, in a period of from 740 to 750 years, be almost 19 million elephants alive, descended from the first pair. Darwin cited some actual instances of "population explosion" among species under favorable environmental conditions, when natural enemies or other checks had been removed.

However, in spite of the tendency to multiply, species generally have fairly constant populations. Their numbers are, in fact, held in check by the universal struggle for life and by the fact that while a species may multiply, its available food supply is apt to remain constant. Since many individuals in every species perish, favorable variations of any sort must greatly enhance an organism's chances of survival and reproduction. Thus Darwin would explain the long necks and forelegs of giraffes, not in terms of their straining up to nibble lofty leaves for many generations but in a quite different manner, reasoning that if some members of the species were born with longer necks and forelegs than others, this might be a favorable selective difference which would give them a greater chance to survive and propagate than their shorter-necked contemporaries. Over a period of time, the long-necked variety would therefore increase at the expense of the short necks, culminating, as an evolutionary end product, in the giraffe which we know today.

To take another example, consider the advantages of protective coloration. There are both brown and green mantises. Scientists have performed some experiments with them, tethering both types of mantis in both brown and green grass. In an environment of green grass, the brown insects were soon destroyed by natural enemies, while the green mantises survived. In brown grass, it was the other way around; here the brown mantises were favored and continued to live, while the green ones perished. Thus the protective coloring became an instrument of natural selection.

Adaptations of this sort are complicated by the fact that organisms may move to new environments, or there may be seasonal changes, as in the turning of leaves in autumn. Hence what was formerly protective may become highly unfavorable under changed conditions, and what was unfavorable may become beneficial. Both dark- and light-colored moths are found in the English countryside, but the light moths predominate because they have more protection from their enemies. But during the last 100 years dark, almost black moths have become much more numerous than light ones in the sooty industrial cities of England. The dark moths are hardier, but they had formerly been exposed to their enemies when seen against light-colored tree bark covered by lichens. Now, in a new environment of gray towns and factories, as well as in rural areas with soot-covered tree bark, they have flourished.

Darwin did not know how new variations arise in an organism; that was later to be shown by geneticists. But he argued that once a new feature, such as a change in color, size, or whatnot appears, it may either help or hinder the organism in its adaptation to the environment. If it hinders that adaptation, the organism will be less apt to survive and reproduce, and the new feature will not be perpetuated. But if it enhances the organism's chances of survival and reproduction, the new feature will be maintained, and organisms possessing the trait will flourish at the expense of those not having it. In this way, changes gradually take place in the appearance and structure of an organism. Since organic forms have been living for many millions of years, there has been plenty of opportunity for plants and animals to adapt to many different environments, progressively deviating from parental forms as they establish more appropriate adjustments to their surroundings.

After the publication of *Origin of Species*, Darwin's work was criticized on various grounds. Darwin and his supporters were able to answer most of his critics. But there was one criticism which shook Darwin's faith in his own theories. The question was raised: If an organism appears with a new trait which has survival value, how can it be maintained? If it is to reproduce, the organism must mate with other members of its species which are apt to lack the new variation. Within a few generations the new trait will be swamped and should disappear. It could only be maintained if several organisms were to simultaneously vary in the same direction. But acceptance of this possibility would involve an orthogenetic view of evolution lacking the fortuitous character of natural selection.

To cope with this objection Darwin developed a complex theory of inheritance, which has since been shown to be inadequate. Darwin might have solved the problem if he had known about the work of his contemporary, Gregor Mendel. But although Mendel gave two reports dealing with his findings before the Brünn Society for the Study of Natural Science in 1865, and although he published his paper the following year in the *Proceedings* of that society, Mendel's work was, for all practical purposes, unknown in the Europe of his day. The few people who heard or read Mendel's report in 1865 and 1866 evidently did not understand it or grasp its significance. It was not until 1900, 16 years after Mendel's death, that his forgotten treatise was simultaneously discovered by three scholars in three different European countries. And then the science of genetics was born.

Gregor Mendel's experiments

Gregor Mendel (1822–84) was an Austrian monk who, over a period of eight years, performed some careful experiments with plants in a patch of garden beside his monastery. His most important work was done with garden peas. One reason for his success in these experiments was that he crossed strains of peas which differed from each other in one definite character. Some had round seeds; others had wrinkled ones. Some were yellow, others green. Some of the plants were tall, others short. Mendel took pollen from a plant that regularly produced round seeds and placed it on the stigma of a plant that produced wrinkled ones. In the same way he crossed the yellow with the green plants and the tall with the short. He did this with seven pairs of contrasting characters.

Another reason for Mendel's success in these experiments is that he kept quantitative records of the appearance of his plants in each generation. Moreover, he kept records of large numbers of plants, so that accidental variations present in groups of small numbers did not significantly influence his findings. After crossing the peas with the round and wrinkled seeds, Mendel found that the peas of the offspring were all round; none were wrinkled. In the yellow-green cross, the peas of the offspring were all yellow. In the tall-short cross, the offspring were all tall. These results were surprising, for one might have expected to find some blending of the contrasting traits. Instead, in each case, one factor appeared to be dominant over the other. However, the submerged (recessive) factor did not disappear. This was shown when Mendel next cross-pollinated his hybrid plants. This time the round-wrinkled hybrids produced about three round peas to every wrinkled one; apparently the wrinkled factor of one of the grandparents had not been lost. The same 3–to–1 ratio was found for the other factors as well. The recessive traits for greenness of the pea, for shortness of the plant, and the other recessive traits were all preserved.

Mendel found that when the peas were allowed to reproduce by self-fertilization the wrinkled-seed plants always had wrinkled peas, and pure strains of the round-seed type always produced round peas. But the hybrids produced three round seeds to one wrinkled one. We shall return later to the question of why this 3–to–1 ratio appeared.

The term *genotype* has come to be used for the genetic constitution of an organism, while *phenotype* denotes its observable appearance. Phenotypically, members of the first generation of Mendel's round-wrinkled hybrids were all alike; all their peas were round. But the underlying genetic makeup of the hybrids was different, as was shown by the reappearance of the recessive factor in the following generation.

Mendel concluded that heredity is determined by discrete units which retain their original character for generation after generation. Nowadays we call these units genes.

Genes and chromosomes

Since Mendel did not work with a microscope, he could not observe the inner structure of cells. His conclusions were drawn from observation and mathematics. Later, microscopes with great power and efficiency became available, and today we now know a great deal about the composition of cells that was unknown in Mendel's day. In the nucleus of a cell, there are some rod-shaped bodies which can be seen much more clearly through the microscope if they are stained. Hence they have been called *chromosomes,* or colored bodies. These structures cannot be the genes themselves, because there are too few of them. There is an intestinal worm which has only two chromosomes. The fruit fly, *Drosophila melanogaster,* has eight. The dog has 78. There must be thousands of times as many genes as chromosomes.

It was concluded that perhaps the genes are located on the chromosomes. This conclusion has been borne out by experiments, although it now appears that there are also genes which are not located on chromosomes; indeed, in some species, such as those in the genus *Paramecium,* some genes are found in the cytoplasm instead of in the nucleus of the cell.

Drosophila melanogaster has very large chromosomes in its salivary glands during the larval stage. Through observations on the effects of radiation, the scientists who have worked with the fruit fly have been able to make detailed chromosome maps, showing at exactly which part of a chromosome a particular gene is to be found. The genes themselves, however, are too small to be seen through a microscope. It is perhaps best to think of them as positions on a chromosome.

The genes on the chromosome are formed in pairs, which may be either of the same or of contrasting type. These partner genes are called *alleles*. A pair of alleles is found across from each other at the same position on a pair of homologous chromosomes. When the alleles are of the same type, the organism is said to be *homozygous* for that trait. For example, if both genes cause roundness in peas, or if both cause wrinkledness, they are homozygous. But if one allele causes roundness and its partner causes wrinkledness, they are *heterozygous*.

All cells undergo the process of cell division, or *mitosis,* which creates new cells. In this process the chromosome divides so that each cell has the same number of chromosomes with the same genes. The new cells are exactly like the parent cells. A somewhat different process takes place in the reproductive cells which develop into the egg and sperm. In their cell division, called *meiosis,* the daughter cells have only half the traditional species number of chromosomes. There is one member present from each chromosome pair, not just any half. The alleles, or gene pairs, separate, with one going to each daughter cell. The maternally and

Diagram of a "typical" animal cell.

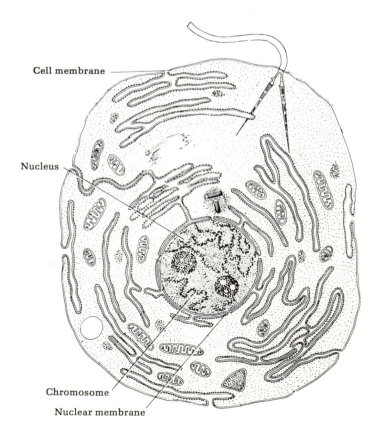

Cell membrane

Nucleus

Chromosome

Nuclear membrane

paternally derived chromosomes assort randomly, making a great number of combinations possible. Thus, when the egg and sperm unite in fertilization, each brings half the normal number of chromosomes, and in their fusion the full number of chromosomes characteristic of the species is provided for the embryo.

The combination of genes that take place at fertilization is a matter of chance. This can be shown if we return to Mendel's experiment with the round and wrinkled peas. We are now in a better position to understand the 3–to–1 ratio which Mendel discovered in his third generation of plants. Mendel began with a pure round strain, containing two alleles for roundness, and a pure wrinkled strain with two alleles for wrinkledness. Every offspring of this cross must contain both a round and a wrinkled gene; they are all heterozygous. Phenotypically their peas are all round, since roundness is the dominant trait.

Consider now what happens when two of these heterozygotes are crossed. At fertilization the dominant round gene of the first pair of alleles could either join up with the dominant round gene or with the recessive wrinkled one of the other pair. The recessive wrinkled allele of the first pair could either join up with the dominant round gene or with the recessive wrinkled one of the other pair. We thus have four possibilities: round-round, round-wrinkled, wrinkled-round, and wrinkled-wrinkled. Since the first three combinations all contain a round allele, these will all appear round. Phenotypically, then, we have a 3–to–1 ratio.

It should be noted that a 3–to–1 ratio does not always obtain in the crossing of heterozygotes, for traits are not always clearly dominant or recessive, and genes that are dominant under some conditions may be recessive in others. There are cases where a kind of blending takes place, as in the skin color of mulattos.

Another qualification which needs to be made about Mendel's findings has to do with the implication that a single gene always affects a single trait, such as the roundness or yellowness of peas. We now know that a particular trait may be influenced by several genes, and that linkages may occur among genes, as among those found on the same chromosome. For example, hemophilia and color blindness are called sex-linked traits, because the genes responsible for them are located on the X chromosome, one of the two chromosomes which determine sex.

In the preceding paragraphs, we have been considering processes involved in sexual reproduction, which is characteristic of the majority of plants and animals. But not all plants and animals have sexual reproduction; many reproduce asexually by mitotic cell division. The more common and more complex processes of sexual reproduction must have been favored by natural selection. Their advantage evidently lies in the variety made possible by the genetic recombination in sexual reproduction. In mitosis each new cell gets a set of chromosomes just like the parental set;

thus asexual reproduction provides little opportunity for variation and for evolutionary change. Genetic recombination, however, does provide variety in the raw material upon which natural selection acts.

Another source of variation and evolutionary change is a change in the number of chromosomes. The separation of chromosomes in the process of cell division does not always take place normally, and it may happen that a daughter cell acquires twice the normal number of chromosomes. The condition of having more than two complete sets of chromosomes is known as *polyploidy;* it has often occurred among plants but rarely among animals and has probably not been important in the formation of new animal species.

Mendel's Three-
to-One Ratio.

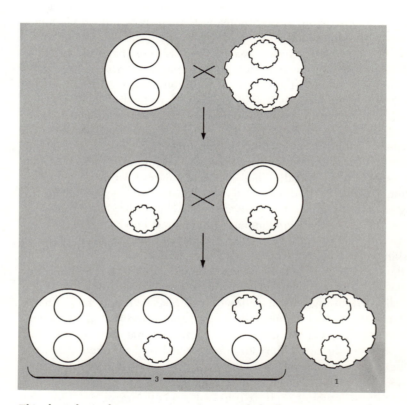

This chart shows three generations of peas, with the first generation on the top row. On the top left there is a pure round pea, having two genes for roundness, represented by the two smaller circles inside. On the top right there is a pure wrinkled pea having two genes for wrinkledness. When these two peas are crossed, each member of the next generation (second row) is heterozygous, having received one of the two genes for roundness-wrinkledness from each parent. Although they each have a gene for wrinkledness, they all look round, since roundness is a dominant trait. When members of this second generation are crossed, there are four possible combinations in the third generation (third row). Since the first three peas all have a gene for roundness, they all look round. The fourth, being pure wrinkled, looks wrinkled.

Changes may also take place in the structure of chromosomes through deletion (loss), duplication, inversions, or translocations. An inversion may occur when a chromosome breaks in two places and a segment between the breaks is turned around. Translocations may occur when two nonhomologous chromosomes simultaneously break and exchange segments.

Genes seem to be remarkably stable. They are always making faithful copies of themselves and so continue for generation after generation. But sometimes an inheritable change takes place in the structure or the chemistry of a gene. This is called a mutation. A new gene, in effect, has appeared, which may result in a difference in coloring, size, or other attribute of the organism. Most such changes are harmful to the organism and may lessen its adaptability. This is because every organism has established a *modus vivendi;* it has acquired successful means of coping with the world. An innovation is more apt to be harmful to it than helpful. Harmful genes tend to disappear before long, since the carriers may either die out or fail to reproduce.

Mutation

Sometimes mutations occur which have no apparent effect for generations. New recessive traits may be masked for decades and only become manifest if mating takes place between two carriers of the trait. To give an example of a recessive trait resulting from mutation, in 1931 a Wisconsin mink rancher found a light-furred female in a batch of otherwise normally dark-furred offspring. The light color was a recessive characteristic due to mutation. The rancher crossed the female with one of her offspring. In this way, a homozygous strain was developed which bred true—a kind of homogenized mink. In the wild state such a mutation might not have had much survival value. Under domestication it was profitable, at least, to the mink rancher, who introduced platinum mink to the world. Naturally, it was preserved and perpetuated.

Not all types of mutations are possible, and there are some which no doubt recur again and again. Very likely, light-furred mink have often been born in the past, but they were not favored by natural selection. Mutations leading to blindness are, of course, harmful to the organisms affected and tend to be weeded out, but in cave fish living in the dark, such mutations make no difference and may therefore accumulate—an interpretation to be contrasted with Lamarck's notion of atrophy through disuse.

Mutations occur with some regularity, although with relative rarity, in all species. The rates of mutation may be increased by exposure to X ray or cosmic radiation and by exposure to some chemicals or to heat. Although most mutations are harmful, it sometimes does happen that a favorable mutation occurs—one which enhances the survival and breeding potentialities of the organism. An example was given earlier of the dark-colored moths in the industrial areas of England. Mutations toward dark pigmentation must often have occurred among these moths in the past, but they did not prove to be useful until parts of England became sooty enough to favor their selection.

Isolation

Evolutionary change has also been fostered by geographic and reproductive isolation. If a species comes to occupy various environments and undergoes different adaptations to these environments, it may become a *polytypic* species characterized by different races or subspecies. Barriers to the exchange of genes, known as isolating mechanisms, may then lead to the formation of separate species. Some isolating mechanisms are: *ecological isolation,* occupation of different habitats; *seasonal or temporal isolation,* mating or flowering periods coming at different seasons; *mechanical isolation,* noncorrespondence of genitalia or floral parts; and *hybrid inviability or sterility.*[3]

DNA

The new field of molecular biology has provided much information about the structure and chemistry of genetic material. As a result, we are now hearing a bit less about genes and a good deal more about "coding." Chromosomes consist partly of chains of DNA (deoxyribonucleic acid) molecules and partly of protein. A DNA molecule is believed to consist of two intertwined sugar-phosphate strands, shaped like a spiral staircase. The nitrogenous bases, adenine, guanine, cytosine, and thymine, form internal links like steps in the staircase. The DNA of all plants and animals seems to have this structure and chemical composition, but variety is made possible by variations in the four kinds of "steps." A thread of DNA has been compared with a recording tape which codes instructions. These instructions are issued in the form of chemicals. A gene may be considered as a position on the tape which issues a particular kind of message.

In addition to DNA, all plant and animal cells contain a similar substance called RNA (ribonucleic acid), which contains a sugar called ribose. (The ribose of DNA has one less oxygen atom; hence the "deoxy" in its name.) DNA is always found in the nuclei of cells; RNA is usually found in the cytoplasm. Within the nucleus, DNA transmits messages concerning protein manufacture to various forms of RNA called "messenger RNA." The essential business of life, the determination of heredity and the manufacture of proteins necessary for life, is therefore carried out by these minute molecules.

A failure in the coding process may result in a mutation. An example

---

[3] For a fuller list and a detailed discussion of isolating mechanisms, see Theodosius Dobzhansky, *Genetics and the Origin of Species* (3d ed.; New York: Columbia University Press, 1951), Chapter 7.

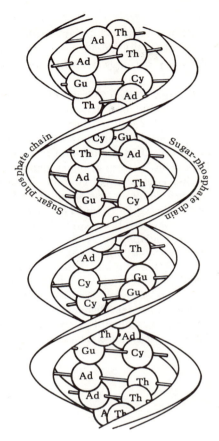

The double helix, or Watson-Crick, model of a DNA molecule.

is sickle-cell anemia, which results from failure of the organism to pro-duce a particular amino acid. This ailment will be discussed in Chapter 12.

This chapter has dealt with the problem of how evolutionary changes are brought about in plants and animals.

Darwin's concept of natural selection, when combined with modern knowledge of genetics, gives an understanding of how evolutionary changes have come about. Genetic variability is provided by genetic re-combination, changes in chromosome structure and number, and gene mutation. Geographic or reproductive isolation allows for the operation of natural selection upon a particular species in different environmental settings, leading to species differentiation.

Knowledge of genetics has helped to solve some problems which Darwin could not answer and to explain why a new variant form need not be "swamped" through matings with organisms which do not have the trait in question. In the following chapters, we shall trace sequences of evolutionary development which led to man. At each stage, at every moment in this evolutionary process, the mechanisms discussed in this chapter must have been in operation.

Suggestions for further reading

Charles Darwin's *Origin of Species* (1859) still makes interesting reading. It is available in a Modern Library edition, along with Darwin's *The Descent of Man* (1871). For a history of evolutionary theory, see Loren Eiseley, *Darwin's Century: Evolution and the Men Who Discovered It* (New York: Doubleday & Co., 1958), and John C. Greene, *The Death of Adam: Evolution and Its Impact on Western Thought* (Ames: Iowa State University Press, 1959). For a critical discussion of vitalism, finalism, and orthogenetic theories, see George Gaylord Simpson, *The Meaning of Evolution* (New Haven, Conn.: Yale University Press, 1949), and *This View of Life: The World of an Evolutionist* (New York: Harcourt, Brace & World, 1964).

For readable works on genetics and related topics, see Ashley Montagu, *Human Heredity* (New York: New American Library, 1960); Hampton L. Carson, *Heredity and Human Life* (New York: Columbia University Press, 1963); and Ruth Moore, *The Coil of Life: The Story of the Great Discoveries in the Life Sciences* (New York: Alfred A. Knopf, 1961). For a classic but more difficult work, see Theodosius Dobzhansky, *Genetics and the Origin of Species* (New York: Columbia University Press, 1951). See also G. Ledyard Stebbins, *Processes of Organic Evolution* (Englewood Cliffs, N.J.: Prentice-Hall, 1966).

Chapter 4

Man's classification among the vertebrates

Early in the first chapter, it was stated that man is a vertebrate, a mammal, and a primate. These categories represent progressive refinements of classification. Let us consider each category in turn, and in doing so trace man's evolution from simpler forms of life.

Vertebrates are bilaterally symmetrical animals which have segmented backbones. Running through the backbone is a spinal cord connecting with the brain, which is usually enclosed in a skull. Thus the brain and central nervous system are well protected. The backbone is flexible, since it is made up of a series of bony rings.

Characteristics of vertebrates

The head of the animal contains sense organs, such as nose, eyes, and ears, and a mouth sometimes equipped with teeth. A heart pumps blood containing food, oxygen, and other substances to all parts of the body. A liver stores food, and a urinary system eliminates wastes. These characteristics, as you must recognize, are true of man. They are also true of fishes, amphibians, reptiles, birds, and all the mammals.

The features just mentioned have some advantages over the body plans of the invertebrates—such literally spineless creatures as worms, mollusks, insects, starfish, and octopuses. Some invertebrates are held together by external armor, but this is not as efficient and mobile a system as an internal skeleton. Vertebrates are generally able to move about quickly. They can readily mobilize energy and have well-developed nervous systems. Because of these advantages some vertebrates have attained huge size, like the whales and elephants of the present day. Although man is much smaller than they, he is much larger than the vast majority of animals. Relatively speaking, man is a giant. Large size may sometimes be disadvantageous, but it also has some advantages. Bulk may be useful in defense or attack. And since larger animals tend to have slower rates of metabolism, they tend to live longer than small animals, whose internal organs wear out more quickly.

The first vertebrates, which appeared about 480 million years ago, were water dwelling, for life originated in the waters of the earth, and it was only gradually that first plants, and later animals, appeared on land and made their ways inland. The first vertebrates, moreover, were probably freshwater fish rather than inhabitants of the sea. Zoologists have reached this conclusion from a study of the kidneys of fishes. Both freshwater and saltwater fishes have a type of kidney that is well adapted to a freshwater environment but less well suited to the salty sea. Marine fishes have developed some specializations to counteract the attendant disadvantages, but they have retained the freshwater type of kidney. Hence it is thought that the ancestral vertebrates must have lived in inland streams rather than in the ocean.

The first vertebrates were jawless. Acquisition of jaws, derived from gill arches, was an important innovation which opened up new possibilities for adaptation and mastery. Grasping and biting of food was thus facilitated. Associated with the jaws of all vertebrates, moreover, are the three semicircular canals which give a sense of equilibrium. Still another significant development in the evolution of early vertebrates was the appearance of median and paired fins which helped to propel the fish through water.

The amphibian stage

Amphibians, such as frogs and salamanders, are vertebrates who have half climbed out of the water, so to speak. In their adult forms they move about readily on land, but they first pass through a fishlike tadpole stage in the water. Their method of reproduction is also like that of most fishes, for their eggs must be laid in water. As tadpoles, frogs have gills through which they breathe, but in the adult stage they develop lungs and breathe air much as the higher land-dwelling vertebrates do. They also develop two sets of limbs, so that the skeleton of an adult frog has many resemblances to that of a human being. The frog, which has developed hopping as a form of locomotion, has a very specialized skeletal structure. Early ancestral amphibians probably had limbs that did not raise the animal off the ground; they helped to drag him along in water, mud, and on dry land. The limbs have three segments each. First, there is a single bone (like the humerus, upper arm, or femur, thigh bone); then there are two parallel bones (like the radius and ulna or the tibia and fibula); then there are the bones which make up the hands and feet with their separate digits. Our limbs are based on the same plan as that of the early amphibian limbs. In this respect man has remained very conservative, while animals such as

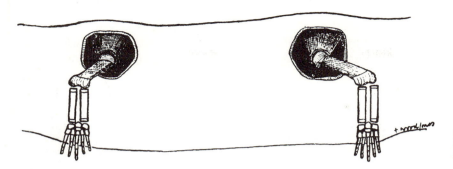

Diagrammatic
drawing of early
amphibian limbs.

horses and cows have limbs which deviate a great deal from the early
amphibian type of limb.

The earliest fossil amphibians which have been found had relatively
small limbs, as one might expect. These replaced the lateral fins which help
to propel and balance fish. Some early amphibian remains have been recovered from Devonian strata dating from about 360 million years ago.
Zoologists think that these creatures developed from lobe-finned fishes
called Crossopterygii, which had air bladders that functioned like lungs,
as among the lung fish of the present day. Crossopterygian fins were
thickened and had skeletal elements which could have provided a base
for the development of limbs. Some fishes of the present day can even
climb trees with their fins. Thus we can understand how some early air-
breathing fish which began to live temporarily on land could have given
rise to the class of amphibians.

Some new problems faced the first amphibian land dwellers. One was
to avoid drying up. This could be partly solved by keeping close to the
water, but there is evidence that some of the early amphibians also developed tough skins. Another problem was the effect of gravity, which was
experienced with much more force on land than in the water. In this case,
adaptations were made in strengthening the limbs and spinal column.

**The reptile
stage**

The amphibians were pioneers, but they were neither fish nor fowl, so
to speak, having made only a partial adaptation to life on land. A new
set of developments took place among some creatures which gave rise to
the class of reptiles. The most dramatic innovation was a change in the
method of reproduction. Amphibians and most fishes, as we have seen,
lay their eggs in water, where they are fertilized. (Some fishes, however,
are viviparous—produce living young instead of eggs from within the
body.) Most of the fish and amphibian eggs fertilized in water die off or
are eaten by other animals, but enough survive to continue the species.
The new development, associated with copulation as the means of fertilization, was the laying of eggs encased in a hard shell. Such eggs could be

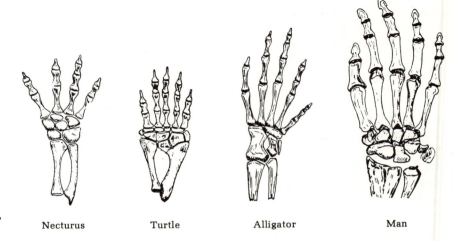

Right hand of
Necturus, turtle,
alligator, and man,
from dorsal view.

| Necturus | Turtle | Alligator | Man |

laid on land, for the watery medium required by the embryo had now
been transferred from the outside world to the inside of the shell. The shell
was strong enough to protect the embryo from at least some of its enemies.
It was porous enough to permit respiration. Food was available in a yolk
sac, which enabled the embryo to take nourishment and to grow in a
protected environment. When the young animal was strong enough to
break the shell, it could step out onto dry land. Thus, for the first time, a
purely terrestrial way of life was made possible.

Reptiles also became equipped for life on land by the development of
stronger limbs, which in some cases raised the body off the ground. Several extinct forms of reptiles, including some of giant size, ran about
on their hind legs. Although the snakes eventually lost their limbs, primitive reptiles generally had limbs containing the same number of fingers
and toes as we have. Reptiles had more efficient lungs and circulatory
systems than amphibians.

The transition from amphibian to reptile took place about 260 million
years ago. Since they were better adapted to life on land than the amphibians were, the reptiles increased and radiated, or diversified, at a
great rate, particularly during the Mesozoic period, which has been called
the Age of Reptiles. The amphibians, sticking close to their watery habitat,
did not, however, become extinct. For about 120 million years, reptiles
dominated the earth. They invaded various ecological niches. Some took
to the air; some returned to aquatic life. Some became vegetable feeders;
others were carnivorous. There were huge dinosaurs, flying pterodactyls,
and many other forms. Human beings never saw living dinosaurs and
pterodactyls, for these creatures became extinct before we appeared on
the scene.

Just why so many of the reptiles became extinct is not clear, but it was probably because of changes in climate and temperature toward the end of the Mesozoic period about 63 million years ago. Despite their improved adaptations, reptiles have some weaknesses. Since they are not warm-blooded animals, they can be active only in warm weather. They slow down and may have to assume a state of suspended animation when it gets cold. Overexposure to the sun may also be fatal. The reptiles' range of movement is therefore restricted, and the giant forms of the Mesozoic must have been particularly vulnerable to changes in climate. Many of the dinosaurs lived in swamps and lagoons, which drained and dried up toward the end of the Mesozoic, when new mountain ranges, such as the Rockies, thrust themselves upward. It has also been suggested that with the rise of the flowering plants (discussed in the following section), there was an increase in pathogenic fungi and parasites which may have spread epidemics among the reptiles. Some of the early mammals, including primates, may have found nourishment in eating reptile eggs and may thus have contributed to the extinction of some species.[1]

At any rate, as the giant reptiles left the scene, some less impressive but ultimately more successful creatures began to increase in number. These were the birds and mammals, both of which evolved from reptilian ancestors and developed warm-bloodedness. The birds retained the reptilian method of reproduction of laying eggs, and they developed feathers, their most distinctive feature. Both birds and mammals benefited from some remarkable changes in the plant world which took place about 150 million years ago.

Loren Eiseley has described these changes in his beautifully written book, *The Immense Journey.* In a chapter entitled "How Flowers Changed the World," Eiseley writes of the appearance of the angiosperms, or flowering plants, toward the end of the Mesozoic. Before that time there were no grasses or flowers, although there existed great forests of spruce, pine, and sequoia trees. Then came the flowering plants.

Flowering plants and their significance for mammalian evolution

. . . the true flowering plants (angiosperm itself means "encased seed") grew a seed in the heart of a flower, a seed whose development was initiated by a fertilizing pollen grain independent of outside moisture. But the seed, unlike the developing spore, is already a fully equipped *embryonic plant* packed in a little enclosed box full of nutritious food. . . . In a movement that was almost instantaneous, geologically speaking, the angiosperms had taken over the world. Grass was beginning to cover the bare earth until, today, there are over six thousand species. All kinds of vines and bushes squirmed and writhed under new trees with flying seeds.

The explosion was having its effect on animal life also. Specialized groups of insects were arising to feed on the new sources of food, and incidentally and

[1] John E. Pfeiffer, *The Emergence of Man* (New York: Harper & Row, Publishers, 1969), p. 19.

unknowingly, to pollinate the plant. . . . A new world had opened out for the warm-blooded mammals. Great herbivores like the mammoths, horses and bisons appeared. Skulking about them had arisen savage flesh-feeding carnivores like the now extinct dire wolves and the saber-toothed tiger. Flesh eaters though these creatures were, they were being sustained on nutritious grasses one step removed. Their fierce energy was being maintained on a high, effective level, through hot days and frosty nights, by the concentrated energy of the angiosperms.[2]

Man is a mammal

We now come to the mammals, the class of vertebrates to which man belongs. Archaic mammals appeared in the Mesozoic about 160 million years ago. Eutherian or placental mammals, a higher form of mammals, date from the end of the Mesozoic era. The first of these to appear were insectivores, which are believed to be ancestral to the other orders of eutherian mammals. The Primate order, to which we belong, is closely related to the insectivores; it is thus a relatively old and conservative mammalian order.[3]

Mammals are warm-blooded creatures which are able to maintain a constant high body temperature. They are thus less at the mercy of the environment than are the cold-blooded amphibians and reptiles. Mammals live in diverse parts of the world, even in the Arctic where one finds representatives of different mammalian orders, including seals, polar bears, whales, and man. Mammals radiated like the reptiles before them, some becoming aquatic, like the whales, some flying, like the bats. But most became either terrestrial or tree dwelling.

Mammals have an efficient circulatory system powered by a four-chambered heart. They generally have a covering of hair or fur, and a skin equipped with sweat glands. All of these features have to do with regulating the temperature of the body. They also have a diaphragm which separates the thoracic from the abdominal parts of the body and helps to draw air into the lungs. The lower jaws of reptiles consist of several bones, but in mammals there is only one on either side; it articulates directly with the skull.

Mammalian dentition is said to be *heterodont,* having different kinds of teeth with different shapes and functions, as opposed to the *homodont* dentition of reptiles. Reptile teeth, which are often incurved, serve to grasp or trap food, and have the same general appearance and function. The mammalian jaw became stronger in the course of evolution, and teeth became specialized for different functions, with incisors for cutting, canines for grasping and piercing, premolars and molars for crushing and

---

[2] Loren Eiseley, *The Immense Journey* (New York: Random House, Modern Library, 1957), pp. 71–74.

[3] Our order also has some features in common with those of the bats and the edentates, an order which includes the tree sloth, anteater, and armadillo. The four orders (insectivores, primates, bats, and edentates) are grouped together by George G. Simpson in one of four "cohorts" into which he divides the class of mammals.

grinding. Different kinds of tooth specialization developed as animals came to specialize as carnivores or herbivores. Some mammals underwent a loss of teeth; cows lost their upper front teeth and whalebone whales lost them all, but for most mammals the heterodont dentition remained an important adaptation:

... the heterodont dentition released to mammals the full food value locked up within the hard outer skeleton of insects and in plant-food storage organs (such as nuts and other seeds). The densely packed carbohydrates and fats of seeds, the sugars and starches of underground tubers and roots, and all the plant proteins locked up in tough vegetation were released to mammals by the chewing and grinding action of their teeth, thus making possible the maintenance of constant body temperature and more or less continuous activity.[4]

The eutherian or placental mammals have two sets of teeth. In the young animal there is a temporary milk set of teeth. When the jaw is more fully formed, the permanent teeth appear. The ancestral mammals are believed to have had 44 teeth, but present-day species have lost some of them in the course of evolution. Human beings usually have 32 teeth, which is more than most mammals have. (Many people, however, have only 28 teeth, and many have impacted third molars.)

The mammalian system of reproduction is quite different from those of fishes, amphibians, reptiles, and birds. Mammals do not lay eggs, except for the duckbill platypus and the spiny anteater or echidna. In all the other mammals, the embryo remains within the mother's body for a time and is born in a more or less helpless condition. It then receives nourish-

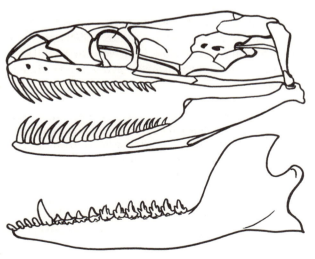

Reptile homodont teeth.

Mammalian heterodont teeth.

[4] Bernard G. Campbell, *Human Evolution: An Introduction to Man's Adaptations* (Chicago: Aldine Publishing Co., 1966), p. 41.

ment from the mother's breasts (*mammae*) from which the class gets its name.

Among the marsupials or pouched mammals, like the kangaroo and the opossum, the embryo does not remain long in the mother's body; after birth it is shifted to a sort of incubator in the mother's pouch, located near the nipples.

The eutherian mammals have evolved a better system. There is an organ in the maternal uterus known as the placenta, from which the foetus gets nourishment and oxygen. This is missing or weakly developed among the marsupials. The placenta makes it possible for the embryo to stay and grow for a long time in the mother's body.

Most adult male mammals have scrotal testes. This feature represents an adaptation to high body temperature. If the testes were to remain within the body, where they are first formed, the internal body heat would be too high for the production of sperm.

Mammalian reproductive processes are controlled by a complex endocrine system, operating through hormones, chemical substances which are carried in the bloodstream to different parts of the body.

Some other general characteristics of mammals include: much larger brains than those of lower vertebrates; eardrums set deeper in the skull than in reptiles, with an outer earflap for concentrating sound waves; separation of nasal and oral passages; and the presence of seven cervical (neck) vertebrae. Human beings have all the features mentioned above. Hence among the vertebrates man is classified as a mammal and not as a fish, amphibian, reptile, or bird.

This chapter has reviewed the general characteristics of vertebrates and, within that classification, particular features characteristic of fishes, amphibians, reptiles, and mammals, which appeared in that order. Transitions from one stage to the next were presumably brought about by the operation of the mechanisms of evolutionary change discussed in the last chapter.

Suggestions for further reading

For authoritative works on vertebrate evolution, see Alfred S. Romer, *The Vertebrate Story* (Chicago: University of Chicago Press, 1959), and Edwin H. Colbert, *Evolution of the Vertebrates: A History of the Backboned Animals Through Time* (New York: Science Editions, 1961).

For a work which deals mainly with man but which also includes good chapters about earlier vertebrate stages of evolution, see Frederick S. Hulse, *The Human Species: An Introduction to Physical Anthropology* (New York: Random House, 1963).

For a well-executed blend of lyricism and science concerning evolution, see Loren Eiseley, *The Immense Journey* (New York: Random House, Modern Library, 1957).

The primates

III

Chapter 5

Man is a primate

Within the grouping of eutherian mammals, man belongs to the mammalian order of Primates. The Primate order includes the lemurs, tarsiers, monkeys, apes, and man. Some authorities include the tree shrews within the order, while others classify them as insectivora.

Primate traits

The outstanding characteristic of the primates is their prehensile (grasping) five-digited hands and feet. In discussing the amphibian stage of evolution, attention was drawn to the conservatism shown in the structure of human limbs. Both arms and legs are characterized by having first a single upper bone, then two parallel bones, then wrist or ankle bones, and then five digits. This limb structure is a very ancient one. Very ancient also is the structure of the human hand, which remarkably resembles those of some tortoises. Terrestrial pronograde animals (ground-dwelling animals which go on all fours) have limbs which differ greatly from the early amphibian limb. In the horse the parallel bones have become fused, and only one functional digit remains. The horse depends upon his limbs for locomotion and nothing else. Such limbs cannot grasp anything, and they lack the mobility and flexibility of early amphibian limbs. Primates have retained this mobility and further developed it. Their forearms, for example, possess the power of pronation and supination, that is, the ability of the forearm to turn over and back again without moving the upper limb.

The hands and feet of many primates also have opposable digits in the thumb and big toe. The thumb can touch the other digits. When you grasp a branch, the thumb goes around one side, while the other four fingers wrap around the other. We cannot do this with our toes, because our feet have become specialized for support and locomotion. Our big toes are in line with the other toes and not set apart from them as the thumb is set apart in the hand. The other primates, however, can generally grasp as well with their feet as with their hands, and their big toes are opposable.

Another feature of primate hands and feet is the presence of flat or slightly curved nails on the digits. Some of the lower primates have claws on some of their digits, but not the higher primates.

How have the primates been able to retain the early amphibian-reptilian type of hand? The answer must be that our early mammalian ancestors did not take to pronograde terrestrial life, as did the ancestors of the ungulates, or hoofed mammals. It is believed that the first mammals were arboreal, or tree dwelling. Most of the primates of the present day still live in trees. Only a few, such as the baboon, gorilla, and man, move about on the ground. The grasping hands and feet of the primates are admirably suited to life in the trees, and it must have been their adaptation to such an environment which preserved the mobility and flexibility of the limbs and maintained their original structure with so little change.

Another important function of the grasping hand and foot is seen in

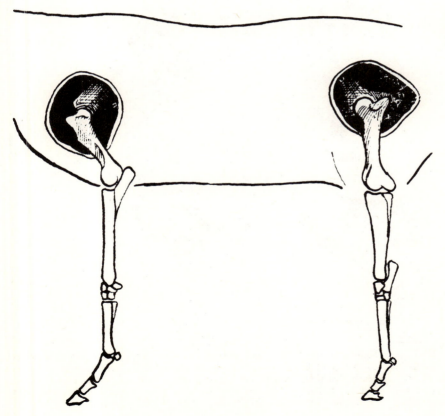

Diagrammatic drawing of stabilized supporting limbs.

the clinging of a monkey infant to its mother. All monkeys are born with a clinging reflex. The infant hangs onto its mother's fur. The mother must often be very active, moving about through the trees, with hands and feet occupied in locomotion and exploration. If the infant could not hang onto its mother, it would die. The grasping primate hand is therefore essential to survival in such species.

Another feature of the primate skeleton, useful in an arboreal habitat, is the clavicle or collar bone. This, again, is an early structure found in some amphibians but missing in many pronograde mammals. It serves as a strut to keep each forelimb at the side of the body.

Most primates, then, became adapted to life in the trees, and this adaptation enabled these mammals to maintain some features of the early amphibian-reptilian skeleton which have been lost by mammals which became adapted to other environments.[1] The teeth of primates are less specialized than those of most other mammals. Their jaws are generally

Comparison of primate power and precision grips.

Tree shrew

Tarsier

Macaque

Human

---

[1] The whales and porpoises, which returned to life in the water, lost their collar bones, pelvis, and hind limbs. The sirenians (manatee and dugong), who are also aquatic, similarly lost their hind limbs. The carnivores (cat and dog families, bears, and seals) have lost their collar bones, as have the ungulates, four-footed ground dwelling, usually herbivorous animals, including deer, cattle, and horses.

rather short, and they have short faces in contrast to the long-snouted terrestrial quadrupeds.

Life in the trees demands good eyesight, but a sharp sense of smell is not so important. For ground-dwelling nocturnal animals, on the other hand, a keen sense of smell may be more important than good vision. It is not surprising to find the sense of smell deficient in primates, especially among the higher ones, in contrast to most terrestrial pronograde animals. Many terrestrial animals have eyes set on either side of a snout, so that they do not have overlapping stereoscopic vision. But most of the primates, whose eyes are set close together on the frontal plane, do have this feature, which gives them a better conception of depth, so important for life in the trees. Moreover, the higher primates also have color vision.

An arboreal habitat is demanding. Leaping from branch to branch requires agility and good timing. The primates, therefore, are generally rather intelligent, high-strung creatures, and their brains are relatively large in proportion to body size. Most of the primates are quite small. Bulk is not suitable for life in the trees. Man seems to have acquired his large size after he adjusted to life on the ground. The gorilla, a large and heavy primate, also spends much of his time on the ground.

An arboreal habitat had many advantages for the primates:

An enormous proportion of the energy received from the sun is converted into trees, as distinct from herbs, and the primates were able to consume not only the foliage but also the fruit and seeds of the forest. Fruit and seeds have high food value, and arboreal animals obtained access to food resources of quite a different order of richness from those available to the grazing animals of the plains.[2]

Color vision helped the primates to identify fruits and seeds.

By taking to the trees, the primates were able to escape from the competition of terrestrial rodents, carnivores, and other rival species. The trees provided a refuge area rich in stimulating challenges for the inquisitive, exploratory primates.

Although most primates are pronograde, they are capable of sitting or standing in an upright position. When climbing, their bodies are vertical. Their forelimbs and hindlimbs have become differentiated, with the forelimbs being used for exploration and the lower limbs for support. Monkeys pick up objects with their hands and examine them. They also feed themselves with their hands, unlike long-snouted pronograde animals which have to close in on food with their large jaws. Primates have flatter faces than such animals.

Primates usually bear only one offspring at a time, and the females

---

[2] Bernard G. Campbell, *Human Evolution: An Introduction to Man's Adaptations* (Chicago: Aldine Publishing Co., 1966), p. 171.

Primates: (Top, from left) lemur;
marmosets, New World
monkeys; Gelada baboon, Old
World monkey; gibbon. (Bottom,
from left) orangutan;
chimpanzee; gorilla.

usually have only one pair of breasts, although there are some exceptions among the lower primates.

The order of Primates is subdivided into two suborders: the Prosimii and the Anthropoidea. The Prosimii include the lower primates such as the lemurs and the tarsier. The tree shrews, which are sometimes included in this group, represent a form transitional with the Insectivora.

The lower primates

Although it may be best to omit the tree shrews from consideration as primates, they deserve a brief description here. The tree shrews, or the *Tupaia,* are not really shrews and do not spend much of their time in trees. They are small, omnivorous animals with long, moist muzzles, found in India, Malaya, Indonesia, and the Philippines. They have claws, rather than nails, on their digits, which are not truly opposable. Another feature which characterizes tree shrews is the presence of a sort of second tongue, consisting of cartilage, underneath the main tongue. They are very active, inquisitive animals which make a great variety of noises. Tree shrews may give birth to litters of from two to five young at a time, although sometimes only one offspring is born. They may have two or three pairs of mammary glands. Related to the tree shrews is a similar species called the feathertail, found in Southeast Asia. Although primitive in appearance, the feathertail has prehensile hands and feet with apparently opposable thumbs and big toes, like those of higher primates. Since the *Tupaia* have eyes set on either side of the snout, they do not have the stereoscopic vision characteristic of most primates, whose eyes are both on the frontal plane.

Lemurs and lorisoids have relatively long snouts. The true lemurs are found only on the island of Madagascar, but the term *lemur* is also used to include such animals as bushbabies, lorises, galagos, pottos, and some other species. Lemurs have heavy coats of fur and bushy tails. Like the tree shrew, they may give birth to two or three offspring at a time and have an extra pair of breasts to accommodate them. They have a second cartilaginous tongue, like that of the *Tupaia,* which is used along with their lower front teeth as a comb in currying fur. While the tree shrews move about during the day, lemurs are generally nocturnal. Thus they do not come into competition with the diurnal monkeys who live in some of the same regions.

Some prosimians, like the dwarf lemur, have weakly developed mechanisms for the temperature regulation of the body and are so much affected by climatic conditions that they fall into states of suspended animation in seasons of cold weather, when they depend upon reserves of fat stored up in their tails.

The tarsier, which is found in Borneo, Sumatra, parts of Indonesia and the Philippines, is a more advanced creature than the other prosimians and has many features in common with the higher primates. The tarsier is very small in size. He has a large head and brain in proportion to his body, large ears, and very large eyes, which are set close together, so that he has stereoscopic vision. In that respect, the tarsier resembles the higher primates, but he does not have color vision, as they do. Nor does he need it, being nocturnal. Like the higher primates, the tarsier has eyes that are set in a bony socket, in contrast to the other prosimians, whose eyes are enclosed by a ring of bone lacking a back wall. The tarsier's feet are adapted for hopping and leaping, which he does with great speed. His legs are extremely long in proportion to his body. Insects form the tarsier's main diet, but he also eats tree frogs, snails, and other small animals.

The Primate suborder to which we belong is the Anthropoidea, which also includes the platyrrhine and catarrhine monkeys and the apes. Members of this suborder have eyes set in the frontal plane, so that they have stereoscopic vision. Both eyes can focus on the same object in front of the face, and since each eye sees it from a slightly different angle, there is a heightened sense of depth. Moreover, members of the Anthropoidea have color vision. In this respect, they differ from some of the lower primates. Stereoscopic and color vision used to be considered as traits which distinguished the Anthropoidea as a group from the prosimians, but it is now recognized that many prosimians have these features. John Buettner-Janusch has written. "The prosimians are usually listed as not possessing either color or stereoscopic vision. The latter is very obviously present in most of the diurnal genera, and the former probably is also. There is no conclusive evidence that color vision is not present."[3]

The higher primates

Color vision has been found in some fishes, insects, and birds but not in most mammals. The higher primates have the best-developed color vision in this class of vertebrates. Among the Anthropoidea, there is a back wall to the eye socket. Brains are larger and more highly developed than those of the Prosimii, with the occipital lobes overhanging the cerebellum. There is only one pair of breasts, set high up on the chest.

A traditional scheme of classification has been to divide the suborder Anthropoidea into two infraorders, the Platyrrhini, or New World monkeys, and the Catarrhini, comprising Old World monkeys, apes, and man. A more recent alternative way of classifying, following George G. Simpson and John Buettner-Janusch, is to divide the Anthropoidea into three superfamilies: Ceboidea (New World monkeys), Cercopithecoidea (Old World monkeys), and Hominoidea (apes and man). This system will be followed here.

The Ceboidea are the platyrrhine ("broad-nosed") monkeys of Central

---

[3] John Buettner-Janusch, *Origins of Man: Physical Anthropology* (New York: John Wiley & Sons, 1966), p. 330.

and South America, having nostrils separated by a broad nasal septum. Some of them, including the howler and spider monkeys, have prehensile tails. They can wrap the tail around a branch and hang from it. None of the Old World monkeys have developed this feature, which is found, however, among some other orders of mammals. Spider monkeys *brachiate,* or swing from limb to limb with their arms, a technique which was also developed by some of the apes in the Old World. The spider monkey has many resemblances to the gibbon, the expert brachiator of the Old World. These similarities are due to parallel evolution, another example of which is the appearance of stereoscopic and color vision in both the New World and Old World primates.

The New World primates have a different dental formula from that of the Old World monkeys, apes, and man. Among the latter, the characteristic dental formula is $I\frac{2}{2} C\frac{1}{1} P\frac{2}{2} M\frac{3}{3} \times 2 = 32.$

This means that in the jaws of either side, above and below, one will find two incisor teeth, one canine, two premolars, and three molars. Among lemurs and New World monkeys there are three premolars instead of two.

The Cercopithecoidea or Old World monkeys have a two-disk placenta in contrast to the apes and man (or woman), who have a single disk. A notable feature of the Old World monkeys is the presence of *ischial callosities*—bare patches of calloused skin on the buttocks. These are thought to provide some protection for the monkeys when they spend the night sleeping in a sitting position in the fork of a tree. Old World monkeys may also have a sexual skin which sometimes becomes brilliantly colored. Some of these monkeys, like the baboons, have cheek pouches which can be stuffed with food, to be subsequently digested.

The Old World monkeys are divided into two subfamilies having different types of digestive systems: the Colobinae (langurs and colobus monkeys), who eat huge quantities of leaves and little else and who can go for months without drinking water, and the Cercopithecinae, including all other Old World monkeys, such as baboons, macaques, and rhesus monkeys, which have a more varied diet. Since they are leaf eaters, the langur and colobus monkeys are more strictly arboreal than the baboons and macaques, who spend much of their time on the ground.

There are interesting differences in temperament between langurs, rhesus monkeys, and baboons. Phyllis Jay, an anthropologist who has made field studies of langurs in India, has described langur groups as peaceful and relaxed. There is little fighting among them, and dominance hierarchies are not as noticeable as among baboons. Rhesus monkeys engage in more fighting and squabbling and bear more scars than do langurs. Dominance-submission is more fully developed among baboons, but, despite the aggressive character of male baboons, there is relatively little ingroup aggression. Their aggressive character, together with the males' long, sharp canines, serves to defend the group from the attacks of predators. The more arboreal langurs save themselves by individual escape to the tree tops.

In contrast to the leaf-eating langurs, ground-dwelling baboons have a varied diet consisting of many kinds of vegetable foods, seeds, flowers, grasses, leaves, roots and bulbs; but they also eat insects, scorpions, and lizards. Baboons that live along the seacoast consume mussels, crabs, and limpets. Inland baboons in Kenya have been known to sometimes catch and eat hares, birds, small gazelles, and vervet monkeys. Such carnivorous behavior is rare, however. It is always an individual activity, not a group enterprise, and it seems to be more common in some baboon groups than in others. Predation of this sort appears to be more common in the rainy season, when many animal species drop their young.

Most monkeys, both Old and New World, have an essentially pronograde manner of locomotion, making their ways along the tops of branches. They have long, narrow trunks like those of dogs and cats.

There are about 150 species of monkeys in the world, as compared with only one species of man. And monkeys are very numerous, outnumbering human beings in many parts of the world. Some monkeys, such as vervets, have a population density which man came to equal only after he had acquired a knowledge of agriculture. The apes, who are more closely related to us, have not been so successful, and their numbers are dwindling.

The great variation among monkey species is best explained by their adaptations to different environments. Arboreal monkeys tend to be divided into more species than terrestrial ones. Ground-dwelling baboons and macaques show less variation. These monkeys are found in large numbers over enormous tracts of territory in Africa and Asia.

The Hominoidea

The superfamily within the Anthropoidea to which we belong is that of the Hominoidea. Its other members are the apes, who differ from the monkeys in lacking external tails and cheek pouches. They usually do not have ischial callosities, although gibbons have them, and they are sometimes found in orangutans, chimpanzees, and gorillas. The last three apes all build nests to sleep in at night, and there may be a connection between this pattern of behavior and the disappearance of the horny seat pads. The apes all have long arms and relatively short legs. Their arms have more mobility than those of the more pronograde monkeys. The apes are not exactly pronograde, nor do they have erect posture, as we do, except for brief periods. When they stand supported by arms and legs, the spine is not parallel to the ground, as in pronograde animals, since their arms are longer than their legs. This gives them a semierect posture. The pelvis of apes is broader and more basin shaped than those of monkeys and more like that of man.

The apes are divided into two subfamilies: the Hylobatinae, which includes the gibbons, concolors, and siamangs; and the Ponginae, which includes the orangutan, the chimpanzee, and the gorilla.

The gibbons range from the eastern Himalayas to Hainan, Borneo, and Java. They are the smallest, lightest, and most acrobatic of the apes, with very long arms adapted to brachiation. The Hylobatinae all have long narrow hands and fingers, to hook onto branches; and their thumbs are rather stunted (and not truly opposable), so that they do not get in the way. Gibbons have relatively longer legs than the other apes and can walk and run with agility on the ground, while holding up their long arms for balance. Gibbons are very vocal and make a lot of noise. In this respect and in their walking ability, the gibbons seem quite human, but in other ways they are less like man than the other apes. What has been said about the gibbons applies as well to the concolors and siamangs. All have heavy coats of fur, unlike the coarse hair of the other apes. Gibbons live in small monogamous family groups consisting of a male, female, and offspring. The monogamous nature of the gibbon family is perpetuated by the aggressive behavior of the male when another male approaches the group, or by that of the female when another female approaches it. Moreover, as offspring mature, they leave the family unit.

The orangutan is also a Southeast Asiatic ape, now found only in Borneo and Sumatra. He weighs as much as a man but is only about 4 feet tall. (Males are twice as big as females). The orang's arms are very long and his legs short. He has a barrel chest and a large abdomen. With a body build like this, it is not surprising that orangutans are rather sluggish, slow-moving creatures, lacking the grace and elan of the gibbons. The orangutan has a rather high, domed forehead with less of a brow ridge than any other ape. Adult males have cheek pads, not found in other apes, and they have air sacs in the throat which are more prominent than those of the other Ponginae. Orangutans hang by their feet a good deal. They lack a ligament, found in other Hominoidea, which holds the thighbone in its hip socket. This gives the leg more mobility. Orangutans are not built to walk with an upright posture. Not much is known about their social life. They are rarely met in groups of over three or four, and sometimes lone males are encountered in the jungle. As among the gibbons, then, the social units seem to be small. In this respect, the Asiatic apes contrast with those of Africa.

More humanlike than the Southeast Asiatic apes are the African apes, the chimpanzee and the gorilla. Both spend a good deal of time on the ground, especially the gorilla, and both can walk erect for short distances.

In contrast to the quiet, sluggish orangutan, chimpanzees are noisy, sociable, and boisterous. Psychologists have worked more with chimps

Chimpanzee. Notice that chimpanzees have large, out-standing ears. The other apes have smaller ears, with rolled helixes, set close to the head. The helix is the curled-over outer margin of the ear. The chimpanzee ear is curled only at the top; the outer sides are flat.

than with the other apes, not because the chimps are more intelligent (which remains to be determined), but because they can be friendly and cooperative. Chimpanzees have been taught to do a variety of things—riding bicycles, opening beer cans, getting water from the tap or food from the refrigerator. Some have learned to work for rewards, earning slugs which must be taken to a slot machine and inserted to get raisins. Some can use keys to open locks. At least one chimp has been taught to hammer nails and to use a screwdriver both to insert and extract screws.

This ability with tools has its foreshadowings in the wild state. Jane van Lawick-Goodall, who studied free-ranging chimpanzees in Tanzania, East Africa, over a period of four years, has observed chimpanzees poking sticks into ant and termite nests. When they pull them out, the sticks are covered with termites, which the chimps lick off and eat. The stick has to be the right length and shape. It if is too long, the chimpanzee breaks off part of it. If there are leaves on the stick, he strips them off. One chimp was seen to carry a stick for half a mile to where some termite nests were located. Chimpanzees also use leaves as a sponge to soak up water for drinking and show their young how to do it. Gorillas have not been seen to use tools in this way. Nor is there any evidence that gorillas eat meat in the wild state. Chimpanzees, however, sometimes eat meat, although fruit constitutes their main diet. They have been known to eat colobus monkey and bush pig. Jane van Lawick-Goodall once saw a chimpanzee attack, kill, and eat a colobus monkey; other chimpanzees joined him in eating the carcass. It is curious that when an adult male has possession of such a chunk of meat, other chimpanzees may sit around holding out their hands as if begging for a handout. Adriaan Kortlandt, who studied chimpanzees in the Congo, has noted this begging behavior among young chimpanzees who want to get food from their mothers. Meat eating and the use of tools have not been reported for forest-dwelling chimpanzees whose behavior has also been closely observed. The apes studied by Jane van Lawick-Goodall live in a rather atypical, relatively open country. Tool use and hunting may, therefore, represent adaptations to particular ecological conditions. Incidentally, Kortlandt states that when chimpanzees use sticks as weapons, they stand erect. These considerations are of interest in relation to man's own evolutionary development.

The social life of chimpanzees is complex and variable. The composition of groups frequently changes. Some bands consist of mothers and young; some have adults of both sexes, with some adolescents; and others consist of adult males only. Such groups may merge, split, or regroup. Adult males seem to do more traveling than the mothers with offspring, whose ranges are more restricted. Chimpanzee mothers seem to be extremely solicitous of their young. According to Kortlandt they carry them around for the first four years of life. The young do not learn to be independent, although they show great curiosity about the environment. Indeed, Kortlandt considered them to be retarded in comparison to chimpanzees raised in captivity. Chimpanzees seem to respect the aged as well as showing solicitude for the young. Kortlandt describes an old chimp whom he judged to be over 40. Despite his infirmities, he was deferred to by stronger and healthier chimpanzees. Chimpanzees that inhabit the forest sometimes make a great deal of noise, hooting, screaming, and drumming on trees. This hullabaloo does not seem to function as a spacing mechanism, like the calls of howler monkeys. Instead, it may be a means of summoning other chimpanzees to an area where there are ripe fruit trees.

The gorillas are the largest and strongest of the apes. In the wild state, adult males weigh between 300 and 450 pounds, while adult females weigh between 150 and 250 pounds. They weigh much more in zoos, where they have nothing to do but sit around and eat, and therefore sometimes attain weights of 500 or 600 pounds. Gorillas have powerful long arms and barrel chests which they beat with their hands to frighten intruders. Their hands and feet are quite humanlike, although the fingers and toes are webbed nearly to the first joint. The foot has something of a heel bone. Another humanlike feature is the presence of mastoid processes at the base of the skull. The adult male gorilla has massive brow ridges and crests on the top and sides of his skull; these sagittal crests serve to anchor his heavy chewing muscles. Gorillas have large interlocking canine teeth. They live on vegetable food and eat from six to eight hours a day. Although gorillas do not eat meat in the wild, they have sometimes become accustomed to eating it in captivity. According to George Schaller, who made a two-year study of mountain gorillas in eastern Congo and western Uganda, gorillas are normally quiet and make few vocalizations, in contrast to the noisy gibbons and chimpanzees. In temperament these large apes are described as being calm, independent, and aloof. Their social groups are more compact and consistent in composition than those of the chimpanzees. A dominant male usually determines the movements of the group, leading the way. Little grooming takes place among gorillas, in contrast with the situation among monkeys such as the baboons, who spend much time in grooming one another.

In this chapter, we have reviewed the general traits of primates and the subdivisions of this mammalian order, ranging from the prosimians to the apes and man. In the following chapter, we shall consider some aspects of the social behavior of primates.

Suggestions for further reading

One well-illustrated general discussion of the primates is *The Primates* by Sarel Eimerl and Irven De Vore (New York: Life Nature Library, 1965). Another is Ivan T. Sanderson, *The Monkey Kingdom* (New York: Doubleday & Co., 1957). The following are also suggested: Cathy Hayes, *The Ape in Our House* (New York: Harper & Row, Publishers, 1951); S. L. Washburn (ed.), *Social Life of Early Man* (Viking Fund Publications in Anthropology, No. 31 [New York: Wenner-Gren Foundation, 1961]); George Schaller, *The Mountain Gorilla: Ecology and Behavior* (Chicago: University of Chicago Press, 1963); Adriaan Kortlandt, "Chimpanzees in the Wild," *Scientific American,* Vol. 206 (1962), pp. 128–138; Charles H. Southwick (ed.), *Primate Social Behavior: An Enduring Problem. Selected Readings* (Princeton, N.J.: D. Van Nostrand, 1963). For Jane Goodall's data on chimpanzee tool using in the wild, see Jane Goodall, "Chimpanzees of the Gombe Stream Reserve," in Irven De Vore, (ed.), *Primate Behavior: Field Studies of Monkeys and Apes* (New York: Holt, Rinehart, & Winston, 1965), pp. 425–73.

Chapter 6

The social life of primates

It is important to note that, with the exception of some prosimian species, the primates are social animals that live in groups the year round. This is not true of all animals. Among the lower vertebrates, which lay eggs, there may be no continuing tie between mother and offspring. This is not the case among birds, which nest and feed their young, but reptiles, after laying their eggs, usually go off and forget about them. The baby reptile that survives steps out of his shell into a world which has no family structure. A baby primate, however, whether he be a lemur, a baboon, or a human being, is born into a social world.

Mother-child relations

It must be kept in mind that primates are mammals. The mammalian pattern of suckling provides for a continuing tie between mother and offspring. While this is true of all mammals, the mother-child relationship is stronger and longer lasting among primates than it is among most of the others. This is because the complex nervous system and brain development of primates requires a longer time to become coordinated. Although the gestation period is longer among more advanced mammals, the young are born in a relatively helpless condition, which increases their dependence upon the mother. There is a great contrast in this respect between primates and ungulates. On the day of birth, a baby deer or antelope can walk about; within a week it can run with great speed. It thus becomes self-sufficient much more quickly than a baby primate. Rodents and carnivores are more helpless at birth than ungulates, but rats and rabbits reach maturity at five or six months and can shift for themselves after a month or so. Baby primates, on the other hand, cling to the mother's body for the first weeks or months of life. Gibbon babies do so for about seven months.

Siamang group.

The interaction between mother and child is not only determined by the helplessness of the child, but also, apparently, by the maternal attitude of the mother. The following is a description of behavior among the langur monkeys of India, which may be more maternal than most:

From the day of birth the infant langur is the center of attention and the source of great interest to almost all the adult and subadult females and the langur female juveniles of the troop. . . . Almost immediately other adult females approach and gather around the mother in an attempt to gain access to the newborn. The mother may be surrounded by from four to five adults and subadults who all want to hold and inspect it. The adult females frequently put their faces to the newborn, smelling, licking, and just nudging gently. . . . When an adult female takes the newborn and moves away from the mother, this female in turn is surrounded by a group of adult and subadult females. When the newborn starts to whine another adult female reaches out and takes the young one. In this manner it may pass from female to female, until as many as four females have held it, before the real mother comes and takes it back. During the time the infant is being carried and inspected the mother keeps constant and close watch on it, although she may remain at a distance of from thirty to forty feet. Should the newborn whine loudly, the mother will quickly retrieve it.[1]

Primate females are not always so "maternal" in their behavior. There are differences in maternal behavior in different species. Howler monkey mothers are said to be relatively indifferent to their offspring. Baboon and macaque mothers will not allow other females to take their offspring away from them during the first month after birth, as the langurs do. Chimpanzee mothers seem to be guilty of maternal overprotection, carrying their children about until they are around four years old and seldom leaving them out of sight.

Male-female relations

Primate social groups contain adult males that remain with the females and offspring the year round. Again, this is not true of all mammals. Among many mammals, the males remain with the females only during a rutting or mating season. Among most of the higher primates, there is no special mating season; females are sexually receptive throughout the year, and pregnancies may occur at any time. But some monkeys do have restricted mating seasons. Among some Japanese macaques, for example, mating is limited to the winter months, particularly January and February, and over 90 percent of the births occur from May to September. Rhesus monkeys isolated on the Caribbean island of Cayo Santiago do not copulate from February to June. During this period, the males undergo testis regression and a cessation of spermatogenesis.

Among monkey groups which have special breeding seasons, the males continue to remain with the females throughout the year. It cannot be sexual attraction which keeps the primate males together with the females in this way. Another function of the continuing social bond is the protection afforded by the social group. There is safety in numbers. Monkeys that stay within a group are more likely to survive. Loners may be picked off by predators. Thus natural selection must have favored a genetic capacity for group life.

Adult male-young relations

Adult males in most primate groups are either tolerant or helpful in their attitudes toward the young. In many species, especially the more terrestrial ones, protective behavior has been reported, and there have been many observations of adult males rescuing or carrying away young

[1] Phyllis Jay, "The Indian Langur Monkey (*Presbytis entellus*)" in Charles H. Southwick (ed.), *Primate Social Behavior: An Enduring Problem. Selected Readings* (Princeton, N.J.: D. Van Nostrand, 1963), pp. 117–18. Copyright © by Litton Educational Publishing, Inc.

animals from danger. Adult male baboons sometimes seem to supervise juvenile play groups and to intervene if the fighting gets too rough. The arboreal langurs are somewhat different in these respects; the males are more aloof and disinterested in the young. Their protective function is not so vital as it is for the ground-dwelling baboons.

Among the Japanese macaques and similar monkeys, whose offspring tend to be born within a particular season of the year, there are "age sets"; that is to say there will be many infants of the same age. As they become older, the juveniles form play groups, chase each other, wrestle, and engage in vigorous play. This is also done among primates that have no breeding seasons. Some juveniles of similar age range are generally available to form play groups of this sort. As the young primate gradually lessens its dependence upon the mother, it spends more and more time with its peers. This shift may be accelerated by the weaning process and maternal rebuffs, particularly after the birth of a younger sibling. But the shift to the play group seems to be a natural transition. Through active play with others, the juvenile not only acquires physical skills but learns to interact with others. In groups where dominant-submissive relations are important, the relative status of individuals may be worked out in the course of rough-and-tumble play.

Young peer relations

We find, then, that most primates live in social groups containing males, females, and offspring. The size and composition of such groups, however, vary a great deal. Gibbons have small monogamous families consisting of one male, one female, and from one to four offspring. Gorilla groups vary from 2 to 30 members, with an average of from 6 to 17. Baboon troops commonly number between 30 and 50 individuals, with 5 to 10 adult males and 10 to 20 adult females. Nocturnal species, for example those of lemurs, tend to have small family groups, while those which are active during the day have larger ones. Terrestrial primates, such as baboons, seem to have larger troops than arboreal species.

Variations in composition of primate social groups

The sex ratio varies in different species. In howler groups there are more than twice as many females as males. A predominance of females is quite common among primates, as is the case among humans, partly because the death rate is generally higher for males. The disparity is more striking in the older age brackets. There are other factors that help to account for the higher incidence of females in such species as the howler monkeys, macaques, and baboons. In these groups the males have a much slower rate of maturation, and some males may live for a while outside the social group. Among Indian macaques, which have a large proportion of females, some males are expelled from the group and form "bachelor" bands on the fringes of the heterosexual group. Such bands include both adolescent young monkeys and old males who have lost their dominant

Order of march in
baboons.

status. Spider monkeys in South America also have small "bachelor" bands, numbering from 3 to 10 individuals. Thus there is considerable variety in the size and composition of primate social units.

Dominance-submission

Different species of primates also vary with regard to the degree of dominance and submission manifest within the group. Something like the pecking order of birds is found in many animal species. Dominant animals are those which display more aggression, win most of the fights, appropriate most of the food if there is a limited amount, and have priority in sexual relations. Where dominant-submissive polarities are found among primates, males are generally dominant over females, and some males are dominant over others.

The dominance of males over females is associated with sexual dimorphism, or the appearance of striking differences in size and strength between males and females. Sexual dimorphism is more marked among terrestrial primates like baboons and gorillas than among arboreal ones like the gibbon. In general, dominant-submissive patterns seem to be associated with terrestrial activity and the defensive functions of the males who, as among baboons and macaques, have developed an aggressive sort of temperament, which helps them to face predators in defense of the group.

The existence of dominant-submissive patterns does not mean that a lot of fighting is always going on among the adult males. On the contrary, fighting tends to be inhibited in such groups, since everyone's position in the hierarchy is relatively fixed and recognized. A threatened individual in a baboon troup may run toward a dominant male for help, as a frightened baboon infant runs to its mother. Dominant male baboons will not let others fight and may dash to the scene of a quarrel to prevent it. There is not much fighting over food resources among baboons in the wild, since the troop is usually spread out over a fairly wide area, with each individual seeking his own food.

Among monkey troops that move about, foraging as they go, there may be some structure to the group. At least this is the case among baboons and Japanese macaques. Dominant males and mothers and infants are usually found in the center of the band and young males on the peripheries. Dominance-submission patterns may therefore contribute to order and stability in the group.

Territoriality

In all classes of vertebrates there are species characterized by territoriality: that is, the pattern of defending a particular range of territory, principally against other members of the same species. This concern may be confined to a particular period, especially the breeding season, or it may be a more permanent preoccupation. Generally, small animals have small territories and large animals have big ones, although carnivorous animals tend to have larger territories than herbivores. A kind of territoriality has been found among many, but not all, primate species. Among some prosimians, urination and defecation help to demarcate the territory, providing boundary stakes, so to speak. Among some of the higher primates, such as the howler monkey and the gibbon, vocalization helps to indicate which group belongs in which part of a forest. Gibbons and howlers both make a lot of noise. Aggressive gestures and cries greet invaders of the territory, who usually retreat.

Terrestrial primates are apt to wander over a wider range of territory than arboreal ones. Baboons, for example, move about 3 miles a day. Baboons seem to stay within a particular range of land, but they do not fight other baboon groups to defend their territory. Similarly, gorillas do not try to defend particular areas. The importance of territoriality therefore seems to differ for different primate species.

Significance of the social matrix

We tend to think of monkey behavior as being largely instinctual. But it is important to realize that monkeys behave differently in different situational contexts. Indian rhesus monkeys that live in temple compounds display more aggression than those who live in the forest. Baboons studied in the London zoo showed more aggression than those observed in the wild state. When C. R. Carpenter transported more than 100 rhesus mothers and infants from India to Puerto Rico, he found that the mothers, cramped in small cages and sparingly fed, fought their own offspring away from the food, and about nine mothers killed their infants. This sort of behavior would not be apt to occur under normal conditions.

What is still more striking is that a rhesus monkey that has been brought up in caged isolation from birth and later, after about a year and a half, introduced to the company of other members of its species, does not know how to interact with them. Mature male rhesus monkeys that have been socially deprived in this way cannot even perform the sexual act. Mature female rhesus monkeys that have been raised in isolation from birth and later impregnated by normal males do not behave in a maternal manner toward their offspring. Indeed, they are quite indifferent toward them, reject them, and often treat them with unfeeling cruelty.

These experiments suggest the enormous importance of adequate maternal care for the normal development of primates. Other such experiments, performed by Harry Harlow and his colleagues at the University of Wisconsin, suggest the equally great importance of peer relations. Infant monkeys which have been deprived of their mothers but allowed to play with other young members of their species for 20 minutes a day seem to develop normally with regard to social and sexual interaction. These experiments show that sexual behavior, which we might have assumed to be instinctive among monkeys, depends upon the development of adequate patterns of social interaction with other members of the species. In the normal course of events, these patterns are learned in play groups. Primates normally live in a social world from birth until death. We cannot understand primate behavior without reference to its social matrix.

Suggestions for further reading

For the social life of primates, see Irven DeVore (ed.), *Primate Behavior: Field Studies of Monkeys and Apes* (New York: Holt, Rinehart & Winston, 1965), and C. R. Carpenter, *Naturalistic Behavior of Nonhuman Primates* (University Park, Pa.: Pennsylvania State University Press, 1964). For Harlow's experiments in social deprivation, see Harry F. Harlow, "The Heterosexual Affectional System in Monkeys," *American Psychologist*, Vol. 17 (1962), pp. 1–9, and Harry F. Harlow and Margaret K. Harlow, "Social Deprivation in Monkeys," *Scientific American*, Vol. 207 (1962), pp. 137–46.

See also Charles H. Southwick (ed.), *Primate Social Behavior: An Enduring Problem. Selected Readings* (Princeton, N.J.: D. Van Nostrand Co., 1963) and Desmond Morris (ed.), *Primate Ethology* (Chicago: Aldine Publishing Co., 1967).

Chapter 7

Evolution of the primates: prosimians to hominids

In the last two chapters, we reviewed the subdivisions of the primate order and the characteristics of primates of today. The present chapter concerns the evolution of the primates. Before tracing this evolution, let us first consider how physical anthropologists go about reconstructing it. We have no time machine and cannot watch evolution unrolling before our eyes; its sequences must be inferred.

This chapter will contain many references to fossil primates which are represented only by teeth and jaw fragments. Teeth, which are so subject to decay in the living human mouth, tenaciously outlast all other parts of the body after death and compared to other body parts are relatively well preserved in the fossil record. For the earlier primates, particularly, teeth are about all the physical anthropologist has to work with. It is fortunate for him if he knows the geological stratum in which these teeth were found and the climatic and environmental conditions it suggests.

Methods of interpreting fossil evidence

The teeth give some indication of the size of the animal, and they may suggest the type of diet to which it was accustomed. Physical anthropologists study living primates as well as fossil forms. A knowledge of the anatomy and physiology of different apes and monkeys helps the physical anthropologist to interpret the skeletal material of extinct species. Where there is much similarity between a living form and a fossil find, some relationship may be inferred.

If limb bones and parts of the vertebral column are present, the animal's form of locomotion may be deduced, whether it went on all fours or with upright posture, or whether it was used to swinging from branch to branch through the trees by brachiation. Some inferences may also be made about the animal's musculature:

We can make deductions about the size and form of the nerves and muscles with which they formed a single functional unit. Muscles leave marks where they are attached to bones, and from such marks we can assess the form and size of the muscles. At the same time, such parts of the skeleton as the cranium give us considerable evidence of the size and form of the brain and spinal cord.[1]

Some further criteria for interpreting the fossil evidence will be given in the pages that follow.

Early prosimians

The earliest primates that we know anything about were small prosimians resembling modern tree shrews or lemurs, dating back to the Paleocene epoch, about 60 million years ago. Lemurs and tarsiers of various kinds had become abundant by the Eocene epoch, about 57 million years ago, when they spread across North America and parts of Eurasia. Then their numbers declined. They continued to exist in parts of the Old World, but by the end of the Eocene they appear to have become extinct in Europe and North America, where their once abundant fossil record comes to an end. This debacle may have been due to the development of competing mammals such as rodents and carnivores, and in the Old World the appearance of higher primates that had evolved from prosimian forms. Increasingly colder weather conditions may also have played a role. Whatever the reasons, the range of prosimians contracted. Although more than 20 different fossil types of Eocene tarsioids have been identified, there is now only one living genus, *Tarsius,* with three living species. Lemurs are now found mainly in Africa and Madagascar but also in Indonesia and the Philippines. This contraction, however, is not the whole story, for the prosimians gave rise to some creatures which ultimately became more successful than themselves.

In the New World, the platyrrhine monkeys evolved from a prosimian base, and in the Old World some prosimian, perhaps tarsioid, ancestors gave rise to the Old World monkeys, apes, and man.

Fossil Hominoidea

The apes of the present day are less humanlike than some of their ancestors, and we are less apelike than ours. Apes and men have adapted to different environments and have evolved in different directions. The ancestral apes had more humanlike limb proportions, lighter brow ridges, and less pronounced canine teeth than their descendants. Like man's

---

[1] Bernard G. Campbell, *Human Evolution: An Introduction to Man's Adaptations* (Chicago: Aldine Publishing Company, 1966), p. 2.

assumption of upright posture, the long arms of the apes may represent a relatively recent development in primate evolution.

The best candidates for the earliest fossil ape discoveries found so far come from Oligocene deposits in the Fayum, Egypt, dating from about 30 million years ago. In those days the Mediterranean reached about 100 miles inland to this area, which was then a border region between sea and jungle. More than 100 specimens of primate finds have been recovered in the Fayum, including the remains of *Oligopithecus*, a foot-high creature on or near the ancestral line of the Old World monkeys. *Oligopithecus* is the oldest known primate having 32 teeth of the catarrhine type. Another find, *Parapithecus*, has an uncertain dental formula; some authorities classify it under the Hominoidea, although William Howells has written that "It is quite likely that he was not a primate at all."[2] Also found in the Fayum were the jaw and tooth remains of *Propliopithecus*, a possible early ape, or perhaps a generalized form in the line of evolution leading to the present-day apes and man. *Propliopithecus* was formerly thought to be a gibbonlike type, perhaps ancestral to the modern gibbon. More definitely gibbonlike is a later fossil, *Pliopithecus*, dating from the Miocene epoch. Remains of this type have been found in both Europe and Africa; it differed from the gibbon of the present day in having arms and legs of nearly equal length, while today's gibbon has much longer arms. *Pithecus*, which appears in most of the foregoing names, means ape.

Many hominoid fossils have been recovered from deposits of the Miocene epoch dating from about 15 million years ago. Various kinds of Miocene apes, generally classified as *Dryopithecus* ("forest ape") have been found in Europe, Africa, the U.S.S.R., India, and China. They are represented mainly by fossilized jaws and teeth, so that it is not possible to get a complete picture of them. The lower molar teeth have what has been called the Y–5 or Dryopithecus pattern, a pattern found also in man, but not among Old World monkeys. The crowns of monkey molars have a cusp at each corner, while the crowns of chimpanzee, gorilla, and human lower molars usually have five cusps. In between the cusps there is a groove which looks like the letter Y. This tooth pattern is found only in the lower molars of chimpanzees, gorillas, and man and some of their precursors.

More complete than the remains of other early hominoid fossils are those of "Proconsul," dating from the early Miocene in East Africa. Here we have not only jaws and teeth but also skull and limb bones. At least three species have been identified, one of which is as small as a gibbon, another as large as a gorilla. Proconsul did not have heavy brow ridges like those of present-day apes, nor did his lower jaw have the simian

---

[2] William Howells, *Mankind in the Making: The Story of Human Evolution* (New York: Doubleday & Co., 1959), p. 103.

shelf, a bar of bone which in modern apes helps to tie the right and left sides of the jaw together. His molars had the Y–5 pattern. His canines were large. Proconsul's arms and legs were rather humanlike in appearance. Indeed, some authorities think that Proconsul may have been in our line of descent. He is not, however, classified as hominid. It must be explained that *hominid* and *hominoid* are different terms. The latter is the broader classification, referring to the superfamily Hominoidea, which includes both the apes and man. The former term refers to the family Hominidae, which includes human beings and their precursors of the Pliocene and Pleistocene epochs.

Early hominids   From some widely separated Miocene or early Pliocene sites in northwest India and East Africa come the fossil remains of jaws and teeth which seem to represent a stage between ape and human. *Ramapithecus* in India and *Kenyapithecus* in Africa both had a parabolic or rather V–shaped jaw like that of man, instead of the narrow U–shaped jaw characteristic of modern apes. Both had small incisor teeth, a *canine fossa*,[3] and a foreshortened face. For these reasons some authorities have classified these teeth as hominid, meaning that they are more human than apelike. There is more than one species of *Kenyapithecus;* there are *Kenyapithecus wickeri,* dated by potassium-argon (see page 169) at about 14 million years ago, and *Kenyapithecus africanus* dated by the same method at about 19 million years ago. *Ramapithecus* is judged to be about 10 million years old.

   The distribution of these finds suggests that toward the end of the Miocene and beginning of the Pliocene epoch a humanlike population of hominoids was found distributed between East Africa and northwestern India. This is not at all unlikely in view of the still wider distribution of *Dryopithecus* fossil finds. The formation of the Red Sea barrier was a fairly recent development, before which many animal populations must have crossed back and forth through this region. Macaque monkeys, which have an enormous range today from northwest India to Indonesia, Borneo, and Japan, and which are also found in northwestern Africa, had an even wider range during the Pleistocene epoch. Many species of mammals were formerly common to both East Africa and India. So it would not be improbable if humanlike creatures ranged between Africa and India in Miocene and Pliocene times. Indeed, their distribution may have been wider still, since similar teeth, dating from the same period, have also been reported from China.

   It has been speculated that maybe these humanlike creatures had upright posture and the use of tools. There is not much evidence to go on here, since *Ramapithecus* and *Kenyapithecus* are represented only by

---

[3] A hollow in the cheekbones on either side of the nose, found in modern man, although missing in some early fossil hominid skulls.

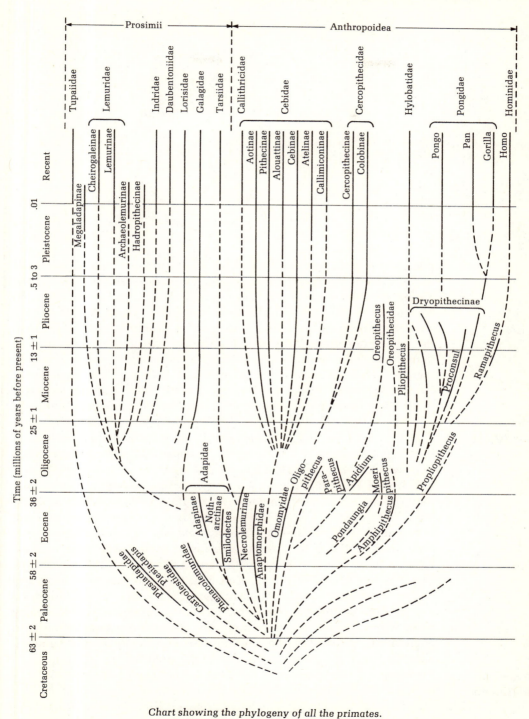

Chart showing the phylogeny of all the primates.

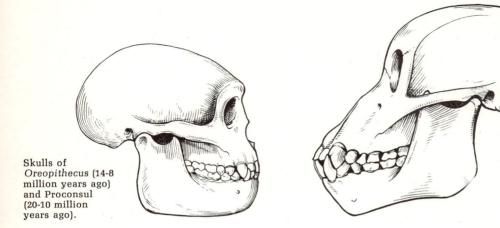

Skulls of
Oreopithecus (14-8
million years ago)
and Proconsul
(20-10 million
years ago).

jaw and tooth remains. The basis for the speculation is the smallness of the canines, which are prominent and sharp in most primates. In the ground-dwelling baboons, the long, sharp canine teeth form an essential weapon of defense and attack. The reduction of the canine teeth may have been made possible by the use of tools or weapons, both for defense and the preparation of food. A similar reduction in size of the canines is later found among the australopithecines, who had upright posture and who seem to have used tools. The argument, then, is that perhaps *Ramapithecus* and *Kenyapithecus* also had upright posture and the use of tools. This is admittedly very speculative and is only mentioned as a possibility.

Oreopithecus   *Oreopithecus bambolii* is another early primate which some authorities have classified as hominid, although most have not. *Oreopithecus* dates from late Miocene or early Pliocene times, about 13 million years ago. Remains of this fossil form, including a complete skeleton, have been found in some coal mines in north central Italy. *Oreopithecus* was about 4 feet tall and weighed about 80 pounds. He had a rather flat face, small canine teeth, and no diastema. (A *diastema* is a gap in the upper-tooth series for reception of the lower canine, found in present-day apes. A similar gap appears in the lower-tooth series.) There was no simian shelf. These are all hominid features. However, the brain case was small and the brow ridges heavy. *Oreopithecus* seems to have brachiated; he did not have upright posture. Moreover, the teeth of *Oreopithecus* differ in many ways from those of man. For these and other reasons some authorities, including Le Gros Clark, declare that *Oreopithecus* was not a hominid. He is generally classified as a member of the Hominoidea.

The Pliocene   While Africa has yielded fossil anthropoids from Miocene and Pleistocene times, we do not have such fossil remains from the intervening Pliocene epoch, which lasted for about 11 million years. No doubt some finds will be made before long. It is understandable, however, that the fossil record should be meager, because the Pliocene epoch in Africa was one of great dryness. Streams dried up and forests contracted.

Perhaps, as the *Kenyapithecus* and *Ramapithecus* finds suggest, man's ancestors had already taken to upright posture by this time. At any rate, they had done so by the beginning of the Pleistocene, when upright ground-dwelling hominids were living in East and South Africa. The fact that the hip bones of the latter were already similar to modern hip bones suggests hundreds of thousands of years of prior adaptation to erect posture or bipedal locomotion. The australopithecines, as these hominids were called, are the subject of our next chapter. Before turning to a discussion of the australopithecines, however, let us first consider the question of what it means to be a hominid.

Man's distinctive traits

Will Cuppy once wrote a book called *How to Tell Your Friends from the Apes.* This is easier to do nowadays than it was in Miocene times, when the ancestors of modern apes and men resembled one another more than pongids and hominids do now. (The pongids include gorillas, chimpanzees, orangutans, and gibbons.) Although they are now classified as hominids, the australopithecines were first considered to be apes, and the first specimen found was given the name of *Australopithecus africanus,* or South African ape. Since specialists have difficulties of classification, even when complete skeletons are available, as in the case of *Oreopithecus,* it is evident that hominids and pongids are closely related.

It must be understood that "hominid," "human being," and "*Homo sapiens*" are not interchangeable terms. The human beings of the present day are all of one species, *Homo sapiens.* We are the only living hominids. But there were formerly other types of hominid in existence, like the australopithecines, which although not human beings, had more in common with us than with the apes.

How do we, after all, differ from the apes and other primates? In answering this question, let us confine ourselves, for the moment, to man and apes of the present day.

Man's most important distinguishing features are his upright posture, his highly developed nervous system, and his large brain. Man's brain is more than twice as large as that of the gorilla, who has the next largest brain among the primates. Compared with the brains of most primates, which are of small size, man's brain is enormous. But this is a relatively recent development in man's evolution, preceded by his assumption of upright posture. We know this because the brains of the australopithecines, who had bipedal locomotion, were little larger than those of apes.

Several of the distinctions between man and other primates have to do with the assumption of upright posture. For example, in the lumbar region in man, there is a forward curvature of the spine which is not

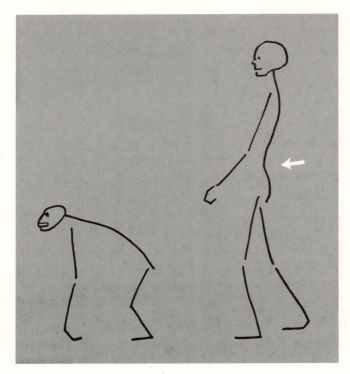

A schematic picture showing (left) the curve of the spine in an ape and (right) the curvature of the human spine, with an arrow pointing to the lumbar curve.

found among other primates. Man has an S–shaped spinal column adapted to upright posture, while other primates have a more bow-shaped spine. Man's pelvis has *ilia* (blades) which are much shorter than those of the larger apes, and they have been bent backwards in the course of time. The pelvis is broad and basin shaped, particularly in females. The *gluteus maximus* muscles of the hip are well developed. Like apes, but unlike the monkeys, we lack external tails, and we have no ischial callosities. In contrast to the ape, man's straight and heavily muscled legs are much longer than his arms. He is a walker, not a brachiator.

Man's feet show a number of specializations resulting from their functions of support and bipedal locomotion. The food is arched from front to back and from side to side and is equipped with a heel. The big toe is not set apart from the other toes, like a thumb, but is lined up with the others, and it is not opposable.

The human face also shows some modifications from an earlier form. Man does not have heavy brow ridges and crests on the skull, as some of the apes do. He has a bony nose bridge with an extension of cartilage, which gives him a more prominent nose than other primates have (except for the proboscis monkey). Beneath the nose there is a groove in the upper lip called the *philtrum*, which is peculiar to man. On either side of the nose, below the eye sockets, is a depression known as the *canine fossa* (see footnote 3). Man's face is relatively lacking in *prognathism*, or facial protrusion.

The mouth and jaws of man have various distinctive characteristics. Man's lips are outrolled, with the membranous red portion showing, in contrast to the thin lips of other primates in which the membranous portion is not easily seen. Modern man has a chin which juts forward, in contrast to the sloping jaw of the ape. There is no simian shelf. The canine teeth do not interlock; so there is no diastema, or gap in the upper row of teeth to receive the lower canine. The jaws flare out and are V–shaped or parabolic, in contrast to the long narrow U–shaped jaws of the apes.

At the bottom of the skull there is a large hole called the *foramen magnum*, through which the spinal cord connects with the brain. This is located at the rear of the skull in pronograde animals. Among apes it is further forward. In man the *foramen magnum* is in the center of the base of the skull, for the skull is balanced on the spinal column. Since it is balanced in this way, we do not need a lot of neck muscles, like those of the gorilla. Our necks are longer than those of the apes.

Man's body is relatively hairless, in comparison with the bodies of other primates, although there are some hairy individuals. But we usually have a lot of hair on our heads. (Again, there are exceptions.) These human patterns are particularly manifest in women, whose head hair is particularly abundant, while their body hair is scanty. The form of human hair shows some specializations; kinky or tightly curled hair like that of Negroes is not found among the other primates.

Man differs from other primates in the appearance of the genitalia and in sexual behavior. The human male has no penis bone. Prosimians, most monkeys and apes, and most carnivorous mammals have a cartilaginous or bony element in the penis. The human male has the largest penis in length and thickness of any primate.

Sexual receptivity in female monkeys and apes is often restricted to a week, or a little more, of their monthly cycle, while the human female may be receptive at any time. Moreover, coitus lasts much longer among humans than among other primates. Among most nonhuman primates, the sexual act is over in about 15 seconds. Human females are unique among primates in their ability to experience orgasm.

The assumption of upright posture and the forward shift of the female genital organs has made it possible for human beings to copulate ventrally, unlike most other animals. A survey in our society has shown that 70 percent of the people follow only this frontal approach in sexual relations, and a cross-cultural survey of nearly 200 societies in different parts of the world has shown that the dorsal approach is not the usual one in any of these societies. There has been some speculation to the effect that the

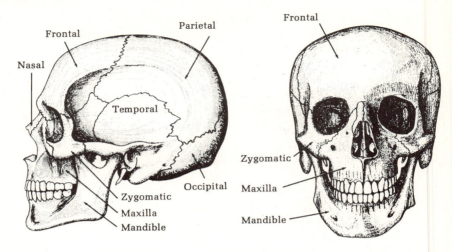

development of the frontal approach has led to a more personal relationship between the sex partners, involving more courtship and sex play than among other primates.[4]

One final point of difference between man and the other primates: man matures more slowly than the other primates, making necessary a longer period of dependency in childhood. This also makes possible a much longer period of learning, which is of importance in the transmission of culture from one generation to the next.

These, then, are the principal ways in which man differs from the other primates. Many of these features, such as the lumbar curve, the characteristics of the pelvis, the long legs, and the specialization of the feet, represent adaptations to upright posture and bipedalism. Some of the differences are matters of degree—larger brains, less body hair. Some of the features mentioned have been acquired rather recently by man and were not characteristic of early hominids such as the australopithecines, Java man, and Peking man. (See pages 86–104) They did not have chins or high nose bridges, and many of them had heavy brow ridges.

The differences which separate us from the pongids are not numerous. The striking thing, perhaps, is the extent of resemblance between the apes and man. This resemblance extends to matters of body chemistry. A number of biochemical studies show that man has more in common with

---

[4] On these matters, see Desmond Morris, *The Naked Ape* (New York: Dell Publishing Co., 1967), Chapter 2; Richard J. Harrison and William Montagna, *Man* (New York: Appleton-Century-Crofts, 1969), Chapter 10. See also Charles F. Hockett and Robert Ascher, "The Human Revolution," *Current Anthropology*, Vol. 5, No. 3 (1964), p. 142; and Weston La Barre's *Comments, ibid.*, p. 149. For a comparative study of sexual behavior, see Clellan S. Ford and Frank A. Beach, *Patterns of Sexual Behavior* (New York: Harper & Bros., 1951).

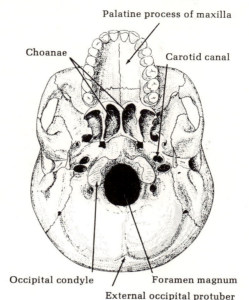

Palatine process of maxilla

Choanae

Carotid canal

(Left) side view
and front view of
skull. (Right)
base of skull.

Occipital condyle   Foramen magnum

External occipital protuber

the apes than he has with other primates. This is true of such features of the blood as purine metabolism, MN blood groups, and gamma globulin. The ABO blood groups are found in the Old World monkeys and the apes as well as in man. Apes and man suffer from some of the same diseases, with similar symptoms, and they harbor some of the same parasites.

The extent of the similarities between apes and man suggests that we share a common ancestry with them. This is what most anthropologists and zoologists believe, but there are some minority views which derive the human stem from other sources. William L. Straus, Jr., has argued that man stems from a generalized catarrhine primate, not an ape. Straus is struck by the fact that man is in many ways more "primitive" and unspecialized than the apes.[5] In an earlier study, Wood Jones suggested that man was derived from an ancestral tarsioid stock.[6] These views raise the question: If we are descended from an early tarsier or generalized catarrhine, how can we explain the numerous similarities between the apes and man mentioned above? Jones and Straus attribute these similarities to parallel evolution rather than to common descent, but in the majority view this solution is unacceptable.

---

[5] William L. Straus, Jr., "The Riddle of Man's Ancestry," in William Howells (ed.), *Ideas on Human Evolution: Selected Essays, 1949–1961* (Cambridge, Mass.: Harvard University Press, 1962) pp. 69–104.

[6] F. Wood Jones, *Arboreal Man* (London: Edward Arnold, 1916).

This discussion, at any rate, shows that man is closely related to all the primates, but particularly to the Old World monkeys and the apes. At the same time, man does have some unique characteristics, particularly in his upright posture, complex nervous system, and large brain. These and the other features discussed above suffice to place man in a separate classification from the pongids: the family of Hominidae.

Suggestions for further reading

For a review of early primate fossil discoveries, see Elwyn J. Simons, "The Early Relatives of Man," *Scientific American*, July, 1964, pp. 50–62.

For an excellently illustrated and well-written text, see F. Clark Howell, *Early Man* (New York: Life Nature Library, 1964.)

On human anatomy and physiology, see *Man* by Richard J. Harrison and William Montagna (New York: Appleton-Century-Crofts, 1969).

Stages of hominid evolution

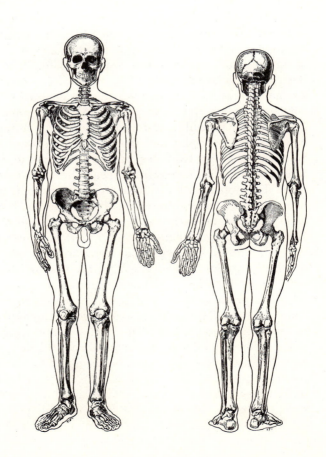

The stage of Australopithecus

Australopithe-
cus africanus

In 1924 Raymond Dart, an anatomist at the University of Witwatersrand, acquired a well-preserved fossil skull which seemed to be that of an immature ape. It came from some limestone bluffs at Taung in Bechuanaland, South Africa. The skull was evidently that of a five- or six-year-old juvenile, since its milk teeth were intact. The first four permanent molar teeth were also present. Although somewhat apelike in appearance, the juvenile's braincase was as large as that of an adult chimpanzee. Dart gave this find the name of *Australopithecus africanus*, or South African ape. However, he drew attention to many humanlike features in the skull. There were no heavy brow ridges or projecting canine teeth. The appearance of the teeth was more human than apelike. The face was quite flat and the skull a bit rounded on top. There were implications of upright posture in the central position of the *foramen magnum.* However, as critics pointed out after Dart published his findings, most of these features are not unusual in immature apes, which have flatter faces, smaller brow ridges, less projecting canines, and higher foreheads than adult apes. But what was unusual, in any case, was the location of this find. The present-day African apes, the gorilla and chimpanzee, live in tropical forests 2,000 miles further north. Taung is in a dry, savannalike environment, and Dart estimated that climatic conditions were not very much different a million years ago, when the Taung child was thought to have lived. His diet must have been quite different from those of chimpanzees and gorillas. Perhaps, like the baboons who now live in such terrain, he ate berries, grubs, lizards, and birds' eggs. He was probably more of a meat eater than most primates, but such shifts of diet are not uncommon in the different orders of mammals. The panda, for example, although classed among the carnivores, has become a strict vegetarian.

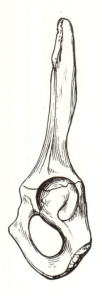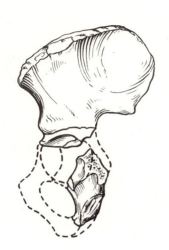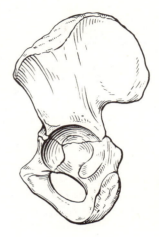

Hipbones (left) in side view, of chimpanzee, *Australopithecus* (Makapan), and man (Bushman).

About 10 years after Dart's discovery, a number of fossils of similar type began to turn up in South Africa; they have come to be known as australopithecines. Their skeletal material, now abundant, consists not only of skulls, jaws, and teeth but of limbs and pelvic bones as well. Remains of over 100 individuals have been found.

With so much material to work with, we now have a fairly clear conception of what these creatures looked like. It seems definite that they had upright posture and bipedal locomotion. Their pelvic bones and limb bones were much like ours. But they had small brains, not much larger than those of present-day apes. This suggests that man assumed upright posture before he developed a large brain. Their brains were, however, quite a bit larger in proportion to body size than those of the great apes. The cranial capacity was between 435 and 600 cubic centimeters.

The later finds generally conform to the picture presented by the immature Taung skull. The australopithecines had large chinless jaws, whose canine teeth were relatively small. There was no diastema. Mastoid processes like those of modern humans appear on the skulls. Some had a good deal of facial protrusion, with heavy brow ridges and crests on top of the skull. These are apelike features, but there is general agreement now that the australopithecines should be classed as hominids; they had more in common with us than with the apes. Some anthropologists assign them to a subfamily of the Hominidae, the *Australopithecinae;* others would classify them as a species of the genus *Homo.* John Buettner-Janusch, who favors the latter view, uses the term *Homo africanus* for this species.

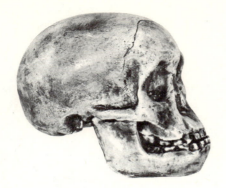
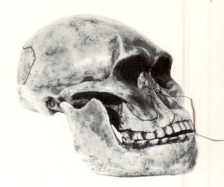

We shall never know whether these particular hominids were actually ancestral to ourselves. The important point is that our ancestors at some point in time must have been much like them and that these South African hominids can be taken to represent a stage in human evolution, just as Java man and Peking man represent the later stage of *Homo erectus,* and Neandertal man is held to represent a still later stage of human evolution.

It was mentioned that the australopithecines have been dated at the early Pleistocene epoch, which Dart took to be about a million years ago, for that was the traditional age formerly ascribed to the beginning of the Pleistocene. Recent dating methods have, however, pushed the Pliocene-Pleistocene boundary back to about 2.5 million years ago, at least in Africa, where potassium-argon dating techniques (concerning which see page 169) have indicated a date of at least 1,750,000 years. Some geologists have dated the Pleistocene epoch at only about 600,000 years ago; it is thought that this may still be applicable to Europe but not to Africa. The age of the australopithecines may thus be two or three times that originally assigned them.

Some recent australopithecine finds have been dated at about 2.5 million years, for example, a fossil arm bone found in Kenya in 1965 and some skull remains found in Kenya in 1970. Other australopithecine remains are still older. An expedition led by Clark Howell of the University of Chicago in 1967–68 found *Australopithecus* teeth and jawbones in the Omo River region of Ethiopia; they are thought to be about 3.5 or 4 million years old.

The Pleistocene epoch was the age in which man's evolution from an apelike creature to *Homo sapiens* was largely accomplished. It was a period of geological upheavals—volcanic activity, the upthrusting of mountain chains, great drops in temperature, and the periodic spreading of ice sheets across the northern continents. "Although permanent ice covers only 10 per cent of the world land surface today, it extended over 32 per cent at the time of maximum Pleistocene glaciation."[1]

The beginning stage of the Pleistocene is sometimes called the *Villafranchian,* a term originally applied to a group of mammals widespread during that period, particularly elephants, horses, and cattle. Bones of Villafranchian fauna have been found in association with the bones of *Australopithecus,* which have so far been found mainly in South and East Africa.

The use of tools

In 1959 Louis S. B. Leakey found the skull of an australopithecine, whom he called *Zinjanthropus boisei,* in association with stone tools in Olduvai Gorge, Tanzania, East Africa. Potassium-argon dates for this site place it at about 1,750,000 years ago. The stones consist mostly of pieces of lava and quartz which must have been brought to the site from about 3 miles away or more; they do not naturally occur at the site itself. Crude, rounded pebble tools called choppers are among the artifacts. But surprisingly advanced-looking tools were also found. Pfeiffer has noted: ". . . a site at the bottom of the gorge contains eleven different kinds of stone implements, such as engraving-gouging tools, quadrilateral 'chisels,' large and small scrapers, and other special-purpose tools generally made of difficult-to-work lavas and quartz."[2]

Leakey's wife, Mary Leakey, has mapped a 3,400-square-foot "living floor" at the Olduvai site within which there is an area with a 15-foot diameter littered with smashed animal bones, which were evidently broken to get at the marrow. The evidence suggests that the Olduvai hominids were both tool users and meat eaters.

The Leakeys first assumed that the tool user was *Zinjanthropus* himself. ("Zinj," incidentally, is a term for East Africa). But the evidence became complicated by the appearance at Olduvai of a more advanced hominid who seems to have lived at the same time as *Zinjanthropus* or even earlier. Perhaps this more advanced form, whom Leakey has called *Homo habilis,* made the tools. The question may not be so important if Leakey's *Homo habilis* is simply a relatively advanced *Australopithecus,* as some physical anthropologists assert. This question is discussed further below.

The Leakeys have also uncovered a semicircular wall at Olduvai which may have served as a windbreak and which has been dated at around 2,030,000 years old, plus or minus 280,000 years—the oldest man-made structure known.[3]

[1] Karl W. Butzer, *Environment and Archeology: An Introduction to Pleistocene Geography* (Chicago, Ill.: Aldine Publishing Co., 1964), p. 96.

[2] John E. Pfeiffer, *The Emergence of Man* (New York: Harper & Row, Publishers, 1969), p. 79.

[3] *Ibid.,* p. 84.

Raymond Dart argued that the earliest tools used by the australopithecines were not likely to have been made of stone but of bone and horn. This contention is still being discussed, and there are some arguments in its favor. Since stone tools last indefinitely, while those of wood and other organic materials decay, archaeologists have focused their attention on man's early stone industries and have developed such terms as Old Stone Age, or Palaeolithic, and New Stone Age, or Neolithic. These rubrics have accustomed us to think that stone was the first material used by early hunters. The early australopithecines might have thrown rocks and stones to defend themselves or to attack animals, and they might have used sharp pebbles to cut up meat, since they did not have large canine teeth to do the job. But in the carcasses of animals, either killed by themselves or by other predators such as lions, the australopithecines would have found sharp, pointed bones and horns useful for piercing and stabbing, and heavy limb bones useful as clubs. Such naturally shaped tools of bone, horn, and antler, may have been the hominids' first weapons. Dart has published photographs of many pieces of bone, horn, and antler taken from australopithecine sites, which he thinks were used as tools. Since they show little evidence of having been worked, this testimony is not convincing by itself. But Dart has made some interesting statistical analyses of this bone material. Ninety-two percent of the bones at the Makapansgat cave in South Africa came from antelopes. Dart concludes that, like most primitive hunters, the australopithecines preferred venison to other meat. The remaining 8 percent included remains of water turtles, birds, moles, hares, pigs, porcupines, hyenas, wild dogs, jackals, horses, leopards, saber-toothed tigers, extinct tree bears, giraffes, a hippopotamus, rhinoceroses, warthogs, and baboons. These include creatures found underground (moles), water inhabitants (turtles), birds of the air, and quadrupedal terrestrial animals. As the list shows, the animals were not all small; some were large creatures.

Dart points out that 82.5 percent of the bone fragments are cranial. A conclusion might be that the australopithecines hacked off the heads of their victims and brought them to the cave, leaving other skeletal remains, including neck vertebrae, behind. Many lower jaws were found of such animals as hyenas, baboons, warthogs, and porcupines, all of which have sharp teeth which could have been used as tools for cutting.[4]

Sherwood Washburn has suggested that the bone accumulation at Makapansgat might have been collected by hyenas rather than by australopithecines and that the latter may have been the hunted rather than the hunters. Making a statistical assessment of recent kills in an African

---

[4] Raymond A. Dart with Dennis Craig, *Adventures with the Missing Link* (New York: Harper & Bros., 1959), pp. 132–46.

game reserve, Washburn found that in a third of the kills the skull and associated parts were all that was left. The kills were presumably made by lions, but the final consumption of the leftover carcasses was probably completed by jackals, hyenas, and other smaller animals. These can consume most of the bones except for the jaws and teeth. This, rather than selective choice by hominids, could account for the preponderance of cranial bones, jaws, and teeth at Makapansgat.[5]

Dart has examined hyena lairs near Kruger National Park, and he reports that they have no bone accumulations. But apparently there are some hyena lairs which do have piles of bones in them. This is true of at least some caves in Devonshire, England, which were inhabited during the Pleistocene by cave hyenas. But most of the bones found there were those of hyenas (110 individuals), while only a minority (20) belonged to other species. This is quite different from the situation at Makapansgat, where there were only 17 hyenas from a total number of 433 animals. Moreover, the bones in Devonshire show many marks of hyena teeth, while those from Makapansgat do not. A specialist on the hyena remains who examined some bones from Makapansgat, said that hyenas had not collected them.[6]

Dart has drawn attention to 42 baboon skulls collected from three different cave sites associated with australopithecine remains. All of the skulls had been bashed in, with seemingly intentional violence; 27 had been struck from in front. In several cases, the blows appear to have been inflicted by a double-headed weapon, which Dart believes to have been an antelope humerus bone, the distal end of which fits into the baboon skull depressions rather well. There is a large percentage of antelope humeri among the Makapansgat bones, and especially of distal ends (336), rather than proximal ends (only 33).

These statistics suggest selection by hominids, but C. K. Brain has pointed out that the distal portions of goat humeri and the proximal portions of their radii fuse before their respective proximal and distal ends and that since the fused portions are more resistant to destruction, they survive longer. Hence no selective choice need be inferred from Dart's statistics.[7]

Some authorities believe that the bones were washed into the cave and were not "accumulated" by any creatures. Carleton Coon has expressed doubt that the australopithecines lived in caves, since cave dwelling was

---

[5] Sherwood L. Washburn, "Australopithecines: The Hunters or the Hunted?" *American Anthropologist,* Vol. 59 (1957), pp. 612–14.

[6] Robert Ardrey, *African Genesis: A Personal Investigation into the Animal Origins and Nature of Man* (New York: Atheneum Publishers, 1961), pp. 309–11.

[7] Donald L. Wolberg, "The Hypothesized Osteodontokeratic Culture of the Australopithecines: A Look at the Evidence and the Opinions," *Current Anthropology,* Vol. 11, No. 1 (February, 1970), pp. 28, 31.

not feasible before the use of fire, of which there is no evidence in australopithecine sites. Without fire, caves are dangerous places, often inhabited by predators or tigers.[8]

Despite his rejection of the significance of Dart's statistics, C. K. Brain believes that hominids did help to build up the bone accumulation at Makapansgat. He bases this conclusion only on the abundance of bone flakes and types of tools which he thinks must have been made by hominids.[9] There is still much controversy about these matters, as may be seen in the conflicting "Comments" added to Wolberg's review article. But, in view of Leakey's discovery of relatively advanced stone tools at Olduvai Gorge, dated 1,750,000 years ago, it seems hard to avoid the conclusion that at least some of the australopithecines were tool users who probably used wood, bone, and horn as well as stone.

Suggested subdivisions of the australopithecines

J. T. Robinson, one of the leading students of the South African finds, has suggested that the australopithecines should be divided into two groups. One genus is that of *Australopithecus;* a second genus is that of *Paranthropus.* According to Robinson, these types were found in different sites and differed markedly in size and weight. *Paranthropus* had about the height of present-day human beings and weighed between 100 and 200 pounds. *Australopithecus* was much shorter and weighed less than 100 pounds. *Paranthropus* had a round, low skull, while *Australopithecus* had a narrow, slightly domed one, and his brow ridges were less prominent. In contrast to *Australopithecus, Paranthropus* had crests on the top of his skull, like those of an adult male gorilla, although less pronounced.

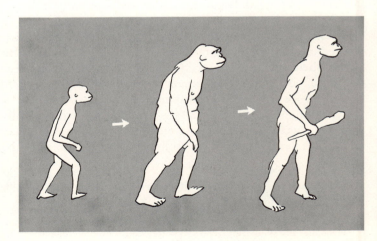

Three theories about the relationship between *Australopithecus, Paranthropus,* and *Homo erectus:*

(Left) *Australopithecus, Paranthropus,* and *Homo erectus* represent successive evolutionary phases, with *Paranthropus* being an intermediate form.

(Center) *Australopithecus* evolved into *Homo erectus,* while *Paranthropus* became extinct.

(Right) *Australopithecus* and *Paranthropus* were members of a heterogeneous population which evolved into *Homo erectus.*

---

[8] Carleton S. Coon, *The Origin of Man* (New York: Alfred A. Knopf, 1962), pp. 236–37.

[9] C. K. Brain, "Comment" in Wolberg, *op. cit.,* p. 31.

Paranthropus had heavy cheek bones, which protruded further forward than his flat nose. But *Australopithecus* had more facial protrusion. *Paranthropus* had much larger molar teeth, but smaller canines and incisors than *Australopithecus*. The contrast in dentition and in the framework of the skull suggest that *Paranthropus* depended more on a vegetarian diet, which required a great deal of chewing and grinding of food, while *Australopithecus* is presumed to have been more carnivorous or omnivorous. *Paranthropus* sites were believed to be later than those of *Australopithecus*. Robinson says that there is good evidence that the climate of the region was much wetter in the time of *Paranthropus* than in that of *Australopithecus*.[10]

As was mentioned earlier, Leakey found a more advanced type (whom he calls *Homo habilis*) coexistent with *Paranthropus* (represented by the

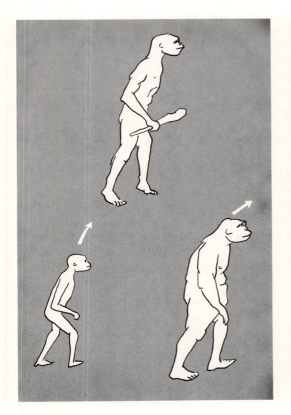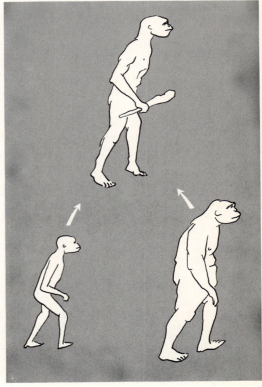

---

[10] J. T. Robinson, "The Australopithecines and Their Bearing on the Origin of Man and of Stone Tool-Making," in William Howells (ed.), *Ideas on Human Evolution: Selected Essays 1949–1961* (Cambridge, Mass.: Harvard University Press, 1962), pp. 279–94.

Zinjanthropus find) at Olduvai Gorge. Together with two associates, Philip V. Tobias and John R. Napier, Leakey has proposed the establishment of a new genus, *Homo habilis,* to represent a hominid stage of evolution between *Australopithecus* and *Homo erectus.* Most authorities seem to disagree with this attempt to set up a new taxon, or grouping of creatures presumably related by descent from a common ancestor, distinctive enough to be given a separate name. They prefer to regard *Homo habilis* as a relatively progressive *Australopithecus.* Many have accepted the divisions made by Robinson. It has recently become a common practice to refer to his two main types as *Australopithecus africanus* and *Australopithecus robustus,* rather than to call the latter *Paranthropus,* but the term *Paranthropus* will continue to be used in the following discussion.

The question next arises: What is the relationship between the two suggested types of hominid, *Australopithecus* and *Paranthropus?* Do they represent different evolutionary stages? Are we derived from one or the other type? Are they really two different genera or species? Different answers have been given to these questions. One is the view of C. L. Brace and Ashley Montagu that *Paranthropus* was derived from *Australopithecus* and represents a stage in human evolution leading to *Homo erectus.* In support of this view, there is, first, the evidence that *Paranthropus* occurs later. Second, he is much bigger. It would seem understandable that an increase in height should take place in a successfully adjusting ground dweller, leading to the height characteristic of *Homo erectus* and *Homo sapiens.* Such an increase would be helpful in defense against other animals. The increased size in the molar teeth of *Paranthropus* may be related to the general increase in body size.

A difficulty with the Brace-Montagu interpretation is that *Paranthropus* generally appears to be more primitive in appearance than *Australopithecus.* He has a lower skull elevation and crests on the skull, which are not present in *Australopithecus.* Brace and Montagu explain the appearance of the crests as being due, once more, to the general increase in body size.

Adult male gorillas have large, heavy jaws and teeth and spend much of their time chewing plant food. The powerful chewing muscles need some locus of attachment. The crests rise along the top of the skull to provide this anchorage. *Australopithecus* did not need such crests, since he was lightly built and did not have very heavy jaws. *Paranthropus* was twice as large and had larger jaws and teeth. His braincase, however, was not much bigger than that of *Australopithecus.* Since the increased musculature involved in chewing did not have a correspondingly enlarged braincase to which to attach itself, the temporal muscles became attached to a saggital crest at the top of the skull.[11]

---

[11] C. L. Brace and M. F. Ashley Montagu, *Man's Evolution: An Introduction to Physical Anthropology* (New York: Macmillan Co., 1965), pp. 227–28.

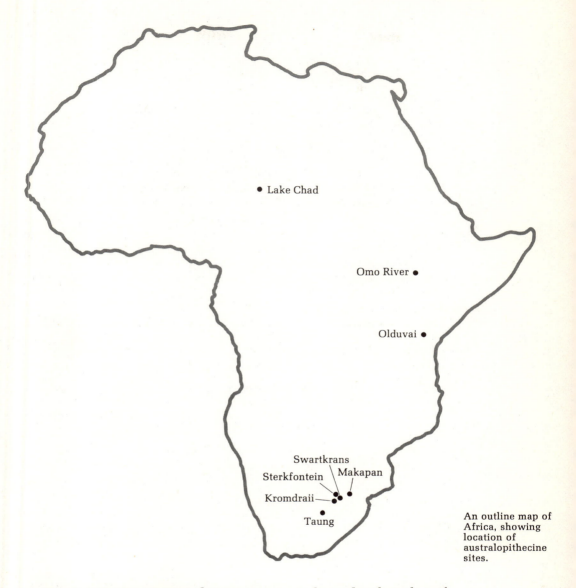

• Lake Chad

Omo River •

Olduvai •

Swartkrans
Sterkfontein   Makapan
Kromdraii—
Taung

An outline map of
Africa, showing
location of
australopithecine
sites.

The distribution of *Paranthropus* appears to be wider than that of *Australopithecus*. Both types have appeared in South and East Africa, but *Paranthropus* has been reported for some other areas. A *Paranthropus*-like fossil has been found near Lake Chad on the edge of the Sahara Desert, and a fragment of fossil jaw with extremely large teeth found in Indonesia and named *Meganthropus palaeojavanicus* (large man of old Java) has been classed as *Paranthropus*. The implication is that the australopithecines originated in Africa and later spread to India and Indonesia, with *Paranthropus* appearing as the longer surviving and more widely distributed type.

The foregoing is a brief statement of the Brace-Montagu interpretation of the relationship between *Australopithecus* and *Paranthropus*. A quite different view has been set forth by J. T. Robinson, who rejects the possibility that *Paranthropus* represents a later stage of evolutionary development than *Australopithecus*. The first lower deciduous molar of *Paranthropus*, Robinson tells us, is immediately recognizable as a *Paranthropus* tooth and is different from the molars of all other hominids. The same tooth in *Australopithecus*, however, closely resembles those of Peking and Neandertal man. This makes it seem unlikely that *Paranthropus* could be an intermediate form. *Australopithecus* has a higher skull elevation and less of a brow ridge than *Paranthropus*, who is more apelike in these respects. It is Robinson's opinion that *Paranthropus* is closer to the original form from which *Australopithecus* was derived. The early ground-dwelling protohominids were probably vegetarian. *Paranthropus* may have remained a plant eater, while *Australopithecus* began to

Time scale for the evolution of the primates

Epoch	Approximate years B.P. (Before the present)	Types of primates
Pleistocene	10,000–2,500,000	Homo sapiens Homo erectus Australopithecus
Pliocene	2,500,000–13,000,000	Australopithecus Ramapithecus Oreopithecus
Miocene	13,000,000–25,000,000	Kenyapithecus Proconsul Pliopithecus Dryopithecus
Oligocene	25,000,000–36,000,000	Propliopithecus Parapithecus Oligopithecus
Eocene	36,000,000–58,000,000	Tarsiers Lemurs
Paleocene	58,000,000–63,000,000	Prosimians like tree shrews or lemurs

specialize as a hunter and carnivore. Robinson believes that it was *Australopithecus* who evolved into *Homo erectus*, while *Paranthropus* was only an aberrant form who finally became extinct.[12] Robinson be-

---

[12] J. T. Robinson, "Adaptive Radiation in the Australopithecines and the Origin of Man," in F. Clark Howell and François Bourlière (eds.), *African Ecology and Human Evolution* (Viking Fund Publications in Anthropology, No. 36 [Chicago, Ill.: Aldine Publishing Co., 1963]), pp. 385–416.

lieves that *Paranthropus* did not use tools, as *Australopithecus* did.

Still another view is that of John Buettner-Janusch. He thinks that the case for distinct species or genera among the australopithecines is very weak. The population is simply a very variable one, just as chimpanzees vary greatly in size and in the appearance of teeth, brow ridges, and other features. Buettner-Janusch denies that the alleged differences in the teeth of *Australopithecus* and *Paranthropus* are significant in differentiating between meat eaters and vegetarians. Moreover, he asserts that it is not true that "*Paranthropus*" lived in a wetter climatic period; "*Zinjanthropus,*" who is classed as a *robustus* or *Paranthropus* form, was not found in a "wet" stratum.[13]

The idea that the australopithecines were a very variable population, including the variation that goes with sexual dimorphism, has also been expressed by Bernard G. Campbell and by C. L. Brace, who now retracts the views expressed in the Brace and Montagu text.

Mention has been made of *Meganthropus palaeojavanicus* (large man of old Java). Robinson has classified *Meganthropus* as a form of *Paranthropus,* for he could find no essential difference between the *Meganthropus* jaws and teeth and those of the large South African hominids. This judgment seems to be widely accepted. *Meganthropus* had one of the largest and thickest primate jaws known.

Large hominids and apes in east Asia

There were other large, powerful hominoids in east Asia, whose fossil remains have been found. These were huge apes, called *Gigantopithecus,* who once lived in southern China. Many remains of these creatures have been found. The first *Gigantopithecus* teeth were discovered by G. H. R. von Koenigswald, who found them, not *in situ,* but in a Chinese drugstore. While on his travels, von Koenigswald had the custom of visiting Chinese drugstores and asking to see the local collection of "dragons' teeth." These are fossilized teeth of various sorts which Chinese customers buy for magical, medicinal purposes. Since fossil primate teeth sometimes appear in these collections, von Koenigswald was always on the lookout for something relevant to hominoid evolution. It was thus that in Hong Kong he acquired three huge molars, which he christened *Gigantopithecus blacki. Gigantopithecus* means "giant ape." *Blacki* does not refer to the presumed color, but was meant as a tribute to Davidson Black, known for his work with the Peking man fossils. The *Gigantopithecus* teeth have a volume five times that of modern human molars. At first it was considered possible that they were hominid molars, perhaps of some giant human ancestor, but the name given to the teeth indicates that they were finally judged to be those of an early ape, a view which has since prevailed. Von

---

[13] John Buettner-Janusch, *Origins of Man: Physical Anthropology* (New York: John Wiley & Sons, 1966), pp. 167–69.

Koenigswald estimated their age at about half a million years and considered them to be contemporaneous with Java man, but the Chinese scholar Pei, an authority on *Gigantopithecus*, believes, on the basis of faunal associations, that they are of lower Pleistocene age.

Since the first appearance of these *Gigantopithecus* teeth, many more have been discovered on the Chinese mainland by Chinese palaeontologists. Some mandibles have also been found, one of which came from a cave high up on the face of a steep cliff accessible only by climbing or flying. The cave was full of bones of Middle Pleistocene animals such as boar, deer, tapir, and elephant, none of which could either climb or fly. No tools or signs of human occupation were found in the cave. It is suspected that the remains of the large animals were hauled up the hillside by the giant ape. It is most unusual for an ape to be a cave dweller and a carnivore. On the other hand, hominids became cave dwellers and carnivores; so perhaps some apes did the same thing as a kind of parallel evolution, although they apparently did not acquire the use of tools.

At the time of the discovery of the giant east Asiatic fossil finds, there was some speculation to the effect that perhaps man went through a giant phase in the course of his evolution. These notions, which seem to have dropped out of currency since the 1940's, were expressed by Franz Weidenreich, one of the leading physical anthropologists of his day. Weidenreich believed that *Gigantopithecus* was not a giant ape but a giant man, as was *Meganthropus*. Weidenreich also held that, although primates were originally small, they became larger in the course of evolution, until man's ancestors reached a giant size before the time of *Pithecanthropus erectus*, and then began to get smaller again. It was in this way that Weidenreich explained the thickness of the human skull. It may seem surprising, but the human skull is thicker than those of the anthropoid apes. Even the bones which make up the gorilla's brain case are thinner than those of modern man. But the bones which make up the skull of *Pithecanthropus* are about twice as thick as modern man's. One of von Koenigswald's *Pithecanthropus* finds, called *Pithecanthropus robustus*, had the thickest human skull then known. Weidenreich argued that the thickness of the *Pithecanthropus* skull and of later human skulls can be seen as a heritage of the giant stage of human development. The *Meganthropus* and *Gigantopithecus* teeth were held to be relics of that earlier stage. Weidenreich was not sure that the whole human species had passed through a giant phase, but he thought that at least part of it had done so.

It will be seen that Weidenreich's theory would fit in with the Brace-Montagu interpretation that *Paranthropus* developed from *Australopithecus*. In the succession *Australopithecus–Paranthropus–Pithecanthropus* we could place the giant stage at the *Paranthropus* level. However, when we speak of "giant stage," this should not be interpreted too literally or sensationally. If the molar teeth of *Gigantopithecus* have five times the volume of modern man's molars, it does not mean that he was five times, or even twice, as large as man, although Pei estimated that the ape was about 12 feet tall. Limb and pelvic bones found among the large-toothed *Paranthropus* remains in South Africa, on the other hand, are of relatively modest size.

Unfortunately for Weidenreich's theory, modern palaeontologists do not agree that *Gigantopithecus* was human; they consider it to have been an ape. (The jaws of *Gigantopithecus* had a simian shelf and a diastema). The line of *Gigantopithecus*, perhaps like that of *Paranthropus*, is thus seen to lead to a dead end. Presumably, human beings, who had the use of tools and who had greater intelligence, were more successful than were the large apes, who became extinct, unless some still survive as "abominable snowmen" up in the Himalayas.[14]

Suggestions for further reading

A lively presentation of Raymond Dart's views is set forth in the book he wrote with Dennis Craig, *Adventures with the Missing Link* (New York: Harper & Bros., 1959). A stimulating, but overly sensational work is Robert Ardrey's *African Genesis: A Personal Investigation into the Animal Origins and Nature of Man* (New York: Atheneum Publishers, 1961).

Excellent drawings of an artist's reconstructions of *Australopithecus, Paranthropus,* and other early hominids may be found in F. Clark Howell's *Early Man* (New York: Life Nature Books, 1964), which was recommended in the preceding chapter.

Two papers by J. T. Robinson are recommended: "The Australopithecines and Their Bearing on the Origin of Man and of Stone Tool-Making," in William Howells (ed.), *Ideas on Human Evolution: Selected Essays, 1949–1961* (Cambridge, Mass.: Harvard University Press, 1962), pp. 279–94; and "Adaptive Radiation in the Australopithecines and the Origin of Man" in F. Clark Howell and François Bourlière (eds.), *African Ecology and Human Evolution* (Viking Fund Publications in Anthropology, No. 36, [Chicago, Ill.: Aldine Publishing Co., 1963]), pp. 385–416.

For a well-illustrated account of some of Leakey's finds concerning *Zinjanthropus,* see L. S. B. Leakey and Des Bartlett, "Finding the World's Earliest Man," *National Geographic,* September, 1960, pp. 420–35.

Franz Weidenreich's views about the presumed giant phase of human evolution are set forth in his book, *Apes, Giants, and Man* (Chicago, Ill.: University of Chicago Press, 1946).

---

[14] Some references to large upright apes in China appear in Chinese literature from as far back as 400 B.C. to as recently as the end of the 18th century. See E. Vlćek, "Old Literary Evidence for the Existence of the Snow Man in Tibet and Mongolia," *Man,* Vol. 59, Article No. 203 (1959), pp. 132–34.

Chapter 9

The stage of *Homo erectus*

Homo erectus represents a stage of hominid evolution beyond *Australo-pithecus,* dating back to between a million and half a million years ago. Fossil discoveries which fall under the heading of *Homo erectus* have been made in Europe, Africa, China, and Indonesia. The principal advance at this level was an increase in height and cranial capacity. *Homo erectus* used tools and must have had a language. The remains of fire have been found in association with some of his skeletal remains, both in Europe and in China. From the neck down, *Homo erectus* seems to have been just like ourselves, and even from the neck up he was not very different. To be sure, he lacked a chin, had heavy brow ridges, and his cranial capacity was relatively small, but there are many people today with similar traits.

Since *Homo erectus* looked so much like us, it seems snobbish not to assign him the status of *Homo sapiens,* but this has not been the custom until recently. John Buettner-Janusch, however, would so classify him.[1] It is only recently that Neandertal man has been admitted to the *Homo sapiens* club. We are gradually extending membership in our species further back in time to our more primitive ancestors.

Hunting-gathering people tend to have larger ranges than nonhuman primates, whose ranges are generally small, with the exception of some, such as baboons, chimpanzees, and gorillas. Man's effectiveness as a hunter must have increased greatly during this period and led to his wider dispersal. Stone choppers or pebble tools, and sometimes hand axes, are found at the *Homo erectus* stage and attest to the deliberate making of tools. Strengthened by these tools and the use of fire, some representatives

---

[1] John Buettner-Janusch, *Origins of Man: Physical Anthropology* (New York: John Wiley & Sons, 1966), pp. 172, 178.

of the *Homo erectus* group were now able to make their way up into cold northerly areas, such as northern Europe and northern China, while others continued to inhabit warmer regions in Africa, south Asia, and Indonesia.

The migrations of *Homo erectus* may have been facilitated by the upheavals and climatic conditions of the Pleistocene epoch. Thus, heavier rainfall in Africa may have led the way to occupation and movement through the Sahara Desert. The locking up of water further north, with the advent of cold Arctic weather, lowered water levels in the Mediterranean and may have provided land bridges, for example at the Dardanelles, permitting the migration of peoples—in the latter case from Turkey into Europe. At any rate, there were hominids in Europe between around 750,000 and 1 million years ago, as evidenced by finds at the caves of Vallonet and Escale in France and Vértesszöllös in Hungary, discussed in a later section.

Java man

The first *Homo erectus* fossil to be found was Eugène Dubois' discovery of what he called *Pithecanthropus erectus,* or erect ape man. Dubois was a Dutchman with a French name, an anatomist and paleontologist with an interest in evolution. Having acquired a medical post in what was then the Dutch East Indies, Dubois used some of his time to search for the "missing link," a hypothetical ancestral form common to both man and ape. He even managed to get some government support to carry out his paleontological research. It seemed to Dubois that Indonesia would be a likely area to yield a missing link, for the somewhat manlike gibbon and orangutan lived there, and Borneo and Sumatra were once attached to the mainland of Asia. Dubois did uncover a good deal of valuable fossil material in Java, including some early hominid skulls, but his principal discovery was a thick-boned fossil skullcap, the part of the skull above the ears. This find was made near the Solo River in 1891. In the following year, Dubois resumed digging near the same spot and this time uncovered a left human thighbone about 40 or 50 feet from where he had found the skullcap. Nearby Dubois also found two molar teeth.

At first Dubois thought that the thighbone and skullcap belonged to two different individuals, but later he concluded that they belonged to the same organism. He was probably right, although this was one point on which Dubois was criticized after he announced his discovery. The thighbone was a straight femur of modern human type with a ridge (*linea aspera*) to which were once attached muscles used in upright locomotion. This was, then, a creature with upright posture, about 5 feet, 8 inches, in height. The skullcap was very primitive in comparison. It was low, had heavy brow ridges, and a cranial capacity of about 900 cubic centimeters. The brain of Java man, as this fossil form came to be known, was therefore intermediate in size between those of the African apes (having about 500 cc.) and modern man (with about 1,400 cc.). Because of the combination of human and apelike features in these fossil remains, Dubois gave his creature the name of *Pithecanthropus erectus*, or erect ape-man, and stated that it was a transitional form of early man.

Publication of Dubois' findings set off a lot of controversy. This was the first discovery of so early a hominid. *Australopithecus africanus* was not known until 1925; the discoveries of Peking man were announced in the late 1920's. Since this was the first reported find of a type more primitive than Neandertal man, it is understandable that there was much skepticism. How, it was asked, could so small a brain go with such a modern femur? Why not assume that the femur was that of a modern man and the skullcap that of a large ape? Perhaps they even came from different time periods.

These were sensible enough objections at the time, but there are now so many australopithecine and *Homo erectus* fossils available for study that we know that Dubois was right. Fluorine tests have since shown that the disputed thighbone and skullcap are of the same age. It is true that we cannot prove that they belonged to the same individual, but there is no longer any incongruity in finding upright posture associated with a small brain. The australopithecines, who lived long before *Pithecanthropus,* were orthograde and had even smaller brains. Besides, four more *Pithecanthropus erectus* skulls have since been found in Java; and near Peking in China the remains of a closely related hominid have been found, which show essentially the same characteristics as those of *Pithecanthropus erectus.* This was a widespread type of early man.

The more recently discovered skulls from Java were found by G. H. R. von Koenigswald in the 1930's. They show the same traits: thick skull walls, heavy brow ridges, and low elevation of the skull. There is no chin. At least some of the Java men had a diastema, or gap in the upper range of teeth for reception of the lower canine. This apelike trait was lacking in *Australopithecus,* so it is surprising to find it in this more advanced form. No tools or evidence of fire have been found in association with *Pithecanthropus erectus,* but it is likely that he used tools and had a culture, for tools have been found in association with several other forms of *Homo erectus.* It was formerly believed that Java man lived about half a million years ago, but more recent dating methods ascribe an earlier date —perhaps around 730,000 years ago for the fossils from the Trinil beds, where Dubois' *Pithecanthropus* was found, and still earlier for the Djetis beds, from which most of von Koenigswald's finds were recovered.

Lantian man   The oldest hominid skull discovered in China is that of Lantian man, found in 1963 in Shensi Province and dated at more than 600,000 years. The skull has low elevation, thick walls, and heavy brow ridges. The skull was found in association with stegodont elephant, an ancient small bear, saber-toothed cat, Sanmen horse, tapir, giant deer, and bison.

An outline map of Africa, Europe, and Asia showing where sites of *Homo erectus* have been found.

Peking man

In the late 1920's, the contents of some limestone caves were excavated at Choukoutien near Peking, China. This rich site yielded the remains of about 40 *Homo erectus* individuals. Their bones were splintered and fragmented, but some fairly complete skulls could be assembled, and limb bones and other skeletal parts were recovered. The individuals were of both sexes and different ages. The cave seems to have been occupied off and on over a period of thousands of years, so the 40 or so persons were not necessarily members of the same family or band.

The physical type represented in this collection was very similar to that of Java man, though with a higher cranial capacity, having a range from about 925 cubic centimeters (in the immature skull of an eight- or nine-year-old boy) to 1,225 cubic centimeters. The larger skulls are within the modern human range. The Peking skulls are low and thick walled, with a slight ridge along the top and heavy brow ridges over the eyes. The jaws and teeth are large. When seen from above, the dental arch is more parabolic or V–shaped than that of apes. The Peking molars have enlarged pulp cavities, a condition known as *taurodontism*, found later in Neandertal man and some modern populations. The upper incisors are "shovel shaped," with the sides seeming to curl inward, a characteristic of modern

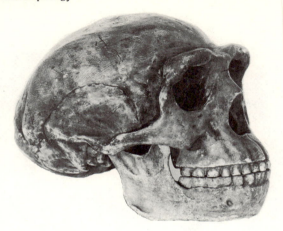

Reconstructed
plaster cast of
skull of Peking Man.

Mongoloid incisors, sometimes also found in non-Mongoloid people. There is no diastema. The jaw has no chin. The nose is broad and low bridged. The men of Choukoutien are judged to have been a little over 5 feet and the women a little under. However, it is not always possible to determine the sex of the bones, especially since they are so fragmented.

Estimating sex and age of skeletal material

Apart from the earlier mention of the youthful age of *Australopithecus africanus*, this has been the first reference to the age or sex of skeletal material. In this context, *age* does not refer to how long ago a person lived but how old he was at the time of death. The estimates are usually rough, and mistakes are always possible, but physical anthropologists do have a number of ways of determining sex and approximate age from bones and teeth. We will return to the subject of Peking man and his culture, but first let us digress and briefly discuss these techniques.

Age may be determined partly from the appearance of the teeth, presence of milk teeth (as in *Australopithecus africanus*) or permanent dentition, the degree of tooth wear and decay, and loss of teeth and the consequent absorption of bone in the jaws of older persons.

In the skull, one indication of age is the degree of closure of the sutures. The skull is not made of continuous bone but of different bones which remain separate in the newly born child, allowing the brain to grow and expand. These skull bones gradually meet, forming irregular serrated edges called *sutures*. In the mature adult the sutures may become obliterated, especially in older persons.

In the 11th prenatal week in humans, there are some 806 centers of bone growth; at birth about 450. These centers "disappear" through union with adjacent centers. Approximate age in the prenatal months and early years may be gauged from the appearance of centers, their union, and the degree of ossification. The right and left hipbones meet in front to form

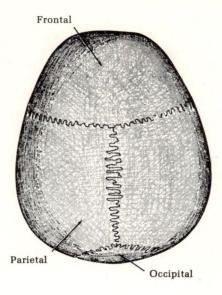

Frontal

Parietal

Occipital

Top of skull,
showing sutures
between the
different bones of
the skull vault.

the pubic symphysis, the appearance of which provides an indication of age in more mature skeletons. Women have a broader and lower pelvic structure, suitable for giving birth to large-brained babies, while men have a high, narrow pelvis.

In "sexing" a skull, size and degree of ruggedness are determining factors. Generally, large skulls are male, small ones female. Female skulls are rounder and lighter boned; they have smoother, more "infantile" foreheads. In males the cheekbones and supraorbital ridges are more fully developed. Males have thicker jaws, broader palates, squarer chins, and larger mastoid processes. The long bones of males are longer and more massive than those of females.[2]

Peking man was definitely a tool maker and user of tools. Stone choppers were found in the cave at Choukoutien. Although their workmanship was rough, they were deliberately flaked. There were also thousands of quartz flakes, which show no sign of retouching, but which must have been used as tools. These pieces of quartz must have been brought to the cave from elsewhere, for no quartz is found within 2 miles of the site. Worked bits of bone were also found.

Charred hearths in the cave provide the earliest evidence in Asia of man's use of fire—perhaps around 500,000 or more years ago. The discovery of the uses to which fire could be put may have made it possible

The culture of Peking man

---

[2] Wilton Marion Krogman, *The Human Skeleton in Forensic Medicine* (Springfield, Ill.: Charles C. Thomas, Publisher, 1962).

for man to live so far north. It seems likely that Peking man cooked the animals he hunted, although the animal bones in the cave show no clear evidence of charring. In any case, fire would have provided protection against predators at night, as well as warmth and visibility. Without fire, cave habitation would be dangerous.

The use of fire must have had some important psychological consequences for early man. A fire provides a rallying point, a center, a circle of warmth in the dark night. Fire must have given early man a greater sense of security and perhaps heightened the feeling of solidarity of those grouped around it. It may also have had aesthetic and religious connotations; for fire, with its warmth and mysterious beauty and its potentialities for both destruction and protection, has always been a source of awe for human beings.

Fire also made possible an extension of man's working hours. He could now sit up late, staring into the embers as we now stare into a television set, perhaps continuing to chip away at some piece of stonework in the artificial light. Animals tend to have built-in time clocks which regulate their sleeping hours. Man has moved away from strict biological controls of this sort. Perhaps this breakaway was encouraged by the regular use of fire with its artificial extension of daytime.

Another use of fire was in the making of tools: splitting stones by heating and sudden cooling, and hardening the tips of wooden shafts.

A more negative note must be added, as far as Peking man is concerned; he was a cannibal and ate other Peking men. This is indicated by the appearance of the bones, which, as already mentioned, were splintered. They were probably broken and split to get to the marrow. Brains seem to have been extracted from the skulls, which were broken in at the base. Cannibalism seems to have been also practiced by Solo man, a later *Homo erectus* related to *Pithecanthropus,* and evidences of cannibalism are also found in Neandertal sites in Europe. This does not mean that all men were cannibals in Palaeolithic times, but evidently many of them were.

Peking man was only a small part of Peking man's diet. Three fourths of the animal bones found at Choukoutien were of deer; so the favorite food of these hunters was venison. Other animal bones found in the cave deposits included boar, sheep, mammoth, water buffalo, bison, camel, ostrich, and otter. Seeds of fruits were also found.

Disappearance of the bones   The bones of Peking man have disappeared. At the time of the Japanese invasion of northern China, an attempt was made to move the Choukoutien material away from possible capture by the Japanese. An American Marine colonel, who was given the valuable fossils, packed them in a footlocker, and on December 5, 1941, they were sent off on a train to the Chinese coast, where they were to be transferred to the American liner

President Harrison. Two days later came the attack on Pearl Harbor; the train on which the bones were sent was captured, and the *President Harrison* was grounded by her crew. Nobody knows what happened to the bones. The Chinese Communist regime has alleged that they have been hidden in the vaults of the American Museum of Natural History; museum officials deny it. Fortunately, photographs and casts were made of the bones, and they were measured and described in detail by Franz Weidenreich; so the loss is not as great as it might have been. Besides, more finds of Peking man, or closely related forms of *Homo erectus,* have been made in different parts of China in recent years, including some very well-preserved bones, such as the Lantian remains.

Reference was made above to the evidence for cannibalism on the part of Solo man. The Solo skulls are much later than those of *Pithecanthropus,* perhaps dating from the Upper Pleistocene in Java. Twelve skulls and two tibia were found together near the Solo River. The skulls were resting on their tops, bases facing upwards. Since only skulls were found, without other skeletal material beside the tibia, and since all of the bases, except two, were broken or partly removed, it looks as though cannibalism was practiced. These skulls are thick walled and resemble those of *Pithecanthropus*. They are often referred to as Neandertaloid, but Carleton Coon classifies Solo man as *Homo erectus,* because the general features correspond and the cranial capacity is equal to that of the skulls from Choukoutien.[3] If Coon is right, *Homo erectus* remained relatively unchanged in some parts of the world long after the time of Java and Peking man.

Solo man

Contemporaneously with Java and Peking man there were evidently similar hominids living in Europe. The earliest evidence of fire from Europe is even older than that from Peking, dating from as far back as 750,000 years ago at the Escale Cave in the Durance Valley, not far from Marseilles in southern France, where hearths of charcoal and ash have been found in caves along with the remains of primitive wolves and saber-toothed cats. Another site of about the same age is the Vallonet Cave in southeastern France on the Mediterranean. Here have been found what seem to be the earliest man-made tools found outside of Africa, dating from between 750,000 to 1 million years ago. Two choppers like those of Olduvai Gorge have been found, along with a few other worked-stone tools, and with the fossil bones of such animals as rhinoceros, elephant, horse, and whale.

At Vértesszöllös in western Hungary, an occupation site roughly con-

Homo erectus in Europe and Africa

---

[3] Carleton S. Coon, *The Origin of Races* (New York: Alfred A. Knopf, 1962), pp. 398–99, 438.

temporaneous with Peking man has been found which shows many parallels with Choukoutien. First of all, the Oldowan-like chopping tools are similar. Second, there is evidence of the use of fire. In this case, it is clear that the animals eaten were cooked; many bones show traces of charring, although there were also many unburned bones. Finally, there is some skeletal material, of which the three teeth of an immature child show similarities to immature teeth found at Choukoutien. On the other hand, there is also an occipital bone (rear part of the skull) which seems more advanced than that of Peking man, although the ridge for muscle attachment is a primitive feature of the skull. An early estimate of the cranial capacity of the Vértesszöllös skull is 1,400 cubic centimeters, which is much higher than that of either Java or Peking man, or any other representative of *Homo erectus.*

The famous Mauer jaw of Heidelberg man is roughly contemporary with Peking man and the Vértesszöllös site. The appearance of this heavy, chinless jaw is similar to those of the east Asiatic pithecanthropines. However, although the jaw is large and thick, the teeth are relatively small, within the range of variation of modern human teeth. No artifacts or other skeletal parts were found with the jaw.

Some interesting finds relating to the activities of pre-Neandertal man, perhaps *Homo erectus,* have been made at two sites in north central Spain, Torralba and Ambrona. Here there is evidence that elephants were deliberately trapped in bogs by setting fire to surrounding grass and driving the animals into the marsh, where they could be attacked when they floundered and sank. There are indications that elephant bones were hacked off and removed. Many artifacts have been recovered at these Spanish sites, which are dated at about 300,000 years ago. Work here has been done by F. Clark Howell.[4] There is evidence that animals were similarly driven into swamps in parts of sub-Saharan Africa during Middle Pleistocene times.[5]

In 1954 and 1955, the French paleontologist Camille Arambourg excavated three hominid mandibles, together with many teeth and a right parietal bone at Ternifine in Algeria, North Africa. The appearance of these bones is, again, like those of the eastern pithecanthropines: thick parietals, no chin, broad ascending ramus of the jaw, big molars with enlarged pulp cavities. Associated with the bones were some roughly made hand axe tools of the type called Abbevillian or Chellean, (see page 179) which is a somewhat more advanced type of tool than the Oldowan chopper, although apparently contemporary with it in some areas.

An incomplete cranium in Bed II at Olduvai Gorge in Tanzania

---

[4] F. Clark Howell, *Early Man* (New York: Life Nature Series, 1964), pp. 85–99.
[5] J. Desmond Clark, "Human Ecology during Pleistocene and Later Times in Africa South of the Sahara," *Current Anthropology,* Vol. 1, No. 4 (July, 1960), p. 314.

and the Telanthropus find at Swartkrans, South Africa, have also been classified as *Homo erectus*. In both cases, hand axes were found in association with the skeletal remains.

All these finds seem to indicate that there was a widespread type of hominid whom we call *Homo erectus* living between a million and half a million years ago, a man who was a hunter and gatherer with a variable stone technology, sometimes using crude choppers and sometimes hand axes. In at least some cases, this type of early man had the use of fire. Groups of such hunting-gathering peoples were distributed from South to North Africa and from Spain, France, Germany, and Hungary to Indonesia and northern China. We must assume that *Homo erectus* spoke a language. His culture had by this time become sufficiently complex to require a language to transmit it. The Choukoutien and Vértesszöllös sites suggest that home bases were in use. This is also indicated by the remains of what seems to be the oldest human dwelling uncovered in Europe. At Nice on the Riviera in France have been found remains of some apparently oval-shaped dwellings about 50 feet long and 12 to 18 feet wide, containing fireplaces. Holes about a foot in diameter are believed to have held upright beams. The site was near a stream running into the sea. Remains of rhinoceros, *Elephas antiquus*, rabbit, deer, and wild boar have been found. This settlement has been dated at about 300,000 years ago. The way of life which it suggests is more sophisticated and advanced than one might have expected of this stage in man's cultural evolution.

The existence of a home base is an important development. Such home bases would provide refuge for the old and sick. The fireplace would be the symbolic center of the group, a beacon by day and by night for the men who had left camp to hunt. At the stage of *Homo erectus*, there must have been some division of labor, with men specializing as hunters and women as collectors and perhaps preparers of food. No doubt the women looked after the children, fetched wood and water, and kept the fire going. Such groups would be apt to split up during the day but have some agreed-upon place to return to in the late afternoon or evening. Planning of this sort requires a language. Primitive though they may have appeared, with their heavy brow ridges, low skulls, and large chinless jaws, these men had relatively large brains, which were often within the range of modern man's. It seems likely that their brains had become sufficiently developed for language to be possible. Everything about their way of life suggests it. Although we must assume that the bands of *Homo erectus* were small and scattered, it is likely that their groups were larger than those of *Australopithecus*. This is suggested, for example, by the evidence for communal action in hunting at Torralba and Ambrona. Such group activity would, of course, be facilitated by language. Cooperation in the

The culture of Homo erectus

hunt would increase the available food resources and strengthen group solidarity, for families that prey together stay together.

Although there is no archaeological evidence to prove it, sharing of meat was probably practiced; it is likely that hunters brought home food for their women and children. This ancient human pattern must have started some time, and it is likely that it was current by the Lower Pleistocene. There is no sharing of food in this manner among terrestrial baboons and other *Anthropoidea,* although something of the sort is implied by the begging gestures of chimpanzees who sit by and watch when a more dominant chimpanzee is eating something.[6]

From the time of *Homo erectus* on there is only one type of hominid. *"Paranthropus"* disappears. Sherwood Washburn has suggested that this lack of speciation is a measure of the effectiveness of culture.[7]

Suggestions for further reading

G. H. R. von Koenigswald has described his own discoveries in *Meeting Prehistoric Man* (New York: Harper & Bros., 1956).

For reviews of the data on early man, see Alan Houghton Brodrick, *Man and His Ancestry* (Greenwich, Conn.: Fawcett Publications, 1964); William Howells, *Mankind in the Making: The Story of Human Evolution* (New York: Doubleday & Co., 1959); and Carleton S. Coon, *The Origin of Races* (New York: Alfred A. Knopf, 1962).

On the Vértesszöllös site, see M. Kretzoi and L. Vértes, "Upper Biharian (Intermindel) Pebble-Industry Occupation Site in Western Hungary," *Current Anthropology,* Vol. 6, No. 1 (February, 1965), pp. 74–87.

On the role of culture in man's evolution, see M. F. Ashley Montagu (ed.), *Culture and the Evolution of Man* (New York: Oxford University Press, 1962); and Charles F. Hockett and Robert Ascher, "The Human Revolution," *Current Anthropology,* Vol. 5, No. 3 (June, 1964), pp. 135–68.

---

[6] See Irven De Vore (ed.), *Primate Behavior: Field Studies of Monkeys and Apes* (New York: Holt, Rinehart, & Winston, 1965), pp. 421, 472.

[7] Sherwood Washburn, "An Ape's-Eye View of Human Evolution," Address, Wenner-Gren Foundation Symposium on the Origin of Man, held at the University of Chicago, April 2–4, 1965.

Chapter 10

The stage of Neandertal man

Neandertal man is considered to represent a stage intermediate between *Homo erectus* and modern man. He was long considered to be a species distinct from modern man and was known by the name of *Homo neanderthalensis*. If *Homo erectus* can be classed as *Homo sapiens,* this classification should certainly also cover Neandertal man, who had well-made stone tools and showed other evidences of culture. This form of man is therefore classified by some authorities nowadays as a subspecies, *Homo sapiens neanderthalensis*.[1] Neandertal men lived in Europe, North Africa, the Near East, and parts of Asia from around 100,000 to around 35,000 years ago.

In between the *Homo erectus* and Neandertal stages there are several finds of early man, some of which show quite modern features. For example, at Steinheim in Germany an almost complete skull, thought to be female, was found, dated as from the second interglacial period, about 250,000 years ago. Some authorities, notably Carleton Coon, see modern features in the appearance of the skull, although it has thick brow ridges, little elevation, and a cranial capacity of around 1,150 cubic centimeters. Coon says that except for some taurodontism the teeth are like those of a modern European woman.[2]

The back part of a young adult skull found at Swanscombe, England, along with some Acheulean stone tools (see page 179) was also dated through associated animal bones at around 250,000 years ago. The bones

---

[1] The spelling "Neandertal" is held to be more correct than the also common form "Neanderthal." However, whenever the taxonomic term is used, it must be spelled *"neanderthalensis."*

[2] Carleton S. Coon, *The Origin of Races* (New York: Alfred A. Knopf, 1962), p. 495.

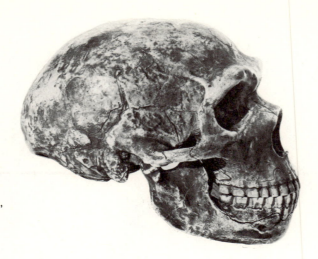

Reconstructed
plaster cast of
skull of a "Classic"
Neandertal Man
(La Chapelle aux
Saints).

of the skull are thick, and the vault is rather low, but some physical anthropologists consider the skull to tend in the modern direction. It cannot be known whether thick brow ridges were present, or what the facial region looked like, since these parts are missing.

The fossil remains of the later stage, Neandertal man, have appeared in Morocco, Gibraltar, Spain, France, Belgium, Germany, Italy, Czechoslovakia, Hungary, Yugoslavia, the Crimea, Uzbekistan, Palestine, and Iraq. Moreover, the vague term *Neandertaloid,* or Neandertal-like, has been applied to fossil finds which cover an even wider range, including a skull found near Ma-Pa in China, the skulls of Solo man in Indonesia, and the skulls of Rhodesian man in South Africa.

The abundance of skeletal material may indicate an increase in population at this time, which is also suggested by the increased number of stone tools. On the other hand, most of the skeletal finds have been made in caves, where Neandertal men often buried their dead under the dirt floor, and this has helped to preserve the bones for their later discovery. Some complete skeletons have thus been recovered, such as that of the man of La Chapelle aux Saints. There is good archaeological evidence that Neandertal men had the use of fire, which made cave dwelling possible.

Some Neandertal men lived in southern Europe at the time of the last glacial advance, when most of Europe was covered by ice. This was a bitterly cold period, when the caves, chilly though they must have been, at least provided shelter. There were also warmer times during the last interglacial period. Different kinds of plants and animals flourished in Europe in the warm and cold periods. During the cold period, there were many mammals with heavy coats of fur, such as the mammoth, wooly rhinoceros, and cave bear. Neandertal men were able to kill these large animals, whose bones have been found in their caves.

Man was originally a tropical primate. During the stage of *Homo erectus,* he ranged as far north as northern Germany and northern China. But in Europe, man subsequently had to endure the long periods of extremely cold weather which came with the last three major glaciations. During the last, or Würm glaciation, the European Neandertalers became confined to the southern parts of Europe. Escape was blocked by the Mediterranean to the south and by glaciers to the north and east, although there was a narrow corridor in central Europe. Meanwhile, other Neandertal men were living in the Near East and parts of Asia, while their Neandertaloid relatives were to be found in Africa, China, Indonesia, and elsewhere.

Two types of Neandertal man have been distinguished by physical anthropologists: a "Classic" and a "Generalized" form. The "Classic" type resembled earlier forms of *Homo erectus* in having thick skulls, heavy brow ridges, low elevation of the skull, taurodont teeth, and not much of a chin. But there was one big difference: his cranial capacity was much larger than that of *Homo erectus* and equaled that of modern man. This may seem paradoxical, since it was just stated that his skull had little elevation. The explanation is that Neandertal skulls were very long, compared to those of modern man, which are rounder and more highly domed. "Classic" Neandertal man's low skull broadened out behind the ears. The frontal part of the skull was not as fully developed as in modern man. The face of "Classic" Neandertal man had a long, massive appearance with a broad nose, large eye sockets, and a forwardly projecting upper jaw. There was no *canine fossa* on either side of the nose, as in modern man; instead there was a slight puffing out of bone in this region. The mouth was very broad, and the neck was thick and heavily muscled.

"Classic" Neandertal man

Neandertal fossils are called "Generalized" if they lack some of the characteristics of the "Classic" form, such as the heavy brow ridges.

It used to be thought that Neandertal man did not stand quite erect and walked with a shambling, shuffling gait, with his head thrust forward. Our cartoon conceptions of Stone Age man are based on this stereotype. One reason for this reconstruction is that some Neandertal leg bones are very bowed. We now know that man had had upright posture since the time of *Australopithecus* and that most Neandertal men must have had a perfectly erect stance; the exceptions were among persons afflicted by arthritis. Another aspect of our cartoon conception of Stone Age man is that he was very hairy, but this cannot be known from the fossil evidence. There is one aspect of the stereotyped picture which does have justification: Neandertal man was barrel chested and had powerfully muscled arms and legs. He was about 5 feet tall, or a little taller.

"Classic" Neandertal man is mainly, although not exclusively, represented by finds in Western Europe, where Neandertal man was first discovered. One interpretation is that "Classic" Neandertal man was a physical type which developed in response to the prolonged cold weather in Europe. The thickset body build, like that of the Eskimo, should have helped to conserve body heat. The puffed-out bone in the region where modern man's *canine fossa* is found may have helped to warm the air he breathed. But it is hard to account for the wide nasal aperture in such Darwinian terms; Eskimos have narrow ones.

There has been much argument among anthropologists about the relationship between modern *Homo sapiens* and Neandertal man. Fossil remains of the latter seem to disappear from Europe after the retreat of the last glaciation. In place of Neandertal we now find man of modern physical type, equipped with a high-domed skull, a chin, and other characteristics of present-day *Homo sapiens*. What became of Neandertal man, then? There are at least three possible answers: (1) Modern man evolved from Neandertal man. (2) Neandertal man became extinct in Europe as men of modern physical type moved in after the retreat of the glaciers. Perhaps the modern types of men wiped out the Neandertalers, or displaced them by being more efficient hunters. (3) Men of modern physical type interbred with Neandertalers. At least some modern Europeans would then be descendants of the resultant hybrid stock.

Many writers on the subject of man's evolution seem to have been reluctant to think that we could have evolved from such brutish characters as "Classic" Neandertal men. They have argued that men of modern physical type already existed at the time of Neandertal man; hence we need not be descended from the latter. Moreover, the disappearance of the "Classic" type and the associated Mousterian culture was rather sudden. There would not have been enough time, it has been argued, for modern man to have evolved from the European Neandertalers. Modern types of men must have been living elsewhere, developing the Upper Palaeolithic culture which they brought into Europe (see pages 183 ff.).

Some current authorities consider the "Classic" Neandertalers of Western Europe to have been a specialized "dead end" stock adapted to the cold weather conditions of glacial times; thereafter that stock became extinct. Those who hold this view derive the modern type of *Homo sapiens* from "Generalized" Neandertalers.

One difficulty with this interpretation is that "Classic" Neandertal men were not limited to Western Europe and must often have lived beyond the confines of the glaciers, as shown by a skull found at Casablanca in 1962 and by the skeletal material at Shanidar, Iraq. Between 1953 and 1960, Ralph Solecki found seven Neandertal skeletons with "Classic" features in a large cave called Shanidar. The deposits have been dated between about 60,000 and 45,000 years ago. One male of about 40 years of age was taller than the European Neandertalers, being about 5 feet 8 inches; he also had an enormous cranial capacity—over 1,700 cubic centimeters. His face resembles that of the man of La Chapelle aux Saints in its length and thick brow ridges. There is no *canine fossa* but some appearance of a chin.

Problems are also presented by the apparent coexistence of Neandertaloid and more modern types of man at Mt. Carmel in Palestine, where a great range of variation appears in the skeletal material. Remains of about a dozen individuals have been recovered from two caves at Mount Carmel, showing a combination of Neandertal and modern human traits. Although all have heavy brow ridges, some individuals have fairly high-domed skulls and some have chins. The caves date from around 40,000 to 35,000 years ago. There seem to be three ways of accounting for the variability of the Mt. Carmel population: (1) This was an area where Neandertal types were evolving into the modern form of *Homo sapiens*. (2) This was an area where two types of man, Neandertal and *Homo sapiens*, came together and interbred. (3) The population was simply characterized by a great deal of variability.

Geneticists are said to disfavor the first view. The second view has the advantage of a certain dramatic appeal and is supported by some authorities. The third view may not seem to be an explanation at all, but it is a fact that higher mammals which have been studied in detail show a great range of variation. Moreover, the only other Neandertal population which has remains of more than 10 individuals (at Krapina in Yugoslavia) shows the same kind of variability as that found in Palestine.[3] It may be that anthropologists have been led to expect too much uniformity in the fossil record and to expect all Neandertals to look like the man of La Chapelle aux Saints. Evolution in the direction of modern man did, after all, take place. It should not be surprising, then, to find a variable Neandertal population in which some persons had chins, high-domed skulls, and other modern features. The division of Neandertalers into "Classic" and "Generalized" types may be a premature ordering of the fossil material, for there must have been a good deal of variation in Western Europe, even in areas where the "Classic" type was prominent.

It may be concluded, then, that modern man is descended from Neandertal man and that there is no reason to rule out the Western European Neandertalers from the human line. The transition of physical type and culture after the Würm glaciation is not necessarily abrupt. At any rate, there is no direct evidence of any clash between Neandertalers and more modern types of men.

The principal evolutionary change between the stages of *Homo erectus*

---

[3] C. Loring Brace, "Refocusing on the Neanderthal Problem," *American Anthropologist*, Vol. 64, No. 4 (August 1962), pp. 730–32.

and Neandertal man was the increase in brain size. Peking man had a cranial capacity of about 1,100 cubic centimeters. European men of the second interglacial period also seem to have had relatively small skulls. Steinheim had 1,150 cubic centimeters. Two skulls from Saccopastore have 1,200 to 1,300 cubic centimeters. But the Monte Circeo Neandertal skull had 1,550 cubic centimeters, the man of La Chapelle aux Saints had 1,620 cubic centimeters; and the man from Shanidar had over 1,700 cubic centimeters.

Neandertal man generally retained various characteristics of the *Homo erectus* stage—thick skull walls and brow ridges, heavy chinless jaws and teeth, and some prognathism, or facial protrusion. The Neandertal facial region is larger and the teeth more prominent.

Such features appear dramatically in the Rhodesian man material. Remains of two individuals have been found in a quarry at Broken Hill, Rhodesia, in South Africa. The skull of the first and more complete find has a very primitive appearance in its low elevation, huge brow ridges, large eye sockets, wide mouth, and long face. The cranial capacity is about 1,300 cubic centimeters. The dating has been placed in the upper Pleistocene, contemporary with Solo man. Both Solo and Rhodesian man have often been called "Neandertaloid," although Coon considers Solo man to be a form of *Homo erectus*. A skull cap similar to that of Rhodesian man and dated at about the same time has been found at Saldanha Bay, about 90 miles north of Capetown; it also resembles a skull from Olduvai Gorge. Apparently this was a widespread type of early man found in southern and eastern Africa.

Man's facial structure underwent an evolution from the large facial region with prominent teeth and heavy brow ridges of "Classic" Neander-

Plaster cast of
skull of Rhodesian
Man.

tal and Neandertaloid types to a reduction of these features. C. L. Brace has argued that early men up to the time of Neandertal man must have used their front teeth as tools for cutting meat or for softening leather as Eskimos do. Such teeth always show considerable wear. Brace believes that with the invention and diffusion of more effective cutting tools in the Upper Palaeolithic, it was no longer necessary for men to have such large teeth and powerful jaws. Their reduction could therefore take place without selective disadvantage; mutations in that direction could occur without detriment to man. The development of cooking and the use of fire to soften meat would also make massive jaws and teeth less necessary.[4] This seems to be a convincing explanation for the modifications in Neandertal man's facial structure in the course of evolution leading to modern man.

Some nonancestors

It was noted earlier that many physical anthropologists have rejected the idea that modern man evolved from Neandertal man on the grounds that men of modern physical type coexisted with, or even antedated, Neandertal man. They have cited modern-looking skulls or skeletons as evidence for this assertion, particularly those of Grimaldi, Galley Hill, and Piltdown. The three latter finds are no longer cited in such arguments, because the first two have been shown to be more recent skeletons, while the third has been revealed as a fraud. These discoveries were made possible by new laboratory techniques which have been of great help in the interpretation of the fossil record.

Since the time of Neandertal man, people in Europe have buried the dead. The question therefore arises when some skeletal material is found: Do the bones date from the stratum in which they were found, or have they been buried and therefore come from a higher level? The Grimaldi skeletons, an adult woman and an immature male, were shown to have been buried from an Upper Palaeolithic stratum. They are therefore later than Neandertal man, not contemporary with him. The same problem concerned Galley Hill man, a complete skeleton found in a terrace of the Thames River near the site of the Swanscombe skull. The stratum seemed to be Middle Pleistocene, but the appearance of the skull was modern, and the completeness of the skeleton suggested that it might be an intrusive burial. Fluorine analysis of the bones proved this to have been the case.

Bones lying in the earth accumulate fluorine from the surrounding soil; the longer they have lain there, the higher their fluorine content will be. This does not provide an absolute chronological age, since different soils contain different amounts of fluorine. However, fluorine analysis can establish an index for the relative dating of bones found within a particular

---

[4] C. Loring Brace, "Cultural Factors in the Evolution of the Human Dentition," in M. F. Ashley Montagu (ed.), *Culture and the Evolution of Man* (New York: Oxford University Press, 1962), pp. 343–54.

site. Bones at the same level should contain about the same amounts of fluorine if they are of equal age. Discrepancies in fluorine percentage indicate that the bones are of different age.

The fluorine content of the Galley Hill bones proved to be very small when compared to those of Middle Pleistocene animal bones found in the same area. Kenneth Oakley, who made the analysis, concluded that Galley Hill man was a relatively recent burial. When the same test was applied to the Swanscombe skull, however, its antiquity was supported by the much higher fluorine content.

The same test, together with other chemical analyses, X rays, and microscopic examination, helped to prove that the famous Piltdown finds were a fraud. Anthropology textbooks always used to have a section on Piltdown man, a controversial fossil discovery. We now know that there never was a Piltdown man, and there is no more controversy about him. When he is discussed in anthropology books today, it is as an object lesson, or to illustrate the role of new laboratory techniques in the analysis of fossil finds.

A lawyer and amateur archaeologist named Charles Dawson announced the discovery of the Piltdown remains in 1912. They came from a gravel deposit in Sussex, in association with some stone tools and the bones of various animals, such as elephant, mastodon, hippopotamus, horse, and beaver. The human remains were parts of a thick but quite modern-looking fossilized skull, an apelike canine tooth, and a very apelike jaw. Some authorities doubted that so humanlike a skull could have belonged with so apelike a jaw, but others argued that this was quite possible. Some judged that the finds were Lower Pleistocene; others held out for Middle or Upper. In either case, it was unusual for the jaw of an ape, otherwise unknown for those geological times in England, to be found in close association with a human skull.

The Piltdown find remained an enigma for many years. As more was learned about the course of human evolution, the Piltdown fossils began to seem more and more peculiar, until finally a British physical anthropologist, J. S. Weiner, hit on the notion that perhaps they were fraudulent. This led to a closer examination of the bones. Oakley undertook a fluorine analysis, which showed that the human skull and the jaw had only about one fifth as much fluorine as the elephant bones in the deposit. They must therefore be much more recent. When Oakley drilled a hole into the jaw to get samples for analysis, he found that the inner bone was white, lacking the deep stain found throughout real fossils. It turned out that the bone had been artificially stained with chemicals. The skull, however, was a real fossil skull, although perhaps not older than Neolithic times. Careful examination of the teeth showed that they had evidently been filed to resemble human teeth. The jaw was that of an orangutan. Not only had the jaw been artificially stained but so had the stone tools.

Oakley tried exposing the fossil material to a Geiger counter. Judging from the responses of the counter, there did not seem to be much uranium in most of the fossils, but the elephant teeth proved to be highly radioactive. This helped to trace the probable point of origin of these teeth; they must have come from a site in Tunisia rich in early elephant fossils. The hippopotamus teeth probably came from Malta. All of these teeth had been stained to the color of the human skull.

This was clearly a very elaborate hoax. We cannot be sure who did it, although suspicion has focused on Mr. Dawson, who made the discovery which bears his name, *Eoanthropus dawsoni*, or Dawson's dawn man. It is hard to understand what the hoaxer's motives may have been. The unraveling of the hoax, at any rate, is testimony to the ingenuity of modern physical anthropology.

Now that Grimaldi, Galley Hill, and Piltdown man have been ruled out as men of modern type who lived at the same time as Neandertal man, the anthropologists who still hold the view that we are not descended from Neandertalers cite other possible *Homo sapiens* ancestors, principally Swanscombe and Fontéchevade, which are, however, incomplete finds.

Suggestions for further reading

The writer has been influenced by the views of C. Loring Brace and has drawn heavily from three of his articles: "Refocusing on the Neanderthal Problem," *American Anthropologist*, Vol. 64, No. 4 (August, 1962), pp. 729–41; "Cultural Factors in the Evolution of Human Dentition," in M. F. Ashley Montagu (ed.), *Culture and the Evolution of Man* (New York: Oxford University Press, 1962), pp. 343–54; and "The Fate of the 'Classic' Neanderthals: A Consideration of Hominid Catastrophism," *Current Anthropology*, Vol. 5, No. 1 (February, 1964), pp. 3–46. The latter article is a polemical one, which perhaps adds to its readability. At the end of the article are rejoinders by some of the writers criticized by Brace.

Detailed descriptions of particular Neandertal finds appear in Carleton S. Coon, *The Origin of Races* (New York: Alfred A. Knopf, 1962).

For a statement of the traditional view about the "dead end" "Classic" Neandertalers, see F. Clark Howell, "The Evolutionary Significance of Variation and Varieties of Neanderthal Man," *Quarterly Review of Biology*, Vol. 32, No. 4 (1957), pp. 330–47. This article also appears in Morton H. Fried (ed.), *Readings in Anthropology*, Vol. I: *Readings in Physical Anthropology, Linguistics, and Archaeology* (New York: Thomas Y. Crowell Co., 1959), pp. 63–83. See also William Howells, *Mankind in the Making: The Story of Human Evolution* (New York: Doubleday & Co., 1959), Chapters 13–16.

Variation in modern man

V

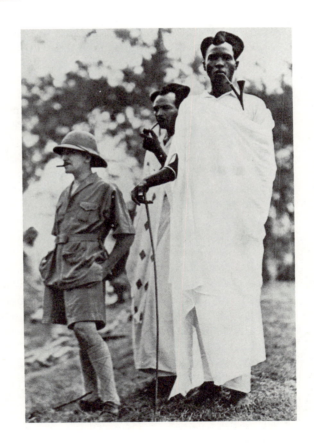

Chapter 11

The concept of race

Variation in early man

The Upper Palaeolithic period, which is discussed further in Chapter 17, was a culturally distinctive period during which men of modern physical type lived between around 30,000 and 11,000 years ago.[1] Although European Upper Palaeolithic skeletal finds have all been classified as *Homo sapiens,* they show a good deal of variation. Some authorities have seen in them foreshadowings of present-day racial groups. For instance, Cro-Magnon man of the Dordogne, France, has been held to be Caucasoid, or "white." Some skeletons from Grimaldi, Monaco, were formerly called Negroid. Although this racial linkage is no longer made, it suggests the variability of Upper Palaeolithic man in Europe.

Various early *Homo sapiens* finds in other parts of the world have been assigned racial affiliations. Franz Weidenreich even saw Mongoloid features, such as shovel-shaped incisors, in pre-*sapiens* Peking man. At a later level, at the site of Choukoutien, parts of about seven skeletons have been recovered which are dated at around 10,000 B.C. Coon considers these individuals to have had Mongoloid traits. At Wadjak in Java, Eugène Dubois, discoverer of Java man, found two skulls which are now held to be Upper Pleistocene and later than Solo man. These are often described as Australoid, resembling the present-day Australian aborigines. It has been suggested that there was an evolutionary progression from *Pithecanthropus erectus* to Solo man to Wadjak man, culminating in the aborigines who migrated from Java to Australia.

Some early skulls found in Africa are said to have Negroid features. For instance, Carleton S. Coon asserts that Upper Pleistocene skeletal

---

[1] These dates, based on radiocarbon dating, refer particularly to central and Western Europe.

materials found at Kanjera, Lake Victoria Nyanza, have Negroid traits. Of course, such racial attributions may be hazardous, since none of the soft parts—hair, skin, or eyes—can be preserved or deduced from the fossil remains.[2]

These racial ascriptions to forms of early man raise the question of whether the human races of the present day developed before or after man reached the level of *Homo sapiens.* Most physical anthropologists regard the differentiation of present-day racial groups as being relatively recent. Coon, however, divides mankind into five racial stocks: Caucasoid, Mongoloid, Australoid, Congoid, and Capoid, which he believes evolved separately to the *Homo sapiens* level.[3] A fivefold parallel development of this kind is regarded as highly unlikely by most physical anthropologists.

We are now faced with the question: What is a race? What, if anything, do race differences signify?

A race may be defined as a human population whose members have in common some hereditary physical characteristics which differentiate them from other human groups. Putting it in more genetical terms, a race is a breeding population which differs from others in the frequency of certain genes. Membership in a race is determined only by hereditary physical traits and has no necessary connection with language, nationality, or religion, although language, nationality, and religion often act as isolating mechanisms which may maintain to some extent the distinctiveness of a racial group. There is no such thing as an Aryan race, a French race, or a Muslim race.

Race defined and questioned

Some anthropologists even argue that there is no such thing as race at all; "races," in their view, are merely products of human imagination and reason which correspond to no reality in the world of nature. This extreme opinion has long been advocated by Ashley Montagu; but it has been adopted by a number of other physical anthropologists, including Frank Livingstone, Jean Hiernaux, and C. Loring Brace.[4]

One reason why these writers reject the race concept is that there is no agreement among physical anthropologists about how many races there are. Most anthropology textbooks list three major racial stocks: Caucasoid, Negroid, and Mongoloid. The Caucasoids are the so-called whites, who seem to have originated in Western Europe and who specialized in light pigmentation, so that some of the more northerly Europeans have light

---

[2] This is not to say that race cannot be deduced from skeletal material. This has often been done successfully. See Wilton Marion Krogman, *The Human Skeleton in Forensic Medicine* (Springfield, Ill.: Charles C. Thomas, Publisher, 1962). The remote age adds to the difficulties in the case of the Kanjera finds.

[3] Carleton S. Coon, *The Origin of Races* (New York: Alfred A. Knopf, 1962).

[4] See Ashley Montagu (ed.), *The Concept of Race,* (London: Free Press of Glencoe, Collier-Macmillan, Ltd., 1964).

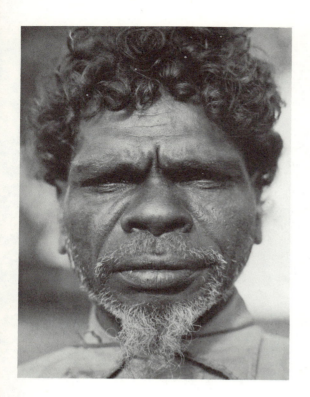

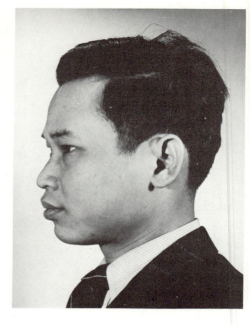

Racial types: (Top) Australian aborigine; Mongoloid, Chinese; Mongoloid, Eskimo; Papuan Negro.

(Bottom) Samoan man; White man (Albanian); and African Negro (Hausa tribe).

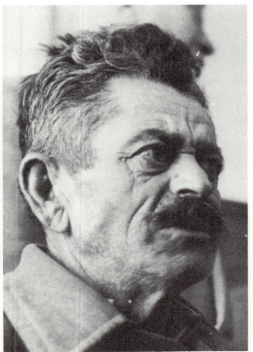

skin, blue eyes, and blond hair, although "Mediterranean" Caucasoids, found on both sides of the Mediterranean and extending eastward through the Near East into India, have dark hair and dark eyes.

The Negroids include the African Negroes; some writers have grouped the dark-skinned peoples of Melanesia with them as "Oceanic Negroes." Negroes generally have dark pigmentation, dark hair and dark eyes, a broad, low-bridged nose, thick everted lips, and kinky or curly hair.

The Mongoloids include the Japanese, Chinese, and other peoples of eastern Asia, the Eskimos, and all the American Indians down to the tip of South America. They are therefore grouped around the Pacific Ocean. Mongoloids generally have straight black hair and dark eyes, with yellowish skin pigmentation. They often have broad cheek bones, low nose bridges, and eyes characterized by an epicanthic fold, a flap of skin which covers the inner pink margin of the eye near the nose. Facial and body hair are usually sparse.

In addition to the three large categories of Caucasoids, Negroids, and Mongoloids, various other groups can be distinguished which have some distinctive physical characteristics. The Bushmen of South Africa are lighter skinned than the Negroes, although they have tightly curled hair of Negroid type, which in their case is often clustered in little clumps on the skull—"peppercorn" hair. They have short stature. Women sometimes have the condition known as steatopygia, a marked enlargement of the buttocks.

The Ainu of northern Japan differ from Japan's Mongoloid majority in having a lot of body and facial hair of a wavy type and large brow ridges.

The Australian aborigines have dark brown skin, abundant body and facial hair, large jaws, and heavy brow ridges. The Vedda of Ceylon and some of the dark-skinned peoples of south India resemble the Australian aborigines in many respects.

The Polynesians are rather large brown-skinned people, who seem hard to classify under any of the three major racial groupings.

In some racial classifications, the groups just mentioned are listed as separate races, apart from the three major ones. Other authorities lump some of them together as subdivisions of the larger ones. For example, Beals and Hoijer characterize the Ainu, the Vedda, "Dravidian" Indians, and the Australian aborigines as possible Archaic Caucasoids.[5]

The Melanesians and Papuans used to be classified with the Negroes of Africa, since they have dark skin, dark eyes, and often kinky hair. But they are a long way from Africa, although there are some intermediate Negroid or Negrito peoples, the Andaman Islanders of the Indian Ocean, who have

---

[5] Ralph L. Beals and Harry Hoijer, *An Introduction to Anthropology* (3d ed.; New York: Macmillan Co., 1965), p. 218.

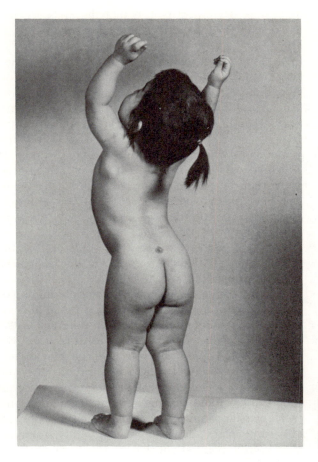

"Mongoloid spot."
Mongoloid babies
often have a bluish
spot near the base
of the spine which
later disappears.

short stature, like the Pygmies of the Congo. There are also many dark-skinned, but not Negroid, peoples in South India, and there are Negritos in the Malay Peninsula.

The question arises: Do the African Negroes and the Melanesians have a common ancestry? Was there once a dark-skinned population somewhere in South Asia which split into two wings, with one moving down into Africa and the other toward New Guinea? Or were there simply two distinct groups of human beings which developed, in some ways, along parallel lines? We will later consider the theory that dark pigmentation confers some benefits in tropical areas. This might also be true of kinky or curly hair and broad nostrils. If these features have survival value in the tropics, it is understandable that they could develop in different trop-ical areas of the world through the operation of natural selection. The more recent view, in fact, is that the Melanesians and Africans are not genetically related, since they differ completely in the composition of their blood groups.[6]

A similar question of classification concerns the African Pygmies and Southeast Asiatic Negritos. The Pygmies of the Congo are short-statured Negroes. There are also short people of Negroid appearance in the Andaman Islands, in the Malay Peninsula, and in parts of New Guinea and the Philippines. Do these scattered groups represent surviving members of an early short-statured Negro population? Or are they different populations which have developed along similar lines? There has been much speculation about this question, but recent blood group studies show that there is no genetic relationship between the African Pygmies and the Papuan Negritos. This is in accord with the general finding about the lack of genetic relationship between Africans and Melanesians mentioned previously. Moreover, in New Guinea, where short-statured persons are found, there is a gradual grade or cline in stature from short to normal-sized individuals, suggesting that shortness of stature is a local development in this area.

These, at any rate, are the problems of lumping or splitting—of grouping together or separating—that face racial taxonomists. Hence the disparity in numbers of races listed in different texts. Some authorities list only three. Coon, as we have seen, distinguishes five major races. Stanley Garn lists 32.[7] Coon and Garn believe that these discrepancies do not weaken the validity of racial classification. They point out that there are large groups, which they call geographical races, and smaller ones which they call local and microgeographical races. Coon and Garn argue that racial classifications have value for the study of evolutionary mechanisms at work in man's adaptation to different environments.[8]

It is often pointed out that zoologists recognize subspecific groupings, variously designated as subspecies, breeds, varieties, demes, or races. Domesticated animals such as dogs resemble man in showing great variations in pigmentation, size, and hair form. In the case of domesticated animals, the breeds are artificially kept "pure" by man; but there also exist some contrasting animal forms in the wild state which could interbreed but usually do not do so, since they have become adapted to different ecological niches. Brook trout and lake trout are an example.[9] If it

---

[6] Coon, *op. cit.*, p. 4 fn.

[7] Stanley M. Garn, *Human Races* (Springfield, Ill.: Charles C. Thomas, Publisher, 1961).

[8] Stanley M. Garn and Carleton S. Coon, "On the Number of Races of Mankind," *American Anthropologist*, Vol. 57, No. 5 (1955), pp. 996–1001.

[9] Ernst Mayr, *Animal Species and Evolution* (Cambridge, Mass.: The Belknap Press of Harvard University Press, 1963), pp. 334–59.

is feasible to classify and study subspecific groups among other animals, what can be the objection to doing the same for man?

In answer to this point, Frank B. Livingstone has argued that zoologists are not in agreement about the usefulness of classifying subspecies of various animals. There is debate in zoology about this matter, just as there is in anthropology.[10]

Another reason why opponents of the race concept criticize current racial categories is that the latter are based primarily on observable and measurable phenotypic traits which give little indication of underlying genotypes. Thus African and Oceanic "Negroids" were lumped together because they looked similar, until the study of their blood group patterns showed that their genotypes differed.

Europe has been the scene of recurrent invasions and migrations. This makes it hard to postulate a "pure" Nordic or other racial stock in Europe. In the United States, there has been much interbreeding between Negroes and whites. Glass and Li have calculated from blood group distributions that North American Negroes have about 31 percent white ancestry. In a later publication, Glass reduced this figure to about 28 percent. In any case, the percentage is substantial.[11] On the basis of a genetic probability table, Robert P. Stuckert has concluded that over 36 million whites in the United States are descendants of persons of African origin and that the majority of persons with African ancestry are classified as white.[12] Should we then abandon the term *race*?

One reason why Ashley Montagu wishes to abolish the word *race* is that it has been used by racists and demagogues to divide the human species and to foster notions of racial superiority and inferiority. The most tragic outcome of such patterns of thinking was the systematic slaughter of 6 million Jews by the Nazi regime in World War II. Ashley Montagu has suggested some substitutes for the term *race*—"ethnic group" and "geno-group"—but it is hard to see how a new label could improve matters. A race by any other name . . . ? A member of the Ku Klux Klan will not feel differently about Negroes if you tell him that Negroes do not constitute a race but an ethnic group or genogroup. And if you tell him that there is no such thing as race, he will think that you are out of your mind. A Black

---

[10] Frank B. Livingstone, "On the Nonexistence of Human Races," in Montagu (ed.), *op. cit.*, pp. 46–60.

[11] Bentley Glass and C. C. Li, "The Dynamics of Racial Intermixture—an Analysis Based on the American Negro," *American Journal of Human Genetics*, Vol. 5 (1953), pp. 1–20; Bentley Glass, "On the Unlikelihood of Significant Admixture of Genes from the North American Indians in the Present Composition of Negroes of the United States," *American Journal of Human Genetics*, Vol. 7 (1955), pp. 368–85.

[12] Robert P. Stuckert, "Race Mixture: The African Ancestry of White Americans," in Peter B. Hammond (ed.), *Physical Anthropology and Archaeology: Selected Readings* (New York: Macmillan Co., 1964), pp. 192–97.

Panther who hates the whites would react in the same way. If we hope to dispel such hatreds, other methods must be used.

There are sociological and psychological forces which lead men to cling to racist attitudes. David Low's Colonel Blimp, who once exclaimed, "Gad, sir, . . . wars are necessary—otherwise how can heroes defend their countries?" might also have said, "Gad, sir, there have to be races; otherwise how can the higher ones keep the lower ones in their place?"

To review some of the points made so far: A race was defined as a human population whose members have in common some hereditary physical characteristics which differentiate them from other groups. Some anthropologists deny the validity and usefulness of the race concept, partly because there is no agreement among physical anthropologists as to how many races there are. Moreover, there is much overlapping, and there has been much interbreeding among human populations. The "no-race" point of view, as it has been called, is a minority one at present in anthropological circles, but it has some able exponents. Later in this and the following chapter, we shall return to some of their contributions. Meanwhile, let us consider some attempts to account for the existence of racial differences. It seems undeniable, after all, that a blond Swede, a Negro, and a Chinese look quite different from one another. How can we explain the development of such racial differentiation?

Pigmentation and environment

Skin color is the most noticeable racial trait. It is degree of pigmentation which most clearly distinguishes Negroes and whites. This is illustrated in Griffin's book, *Black Like Me*.[13] Griffin, a white man, had his skin darkly pigmented through a combination of taking oral tablets and exposing his body to ultraviolet rays. With a dark skin he then traveled about in the South, where he was automatically accepted as a Negro by white men and Negroes alike.

There has been much speculation to account for the extremes of pigmentation found in human beings. Such extremes are also found in some wild animals, such as black bears and white polar bears. They are more common, however, in domesticated forms of cows, horses, pigs, sheep, dogs, and so on. Since man domesticated himself before he domesticated other animals, Franz Boas suggested that such variations in pigmentation, as well as other "racial" differences, may in some way be due to domestication, or the experience of living in an artificially protected environment.[14] It may be argued that black and white forms of animals would be too noticeable for safety in many environments and that mutations in these directions would be disfavored, but under the protection of domestication such mutations could occur without penalty.

---

[13] John Howard Griffin, *Black Like Me* (Boston: Houghton Mifflin Co., 1960).

[14] Franz Boas, *The Mind of Primitive Man* (rev. ed.; New York: Macmillan Co., 1938), p. 99.

A more widely held view among physical anthropologists is that degree of pigmentation is related to climate. Those who advance this view sometimes cite "Gloger's rule," which holds that races of birds and mammals living in warm, humid regions have more melanin pigmentation than races of the same species living in cooler, drier regions. This "rule" was at first meant to account for the color of fur and feathers and had more to do with the effects of humidity than of temperature. But dark-skinned human beings are also found in warm, humid regions, although not all occupants of such regions have dark skins. Dark pigmentation occurs mainly among people who live within 20 degrees of the equator. As we have seen, African Negroes and the dark-skinned peoples of Melanesia have been shown to be genetically unrelated populations. Both groups of tropical peoples therefore developed dark pigmentation independently. It seems likely that such was also the case among the dark-skinned peoples of South India. Dark pigmentation may therefore provide some selective advantage in tropical regions. What advantages can it have?

Negroes and whites differ in the amount of melanin in the skin. The melanin serves to absorb ultraviolet rays. People with very light skin not only suffer more from sunburn than dark-skinned persons, but they also have a higher incidence of skin cancer, especially in sunny southerly areas. Man was originally a naked tropical animal. Mutations in the direction of dark pigmentation would evidently have been favorable for human beings living in the tropical zone, where solar radiation is most intense and subject to little seasonal change.

There are some difficulties with this theory, although they are not necessarily damaging to the basic principle. One difficulty is that many African Negroes live in jungle areas where they are not much exposed to sunlight. Another difficulty is that the American Indian inhabitants of tropical South America and most of the peoples of Indonesia and Southeast Asia are relatively light skinned. The first objection has been met by a historical reconstruction which has not been exactly demonstrated but which seems plausible: that is, the African Negroes are relative newcomers to the jungle area, having formerly lived in more open savanna country. The acquisition of iron tools was necessary to make the forest habitable. Carleton S. Coon has argued that the African Negroes cannot have made their homes in the forest much before the time of Christ. If the ancestors of the modern Negroes lived in grasslands south of the Sahara during Pleistocene times, dark pigmentation would have been advantageous for them. Coon points out that there are other bare-skinned animals living in the same environment which are either black or dark grey in color, such as the elephant, rhinoceros, hippopotamus, and buffalo.[15]

There are two ways of accounting for the relatively light pigmentation

---

[15] Carleton S. Coon, "Climate and Race," in Harlow Shapley (ed.), *Climatic Change* (Cambridge, Mass.: Harvard University Press, 1954), pp. 13–34.

of American Indians in tropical South America. One is that they are relatively late arrivals in this region. The other is that those who live in the tropical forest area are not exposed to much sunlight, while those who live in the highlands wear much clothing and broad-brimmed hats. The light-skinned inhabitants of Indonesia and Southeast Asia are also believed to be relatively recent immigrants of post-Neolithic times.[16]

The solar radiation theory seems plausible. But we must also try to account for the development of light pigmentation. It has been suggested that light pigmentation is favorable in clouded northerly areas, since it allows more ultraviolet rays to penetrate the skin and build up vitamin D. This factor may be significant. But C. Loring Brace has another suggestion; he believes that the use of clothing originated in Western Europe. Neandertal man and his successors had to wear clothes to stay alive during the periods of intense cold weather in Europe. The abundance of scrapers dating from the beginning of the Würm glaciation suggests that animal skins were prepared for clothing, and we know from the presence of bone needles that Upper Palaeolithic Europeans made clothes. Once this pattern began, the presence or absence of melanin in the skin became relatively immaterial (although some parts of the body were still exposed to ultraviolet rays), and mutations in the direction of pigment loss could occur without ill effects. We may assume that this development would be apt to occur wherever human beings wear clothing, but clothes have been worn longest in the area where the lightest-skinned people are found.[17] These speculations seem reasonable, although the absence of proof gives them a tentative character.

Body build and environment

Another "rule," like that of Gloger, referred to in zoology is Bergmann's rule which holds that the smaller-sized races of a species are found in the warmer parts of its range, while the larger races are found in the cooler parts. Julian Huxley has written that most small or moderate-sized species of birds and mammals vary in size with latitude and become larger, the nearer they are found to the poles. He writes:

Thus, for each degree of north latitude, the linear dimensions of puffins increase by over one per cent; with the result that puffins from their furthest north in Spitzbergen have nearly doubled the bulk of puffins from their furthest south on the coast of Brittany. The biological reason for this is that absolutely larger bodies have a relatively smaller surface, and so lose heat less readily.[18]

How well does Bergmann's rule apply to man? In some ways not so well, since man has a culture with which he modifies his environment. He may wear clothes, build a shelter, or crouch beside a fire. Climatic forces

[16] C. Loring Brace, "A Nonracial Approach towards the Understanding of Human Diversity," in Montagu (ed.), *op. cit.*, pp. 118–19.
[17] *Ibid.*, pp. 115–17.
[18] Julian Huxley, *Evolution in Action* (New York: Mentor Books, 1957), pp. 43–44.

do not bear upon human beings as directly and inexorably as they do upon puffins. Nevertheless, Coon, Garn, Birdsell, and others have argued a case for the influence of climate on body build among humans.

The Eskimos are short, not tall, and Coon, Garn, and Birdsell point out that they have chunky bodies, thick chests, short legs and short fingers and toes. Their bodies are thus well constructed to preserve heat. In contrast, the Nilotic Negroes of the Sudan are tall and lanky; they have long narrow chests, long arms, and long legs. Such a body build would be unfortunate in the Arctic, but is well suited to a hot, dry environment, where it is well adapted to shed heat. Not all Negroes have this type of body build. The so-called Forest Negroes are more rugged and stockily built and have shorter legs, and the Pygmies of the Congo are, of course, very short in stature. The Nilotic Negroes, however, are generally long and slender. Caucasoids who have lived in the same environment as these Negroes for many generations have a similar body build. Moreover, many of the mammals who inhabit hot, dry deserts and savannas, such as giraffes, camels, and cheetahs, are also built along lean lines. The Australian aborigines who live in the hot, dry desert regions of northern and central Australia, as pointed out by Coon, Garn, and Birdsell, have slender body builds.[19]

Here one begins to wonder, however. The Australian aborigines, until recently, never wore clothing. Perhaps their slenderness might be appropriate to the heat of the day, but how would it protect them from the coldness of the night? The aborigines sleep naked on the ground, between fires, under conditions which cause extreme discomfort to Europeans.

It must be said that Bergmann's "rule" has been criticized, not only in its applicability to man but in application to animals in general. To quote one critic, Charles G. Wilber:

The barren ground caribou is given as larger than the more southern forest species. The extensive migrations back and forth of these animals should not be ignored and the greater severity of cold in the subarctic forests is a pertinent factor. The penguins of the extreme south are said to be larger than those nearer the equator. But, large and small penguins are found together in some antarctic areas. In all these examples when one examines the basic data, the differences in size and weight are relatively trivial and do not in any clear manner give overwhelming cold survival value to the heavier forms. . . .[20]

Besides, asks Wilber, what about the roly-poly hippopotamus, rhinoceros, and elephant in the tropics?

---

[19] Carleton S. Coon, Stanley M. Garn, and Joseph B. Birdsell, *Races: A Study of the Problems of Race Formation in Man* (Springfield, Ill.: Charles C. Thomas, Publisher, 1950, p. 37.

[20] Charles G. Wilber, "Physiological Regulations and the Origin of Human Types," in Stanley M. Garn, (ed.), *Readings on Race* (Springfield, Ill.: Charles C. Thomas, Publisher, 1960), p. 108.

These criticisms seem to place the burden of further proof on the climatic determinists. Their views have other weaknesses. It is awkward for their theory, for example, that two tribes at Tierra del Fuego, the Ona and Yahgan, differ greatly in stature, the Ona being tall and the Yahgan short. One can straighten things out, perhaps, by arguing that the Yahgan (or the Ona) are relative newcomers into the area, but there is no good evidence for either case. In tropical Africa, one can find both very tall and very short human beings, just as one can find both pygmy chimpanzees and normal-sized ones and pygmy as well as large hippos.

Besides climate, another consideration affecting stature and body build is, of course, diet. In the past 20 or 30 years, Americans have been getting taller and taller. Children tend to be taller than their parents. This development has had all kinds of repercussions in the field of business. Shoe companies have been making more shoes of larger size. Hotels have been installing more longer-sized beds. Movie theaters have been installing wider seats to fit the broadening American posterior. This increasing size is probably due to improvements in nutrition—vitamin-enriched breads, cereals, and other foods. The tendency to grow taller is not limited to Caucasoids, for since World War II the same thing has been happening in Japan where, again, children are often taller than their parents. If this tendency persists, it may work a revolution in the architecture of the low-ceilinged Japanese home.

In the underdeveloped and overpopulated countries of Asia, people are often undernourished. Large body size with its demands for larger food intake would be an unfortunate development in these areas. The advent of economic prosperity in such regions, however, might well be accompanied by an increase in body size, like those now seen in the United States, Europe, and Japan.

Suggestions for further reading

The case for the climatic determinism of racial features in man is best set forth in Carleton S. Coon, Stanley M. Garn, and Joseph B. Birdsell, *Races: A Study of the Problem of Race Formation in Man* (Springfield, Ill.: Charles C. Thomas, Publisher, 1950), and in Carleton S. Coon, "Climate and Race," in Harlow Shapley (ed.), *Climatic Change* (Cambridge, Mass.: Harvard University Press, 1954). "Climate and Race" is reprinted in Morton H. Fried (ed.), *Readings in Anthropology*, Vol. I: *Readings in Physical Anthropology, Linguistics and Archaeology* (New York: Thomas Y. Crowell Co., 1959), pp. 103–20.

For a criticism of such theories, see Weston La Barre, *The Human Animal* (Chicago: University of Chicago Press, 1954), Chapter 8.

For some stimulating hypotheses about the development of diversity in man, see C. L. Brace, "A Nonracial Approach towards the Understanding of Human Diversity," in Ashley Montagu (ed.), *The Concept of Race* (London: Free Press of Glencoe, Collier-Macmillan, Ltd., 1964), pp. 103–52. The latter book presents the views of those who are critical of the race concept.

Chapter 12

The concept of cline
and the study of
single-trait distributions

Frank B. Livingstone has written, "There are no races, there are only clines."[1] A cline is a geographical transition from higher to lower incidence of a biological trait, a gradient in the frequency of a trait over a geographical range. Julian Huxley's example of the size of puffins, cited in the preceding chapter, would be an example. One can follow a gradient in size from large to small as one goes from pole to equator. To take a human illustration: As one moves from northern to southern Europe, one notices a decrease in the frequency of blue eyes and blond hair among the inhabitants. If one took blood samples from the people in the same area, one would find different frequencies of certain blood groups, but cline maps of their distributions would not resemble those for eye color or hair color. For example, the gene for blood group B progressively increases in frequency from West to East.

There is a tendency in present-day physical anthropology to study the distribution of genetically determined single traits. When these are plotted, they often do not coincide very well with traditional racial groupings. Serological studies provide some of the best examples. Knowledge of the different blood groups has great practical importance in relation to blood transfusion. For this reason, abundant records about blood groups are available from populations all over the world. We can therefore trace

---

[1] Frank B. Livingstone, "On the Nonexistence of Human Races," in Ashley Montagu (ed.), *The Concept of Race* (London: Free Press of Glencoe, Collier-Macmillan, Ltd., 1964), p. 47.

the distribution of blood factors A, B, O, Rh, and others in different human populations. Let us consider some of these distributions.

The ABO blood groups

The blood types A, B, AB, and O are the earliest known and most fully studied. If a person has the chemical factor A in his blood, it is said to belong to blood group A. If his blood has another chemical factor called B, it is assigned to blood group B. If his blood has both factors, it belongs to blood group AB. If his blood has neither A nor B, it belongs to blood group O. An individual inherits one blood group gene from each parent, so there are six possible genotypic combinations: OO, AA, AO, BB, BO, and AB. Since neither A nor B is dominant over the other, their combination results in the blood group AB. But O is recessive to both A and B. Thus both AA and AO result in the phenotypic blood group A, and both BB and BO result in the phenotypic blood group B, making four main blood types.[2]

These blood groups have been distinguished because they may not be compatible in blood transfusions. Transfusion of A blood into a person of blood group B, or vice versa, may result in the clumping or disintegration of blood cells. This also happens if an O recipient receives blood of another type. It used to be thought that persons of blood group O were "universal donors" who could give blood to patients of any type, while AB individuals were "universal recipients" who could receive blood of other types without injury. This is not always the case, however; so blood given in transfusions is usually of the same type as that of the person receiving the blood.

Turning now to the anthropological significance of the blood groups, it has been shown that they are not evenly distributed throughout mankind. Although the gene for O is recessive, blood group O has the highest frequency in human populations. Most American Indians belong to blood group O. There is very little B among North and South American Indians, but some northern tribes, the Blackfoot and Flathead Indians of Montana, have surprisingly high percentages of A.

There is a high incidence of A in Western Europe and high concentrations of B in northwestern India, West Pakistan, and northern China and Manchuria. These distributions do not accord very well with traditional racial classifications. The Caucasoids of northwestern India and Pakistan have blood types like those of the Chinese and unlike those of Western Europe, while the Mongoloids of eastern Asia have a different blood type from that of most American Indians.

The significance of these distributions is not yet understood. The factors for A and B have not been brought about by recent mutations,

---

[2] There are two forms of A, which slightly complicates matters, but this does not negate the above.

since the apes also have them, or substances very similar to them, and it is likely that the blood groups are older than *Homo sapiens*. Natural selection may have influenced their distribution. It has been shown that there is some association between blood group O and susceptibility to duodenal and gastric ulcers, and between blood group A and susceptibility to stomach cancer. It is also possible that the different blood groups have been selectively affected by plagues and epidemics.

Analysis of blood types has sometimes been helpful in determining the regions of origin of certain populations. For example, serological analysis has shown that the Gypsies probably did come from India, as their traditions assert and as their language testifies. We have already seen that the Africans and Melanesians have different blood group patterns and are therefore held to be genetically unrelated.

The Rh factor

The chemical factor known as Rh is present in the blood of about 85 percent of Caucasoids. Those who have it are said to be Rh positive. The 15 percent who lack this chemical substance are said to be Rh negative. The significance of the Rh factor lies in the damage to embryos which may occur during prenatal development in Rh-negative women married to Rh-positive men. Mother and foetus have separate circulatory systems, but it sometimes happens that some of the foetus's blood filters through into the mother's bloodstream. Since the foetus manufactures the Rh substance derived from its father's genetic combination (the Rh positive condition being dominant over the negative), the mother's blood produces antibodies which may subsequently filter into the foetus' body and damage its blood cells. The danger is greater in the case of third, fourth, or later pregnancies, by which time the mother may have produced more antibodies, which may then attack the foetus at an earlier stage of development when it is more vulnerable. This resulting ailment is known as *erythroblastosis fetalis*. Fortunately, it is relatively rare, occurring only once in about 200 deliveries in which the mother and father have the relevant blood types.[3]

It is interesting that American Indians have no Rh-negative genes; hence they do not suffer from *erythroblastosis fetalis*. Rh negative is also absent among Polynesians, Melanesians, and Australian aborigines. Its incidence is apparently low among peoples of the Far East. African Negroes and American Negroes have about half the incidence found among whites. The highest known concentrations of Rh negative are among the Basques of northern Spain and southern France, and among some isolated village communities in Switzerland. It may be that Rh

---

[3] In 1968 a vaccine named RhoGAM was developed to curtail an Rh-negative mother's production of antibodies and thus lessen the danger to a future Rh-positive child.

negative originally developed as a mutation in Europe and subsequently spread to other areas of the world.

Much work is currently being done in the analysis of blood chemistry. Various other blood factors have been discovered, such as the MNSU system, the Duffy system, the Diego system, and others. Mapping of the frequencies of these systems will throw more light on the genetic relationships of different human populations.

The sickle-cell gene

Sicklemia is a condition in which a person's red blood cells, when deprived of oxygen, assume a crescent or sickle-shaped appearance instead of the usual round form. This may be seen when a drop of the person's blood is left to stand on a glass slide. The condition of sicklemia is determined by genetic factors and may exist in either a homozygous or

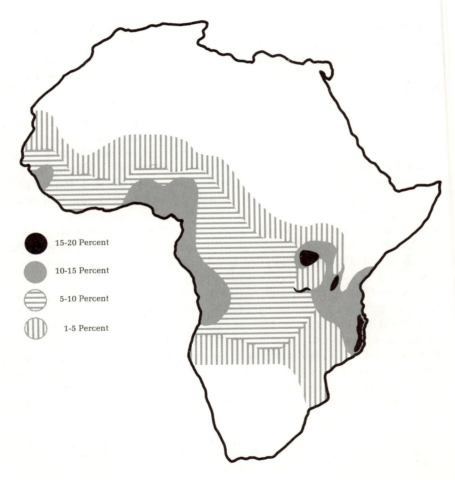

15-20 Percent

10-15 Percent

5-10 Percent

1-5 Percent

Distribution of sickle cell gene. Frequency of the sickle cell gene is plotted in percent on the map of Africa. High frequencies are confined to a broad belt in which malignant tertian malaria is an important cause of death.

heterozygous form. In the former case, the individual produces only the sickle-cell type of hemoglobin, in which oxygen is transported to the various cells of the body. Such individuals suffer from anemia and usually die before maturity. Heterozygotes have both a sickle-cell gene and a normal gene. Since such persons have a fair amount of normal hemoglobin, they may not suffer from anemia, though they sometimes do. In a population in which the sickle-cell allele is present, there are also "normal" homozygous persons who do not have the gene.

Since anemic homozygous individuals usually die without reproducing, one would expect the incidence of the sickling gene to diminish through natural selection; but there are parts of Africa where the gene has an incidence of over 20 percent. Although it has not been found among the Bushmen of South Africa, the sickle-cell is present in most African Negro populations and in about 10 percent of American Negroes. The sickling gene is also found in parts of Sicily, Italy, Greece, Turkey, Arabia, and India, but it is not known to be present in the peoples of eastern Asia, Melanesia, Polynesia, Australia, or the American Indians.

The wide distribution and the sometimes high incidence of the sickling gene suggest that it has some selective advantage. The gene is generally found in malarious tropical regions; apparently the sickle-cell trait provides some protection against falciparian malaria. Just how it does so is not understood, but investigations in Africa have shown that heterozygous persons have much more resistance to the disease than do normal homozygous ones. Anemic homozygous persons die out; normal homozygous ones get malaria. It is the heterozygous persons, therefore, who are favored by natural selection in malarial areas.

This accounts for the persisting incidence of the sickle-cell gene, despite the selective pressures against it. One would expect the incidence of the gene to decline among American Negroes who do not live in malarial regions. One would also expect it to decline in Old World regions where DDT campaigns have helped to eradicate malaria. Meanwhile, it has some survival value in the tropics, although it also poses the threat of anemia.

Frank B. Livingstone has shown how man has fostered the spread of malaria in Africa through his own cultural advance. Here we have an intricate network of factors involving technology, population increase, mosquitoes, and genes. Livingstone points out that the cline in the frequency of the sickle-cell trait coincides with the spread of yam cultivation. Such cultivation is relatively recent in West Africa, having had to wait upon the introduction of iron tools for clearing the forest.

The major local carrier of malaria, *Anopheles gambiae*, cannot breed in water that is brackish, shaded, polluted, or which has a swift current. In former times there were relatively few favorable breeding places in the forest for this mosquito, since the trees provided shade, and there were few stagnant pools. But when man began to cut down the forest and establish farming settlements, swamps were formed, the shade cover was removed, and man's villages, ponds, and garbage dumps provided attractive breeding grounds. Population increase also favored the spread of malaria. It was in this setting, then, that the sickle-cell mutation became favored by natural selection.[4]

Thalassemia

A type of anemia known as *thalassemia* is also common in malarious regions. In this case, the areas involved are the Mediterranean region, Asia Minor, India, Thailand, and Indonesia. Here, again, individuals who are homozygous for the gene which causes the anemia are apt to die young, but those who are heterozygous seem to receive some protection from malaria, although the evidence for such protection is not as clear as it is for the sickling gene.

The present chapter has dealt with an approach in current physical anthropology which places an emphasis on the study of single-trait distributions and clines. A cline is a geographical transition from higher to lower incidence of a biological trait, a gradient in the frequency of a trait over a geographical range. The value of studying clines and frequency distributions lies in the possibility of uncovering the selective factors which affect the incidence of the trait in question. Thus we have seen how, in certain regions, natural selection has favored such apparently deleterious genes as those which cause sicklemia and thalassemia. The study of clines opens up real problems for research in physical anthropology. In contrast, the classification of races seems to be a rather sterile procedure. When plotting the distribution of single traits, it is often seen that they cross traditional racial groupings. The ABO blood groups, for example, are found in different "races," although sometimes in different frequencies. The distribution of the sickle-cell also crosses racial lines. It was formerly believed to be a "Negroid" trait, but we now know that the sickling gene is not limited to Negroes; nor is the gene for thalassemia limited to Mediterranean Caucasoids.

Suggestions for further reading

Two articles by Frank B. Livingstone are recommended: "On the Non-existence of Human Races" in Ashley Montagu (ed.), *The Concept of Race* (London: Free Press of Glencoe, Collier-Macmillan, Ltd., 1964), pp. 46–60; and "Anthropological Implications of Sickle Cell Gene Distribution in West Africa" (see fn. 4). Also see C. L. Brace, "On the Race Concept" with discus-

---

[4] Frank B. Livingstone, "Anthropological Implications of Sickle Cell Gene Distribution in West Africa," *American Anthropologist*, Vol. 60, No. 3 (1958), pp. 533–62; reprinted in both Stanley M. Garn, *Readings on Race* (Springfield, Ill.: Charles C. Thomas, Publisher, 1960), pp. 118–49; and in M. F. Ashley Montagu (ed.), *Culture and the Evolution of Man* (New York: Oxford University Press, 1962), pp. 271–99.

sion and comment by Carleton S. Coon, Earl W. Count, Stanley M. Garn, Julian Huxley, Ashley Montagu, and Andrzej Wiercinski, *Current Anthropology,* Vol. 5, No. 4 (October, 1964), pp. 313–20.

On the human blood groups, see William C. Boyd, *Genetics and the Races of Man* (Boston, Mass.: Little, Brown & Co., 1950), and William C. Boyd, "Four Achievements of the Genetical Method in Physical Anthropology," *American Anthropologist,* Vol. 65, No. 2 (1963), pp. 243–52.

Chapter 13

Race and ability

It is a common characteristic of ingroups such as tribes, castes, and clubs that its members feel that they are somehow better than other such groups. Since racial traits are conspicuous, and since Europeans played a dominant, often exploitative, role in the periods of exploration and colonial expansion, it is understandable that attitudes of racial superiority developed among whites. While such attitudes have characterized many other human groups, racial prejudice took a new turn in 19th-century Europe; it sought scientific justification. By measuring skulls or estimating cranial capacities some 19th-century scholars tried to find evidence for the superiority of the whites.

Skull measurement

It is curious that some of the first work of this kind had an intra-European scope and was concerned with trying to demonstrate the superiority of either broad- or narrow-headed persons. Paul Broca was foremost in this new kind of undertaking. It was under his leadership that an Anthropological Society was founded in Paris in 1859, the year of publication of Darwin's *Origin of Species*. Broca, a great measurer of skulls, believed that city dwellers had rounder, broader heads than people who lived in the country, and that round-headed Frenchmen of Gallic ancestry were superior to narrow-headed Nordics. An opposing view was held by Vacher de Lapouge and Otto Ammon, who did their skull measuring in the 1890's; they believed that narrow-headed Nordics were essentially superior to broad-headed Europeans of Alpine stock.

De Lapouge measured skulls found in medieval cemeteries in Paris and found that in an upper-class cemetery there was a higher incidence of *dolichocephalic* (narrow-headed) skulls than in a lower-class graveyard. Ammon measured the skulls of army recruits in Baden and found that

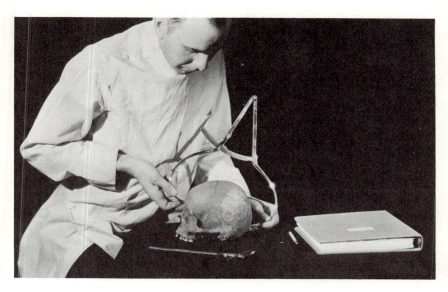

Measurement of
head length of
skull.

men from the city of Baden tended to have narrower heads than those
from the rural districts around the city. This led him to conclude that there
is a selective migration of the more intelligent and adventuresome narrow-
headed persons from the countryside to the city, leaving behind on the
farms a plethora of peaceful, dull-witted, broad-headed peasants.

It was unfortunate for Ammon's theory that an Italian scholar, Livi,
found just the reverse situation in southern Italy, where the rural population around Naples turned out to be prevailingly narrow headed, while
a higher incidence of broad-headed persons was found in the city of
Naples itself.

The situation in both cases can be explained by the fact that cities at-
tract a heterogeneous population from different parts of Europe and not
just from the immediate area. The countryside around Baden has an old,
stable population of broad-headed Alpines, but in Baden itself there are
narrow-headed Nordics from northern Europe and narrow-headed Medi-
terraneans from southern Europe; hence there is a higher incidence of
dolichocephaly in the city than in the surrounding countryside. A similar
situation exists in southern Italy, where the stable rural Mediterranean
population is prevailingly narrow headed. But in the city of Naples there
are more central Europeans of Alpine stock and hence a higher incidence
of *brachycephaly*, or broad-headedness, than in the surrounding countryside.

There is no longer a school of thought which champions the broad-
headed or narrow-headed person as superior. It is nice to know that a racist
view can become extinct. At the time, however, such views were taken

seriously. De Lapouge believed that since the enterprising narrowheads automatically rise to the top, they form an upper-class aristocracy, ruling over the submerged broadheads. De Lapouge predicted an ultimate class war between these two groups and wrote that "I am convinced that in the next century millions will cut each others' throats because of one or two degrees more or less of cephalic index."[1] De Lapouge was right that in the next century millions would cut each others' throats, but he was wrong about the reasons for it.

The notions of Broca, Ammon, and De Lapouge may seem funny to us now, but there was a serious consequence in their head-measuring activities. Racist thinking now sought scientific justification. Broca, Ammon, De Lapouge, and others used methods which were held to be scientific and thus brought the question of racism into the arena of science. Moreover, after the publication of Darwin's *Origin of Species* and the growing acceptance of the idea of evolution, a new type of sanction for the notion of white supremacy appeared. Some writers argued that the whites were the most highly evolved and least apelike of the various races and had the largest skulls and brains.

Race and evolutionary development

Franz Boas in *The Mind of Primitive Man* and Otto Klineberg in *Race Differences* countered these arguments. If one selects certain traits for comparison, they pointed out, a case may be made for the whites being more highly evolved than Mongoloids or Negroids; but it depends upon the traits selected. If one chooses other traits for comparison, Negroids may be seen to be less apelike than whites or Mongoloids. In their dark pigmentation, prognathism (facial protrusion), receding forehead, and low, broad nose, the Negroes seem to be more apelike than the other two major racial groups. But Negroes have some traits which show them to be less apelike than Caucasoids and Mongoloids: in particular the thickness of their lips. Man differs from the other primates in having everted lips in which the mucous membrane can be seen as a continuous red line. The Negroes have the thickest, most everted lips among present-day racial groups. Their hair form is also least apelike, for tightly curled or kinky hair is not found among apes and monkeys. The whites are the most apelike of the three major racial stocks in having more body hair and more of a brow ridge than either Negroids or Mongoloids. However, one cannot say that any one of these three groups is the most highly, or least highly evolved.[2]

---

[1] Quoted in Otto Klineberg, *Race Differences* (New York: Harper & Bros., 1935), p. 7. An almost identical quotation is attributed by Jacques Barzun to Alfred Fouillée. See Jacques Barzun, *Race: A Study in Modern Superstition* (New York: Harcourt, Brace & Co., 1937), p. 176.

[2] Klineberg, *op. cit.*, p. 34; Franz Boas, *The Mind of Primitive Man* (rev. ed.; New York: Macmillan Co., 1938), pp. 100–102.

Racists have sometimes made the claim that whites have larger or more advanced brains than nonwhites. Comparative studies have sometimes shown slight differences in cranial capacity between racial groups, but these do not seem to be significant. Cranial capacity is determined by first plugging up the holes in a cranium to prevent leakage and then filling the inverted skull with seeds, water, or small shot, which are then poured into a graduated container. One comparative study of the cranial capacities of whites and Negroes gives the mean capacity of 1,179 white male skulls as 1,517.49 cubic centimeters and that of 661 Negro male skulls as 1,467.13 cubic centimeters. Thus, the white skulls are larger, but the difference between the two series is only 50.36 cubic centimeters. Some series of nonwhite skulls have yielded larger cranial capacities than the white series with which they were compared.[3]

Brain size and morphology

It must be kept in mind that in many of the non-European groups, the stature is smaller than that of whites. In the preceding chapter, we saw that diet affects stature. An increase in head size accompanies growth in stature. The more favorable nutrition of European and American whites probably affects brain size, but this does not necessarily indicate greater intelligence on their part. Many outstanding persons have had quite small brains. Within the normal human range, mere size is not an indicator of intelligence.

Some American racists of the present day who seek scientific justification for racial segregation argue that whites have more highly developed frontal lobes than Negroes do and that the brains of whites show more fissuration and sulcification. There seems to be disagreement about these points among brain anatomists. Robert Bean is cited for an early study in which he claimed that Negroes tend to have smaller frontal lobes than whites.[4] A later study by Franklin P. Mall did not confirm Bean's findings. He separated the brains of about 100 Negroes and whites into three groups according to the richness of their convolutions. The brains of the whites were not found to be more complex. Mall also weighed the frontal lobes of all the brains. He found that the brains of Negroes were somewhat lighter than those of the whites, but the Negro frontal lobes were relatively as heavy. Mall emphasized the great variation to be found among the brains of both racial groups.[5]

---

[3] Katharine Simmons, "Cranial Capacities by both Plastic and Water Techniques with Cranial Linear Measurements of the Reserve Collection," *Human Biology,* Vol. 14 (1942), pp. 473–98. See also Klineberg, *op. cit.,* pp. 83–87, and Robin Fox, "Chinese Have Bigger Brains than Whites—Are They Superior?" *New York Times Magazine,* June 30, 1968, pp. 13, 23–30.

[4] Robert Bennett Bean, "Some Racial Peculiarities of the Negro Brain," *American Journal of Anatomy,* Vol. 5 (1906), pp. 353–432.

[5] Franklin P. Mall, "On the Anatomical Characters of the Human Brain, Said to Vary According to Race and Sex, with Special Reference to the Frontal Lobe," *American Journal of Anatomy,* Vol. 9 (1909), pp. 1–32.

A more recent work cited in racist literature is Cornelius J. Connolly's *External Morphology of the Primate Brain*, a book which has also been quoted by Juan Comas in a criticism of contemporary racist literature.[6] The fact that both racists and an antiracist find support for their views in the same work suggests that there is some ambiguity in its conclusions; it depends upon which passages you quote. Connolly found somewhat more fissuration among the brains of whites than of Negroes, but he states that no morphological features are exclusively characteristic of the brains of either race. Two of the brains in his collection which had the most "primitive" fissural patterns belonged to Negroes, but Connolly says that further study might show equally primitive brains among whites. "In any case," he adds, "the retention of primitive morphological features is not known to have any mental correlate."[7]

It should be noted that Connolly's sample is quite small, consisting of the brains of 30 Negroes and 30 whites. In view of the fact that great variation has been reported for the brains of both Negroes and whites, this sample would not seem to form an adequate basis for wide-ranging conclusions about the relative aptitudes of Negroes and whites. J. H. F. Kohlbrugge has written:

The comparison of convolutions and sulci does not present constant racial differences. . . . Each variation can be found in different races if one has enough data. . . . Among a group of brains belonging to different races, no one is capable of distinguishing one which corresponds to an Australian from a European, nor one of a genius from that of a man of average intelligence.[8]

Still another work on brain morphology cited in racist literature is F. W. Vint's "The Brain of the Kenya Native."[9] The reason this brief article is referred to in such publications is that Vint, who made a study of 100 brains of Kenya natives, concluded, among other things, that the pyramidal cells of the supragranular cortex are smaller in the brains of Kenya natives than in the European brains described by Von Economo. Racist writers who have made use of these findings consider it to be significant that the African Negro brains studied had thinner supragranular layers of the cortex than European brains. But these writers ignore some qualifications made by Vint himself. Vint pointed out that his collection of brains came from individuals who, while alive, were generally of poor physique. He wrote: "The high incidence of spirochaetal diseases, yaws

---

[6] Juan Comas, " 'Scientific' Racism Again?" *Current Anthropology*, Vol. 2, No. 4 (October, 1961), pp. 303–40.

[7] Cornelius J. Connolly, *External Morphology of the Primate Brain* (Springfield, Ill.: Charles C. Thomas, Publisher, 1950), pp. 258–59.

[8] J. H. F. Kohlbrugge, *Le Cerveau Suivant les Races*, Bulletins et Mémoires de la Société d'Anthropologie, Paris. Série 8, tome 6, p. 82. Quoted in English in Comas, *op. cit.*, p. 308.

[9] Vint, *op. cit.*, p. 216. *Journal of Anatomy*, Vol. 68, Part 2 (1934), pp. 216–23.

and syphilis, must be taken into consideration in any deduction drawn from the findings in this series of brains."[10] The racist writers who cite Vint's study make no reference to this caveat. Moreover, none of the 100 brains came from members of the "so-called educated class." If generalizations are to be made about the brains of Negroes and whites, certain variables should be held constant, if possible, such as previous condition of health, freedom from disease, and the former educational levels of the subjects. One should be certain, moreover, that the techniques used in fixing the brains, preserving and preparing them for examination, are the same for both groups of specimens. This may not be the case when one investigator reports on the brains of one racial group, while another reports on the brains of a different group.

Intelligence testing

In current racist literature, much is made of the fact that whites generally do better than Negroes in intelligence tests given in the United States. This fact has long been known, but the most generally held interpretation among psychologists and other social scientists is that the poorer performance of Negroes on such tests reflects poorer educational facilities for Negroes and a more generally depressing, inhibiting social environment. IQ scores do not reflect native intelligence. Many studies have shown that when children are moved from orphanages to satisfactory foster homes, their IQ scores often shoot up. And IQ scores may also drop if the individual's environment is restrictive and unrewarding.

Klineberg has shown that an individual's performance on intelligence tests is affected by many factors besides intelligence, such as familiarity with the language in which the test is given, motivation, rapport with the investigator, and level of education. He showed that northern Negroes did better than southern Negroes in intelligence tests given to Army recruits in World War I. For that matter northern whites also did better than southern whites. Evidently these differences reflect more adequate educational facilities in the North. What is more, some groups of northern Negroes did better than southern whites. Indeed, on the Beta tests, the Negroes of Ohio did better than the whites of 27 other states.[11]

A recent, sophisticated argument along racist lines is the much-debated article by Arthur R. Jensen, "How Much Can We Boost I.Q. and Scholastic Achievement?"[12] Jensen claims that efforts in compensatory education such as the Headstart program have failed to raise the level of scholastic performance among Negroes. Their inability must therefore be due to a genetic deficiency in intelligence. Some of Jensen's critics have

---

[10] *Ibid.*, p. 216.

[11] Ashley Montagu, *Race, Science, and Humanity* (Princeton, N.J.: D. Van Nostrand Co., 1963), p. 111.

[12] *Harvard Educational Review*, Vol. 39, No. 1 (1969), pp. 1–123.

replied that most programs in compensatory education have not been effectively administered; their alleged failure need not imply any genetic inadequacy on the part of Negroes.

In Chapter 11, reference was made to calculations by Glass and Li that North American Negroes have about 28 percent white ancestry, while over 36 million whites are descended from persons of African origin. Neither Negroes nor whites are genetically homogeneous, as Jensen's generalizations seem to imply.

Jensen and other writers with a racist orientation assert that when Negroes and whites of comparable status and educational level are tested, whites still come out ahead. But in what sense is status comparable? Negroes were slaves little more than a hundred years ago, and in the intervening years they have faced barriers of poverty and prejudice. The U.S. census of 1940 showed that only 2.2 percent of Negroes had finished four years of high school; only 1.1 percent had finished four or more years of college. These low figures cannot be due to intellectual deficiency; more significant, no doubt, has been the low caste position of the Negroes, their poverty, and a consequent lack of motivation. This is suggested by some more recent figures: in 1965 Negro men held a little over 1 percent of the white-collar jobs available to men and 2 percent of the "male technician" jobs available.[13] The 1940 statistics on school and college attendance show that there has been little time in which to establish traditions of scholarship and concern with higher education among American Negroes. Advances in this area have been recent and limited in extent.

Race and crime   Writing in 1940, Ruth Benedict observed, "The racist literature of the United States deals hardly at all with our great national racial problem, the Negro."[14] In the 1960's, however, most racist literature was anti-Negro, an emphasis which developed from the 1954 Supreme Court decision on school segregation and the efforts of many white Americans to resist integration. There is an active committee in the South which has sent racist pamphlets and journals to members of the American Anthropological Association, among others, evidently in the hope of winning some anthropologists over to the cause. This literature attacks the works of Boas, Klineberg, Comas, and Ashley Montagu and presents the arguments about brain morphology and intelligence testing mentioned above. It also cites the high rates of crime found among American Negroes. Thus, an FBI report[15] is cited to show the following ratios of Negro to white crimes;

---

[13] Richard H. Rovere, "Letter From Washington," *The New Yorker,* September 11, 1965, p. 126.

[14] Ruth Benedict, *Race: Science and Politics* (New York: Modern Age Books, 1940), p. 198.

[15] Department of Justice, *Uniform Crime Reports* Vol. 25, No. 2 (1954).

for murder, 16–to–1; for robbery, 13–to–1; for prostitution and "vice," 16–to–1; for rape, 6–to–1.

There are socially disorganized Negro areas where crime seems to be endemic; for example, the Los Angeles community of Watts (90 percent Negro), where violent antiwhite rioting broke out in August, 1965, and again in March, 1966. In three months before the 1965 outburst, the police reported 1,000 crimes in Watts, including 196 murders, rapes, or felonious assaults, and 87 robberies. At the time Watts contained more than 500 parolees from California prisons and many narcotics addicts, prostitutes, and alcoholics.[16]

That this is a grim picture cannot be denied, but there is no reason to conclude that there is something defective about Negro heredity. American Negroes should be seen not only as making up a "race" but, more significantly, as currently constituting a lower caste in American society.[17] Urban slum areas inhabited by whites also have high crime rates. Whites from urban slums have been said to commit twice as many assaults, three times as many larcenies, and four times as many rapes as do whites in rural areas.[18]

Moreover, American Negroes are exceptionally poor. "Except for a small minority enjoying upper or middle class status, the masses of American Negroes, in the rural South and in the segregated slum quarters in Southern and Northern cities, are destitute."[19] This statement, which Myrdal documented in his classic work on the American Negro was made more than 20 years ago, but still holds true.

To understand the low IQ scores and the high rates of divorce, delinquency, and crime among American Negroes, we must look at the social environment and the past history of the American Negro, including the years of slavery and their aftermath, years of poverty and prejudice. One need hardly invoke race to account for such phenomena.

It is striking that, despite the prejudices they have encountered, American Negroes have often been outstanding in the fields where they have been accepted, especially in literature, music, the entertainment world, and athletics.

The discussion of race and ability in this chapter has been largely concerned with some racist attributions of inferiority to Negroes. The at-

---

[16] *New York Times,* August 15, 1965, p. 79.

[17] John Dollard, *Caste and Class in a Southern Town* (New York: Harper & Bros., 1937).

[18] William M. McCord, "We Ask the Wrong Questions about Crime," *New York Times Magazine,* November 21, 1965, p. 146.

[19] Gunnar Myrdal, with the assistance of Richard Sterne and Arnold Rose, *An American Dilemma: The Negro Problem and Modern Democracy* (New York: Harper & Bros., 1944), p. 205. See also Chapter 31, "Caste and Class" for a discussion of the caste position of the American Negro.

tention devoted to this topic may seem disproportionate, but since most racist literature in the past decade has been anti-Negro, and since racist views have such disastrous social consequences, it seems necessary to underline the weaknesses of the racist position.

Suggestions for further reading

On the general subject of race and ability, see Franz Boas, *The Mind of Primitive Man* (New York: Macmillan Co., 1938), and Otto Klineberg, *Race Differences* (New York: Harper & Bros., 1935).

The classic work on the "Negro problem," which might better be called the white-and-Negro problem, is Gunnar Myrdal, with the Assistance of Richard Sterne and Arnold Rose, *An American Dilemma: The Negro Problem and Modern Democracy* (New York: Harper & Bros., 1944). For a more recent study, see Charles E. Silberman, *Crisis in Black and White* (New York: Random House, 1964).

On the historical and comparative aspects of slavery, see Frank Tannenbaum, *Slave and Citizen: The Negro in America* (New York: Alfred A. Knopf, 1947).

For a psychological or psychoanalytic study of the American Negro, see Abram Kardiner and Lionel Oversey, *The Mark of Oppression: Explorations in the Personality of the American Negro* (Cleveland and New York: World Publishing Co., 1962).

On the Jensen article, see Martin Deutsch, "Happenings on the Way Back to the Forum: Social Science, I.Q., and Race Differences," *Harvard Educational Review*, Vol. 39, No. 3 (1969), pp. 523–57, and other articles in the same issue.

On the American Negro, see also Thomas F. Pettigrew, *A Profile of the Negro American* (Princeton, N.J.: D. Van Nostrand Co., 1964); and George E. Simpson and J. Milton Yinger, *Racial and Cultural Minorities* (New York: Harper & Bros., 1953). See also Martin Deutsch, Irwin Katz, and Arthur R. Jensen (eds.), *Social Class, Race, and Psychological Development* (New York: Holt, Rinehart, & Winston, 1968).

Part **TWO**

Archaeology and prehistory

Introduction to archaeology VI

Chapter 14

The historical background of archaeological research

The period of discovery, at the end of the 15th and in the early years of the 16th centuries, when Columbus reached the New World and Magellan circumnavigated the globe, also saw discoveries in time, of the past, with the recovery of much information about the ancient civilizations of Greece and Rome. A forerunner in the field was Cyriacus of Ancona, who was also named Ciriaco de' Pizzicolli. He was born in 1391 and died around 1449. He visited Egypt and Asia Minor, but most of his work was done in Greece, where he examined temples, copied inscriptions, and searched for ancient manuscripts. The material he accumulated in his diaries and commentaries was of great value to scholars of a later day. Among the documents Cyriacus acquired in Greece was a copy of the Histories of Herodotus. Scores of old Greek texts thus found their way into the collections of Italian dukes. When Constantinople fell to the Turks in 1453, many Greek scholars moved to Italy, often bringing more ancient documents with them. There was a great interest in this literature and in information about the classical worlds of ancient Greece and Rome, since the Italians, particularly the Florentines, saw their age as a time of rebirth for Italy, which had been overrun by barbarian Gothic invaders a thousand years before. This interest in the past spread beyond the confines of Italy to courts and centers of learning in other parts of Europe.

By the end of the 16th century and during the 17th, there were many antiquarians, and the collecting of classical statuary had become a hobby of the rich. Wealthy men built up private collections, some of which ultimately became museums. One prominent collector was the Earl of Arundel (1585–1646), who acquired 37 statues and 128 busts, along with sarcophagi, many inscribed stones, gems, coins, and various other objects. Some of the collection finally became part of the Ashmolean Museum in Oxford. The Ashmolean, built in 1683, contained not only objects of classical art but also ethnological curiosities brought back from foreign lands: the mantle of the Indian chief Powhattan, made of deerskin and embroidered with shells, canoe paddles from Polynesia, and ivory spoons from the Congo.[1]

Museums have always been associated with the work of ethnologists and archaeologists. Curators have to sort out and classify their objects in some way. It was a museum curator, Christian Thomsen, who, being obligated to systematize the artifacts in the Danish National Museum early in the 19th century, came up with the Three Ages classification of Stone, Bronze, and Iron. These were in chronological sequence; a long Stone Age preceded an age in which bronze was used, which in turn gave way to an Iron Age. This simple scheme proved to be a very useful framework, later elaborated upon and subdivided.

The interest in classical antiquity which welled up during the Renaissance was maintained in 18th century England, when a Society of Dilletanti was formed to foster this study. The society financed an expedition to Ionia in Asia Minor and published some volumes on Ionian antiquities. Robert Wood published *Ruins of Palmyra* and *Ruins of Baalbek* in the 1750's. Interest in the classical past was heightened by the excavation of Pompeii in 1754. The foremost 18th-century student of Pompeii and Herculaneum was J. J. Winckelmann, who helped to interpret and explain much of the material that was being unearthed.

In addition to the vogue for classical antiquity, there was also a growing curiosity about pre-Roman structures such as Stonehenge and Avebury. These were megalithic monuments—that is, huge simple structures built of undressed stones. William Stukely made careful drawings of both these sites from 1718 to 1725. He was the first secretary of the Society of Antiquarians of London. Although he made painstaking notes and measurements, Stukely became carried away by fantasies about the ancient Druids, who he believed had built Stonehenge. Druidism and enthusiasm for mysterious ruins became aspects of the Romantic movement, and antiquarianism became a fashionable interest for ladies and gentlemen in the 18th and early 19th centuries. On the Continent, nationalistic sentiments also furthered an interest in the past, in the ancient Celts and other ancestral groups.

After the Revolutionary War in North America, settlers moved into the Ohio Valley, where they found large mounds and earthworks. It soon became the custom to attribute these remains to some ancient race which

---

[1] Stanley Casson, *The Discovery of Man: The Story of the Inquiry into Human Origins* (New York: Harper & Bros., 1939), pp. 126–39.

had occupied the area before the coming of the American Indians. There was much speculation about the origins of the Mound Builders and their Indian successors, and they were linked with all kinds of Old World peoples, including Persians, Basques, Welsh, and the Ten Lost Tribes of Israel. In the New World, the time was not yet ready for archaeological research; the Americans were too busy settling their new land.

In 1798 Napoleon sailed for Egypt with 38,000 men. They did not stay there long, but the expedition was of importance to world scholarship, since Napoleon took along 175 savants, who had a firsthand opportunity to learn something about the monuments, temples, and tombs of ancient Egypt. An Egyptian Institute was started in Cairo. Several sarcophagi and statues were shipped back to France. But the most valuable find was the Rosetta Stone from which the linguistic genius, Jean François Champollion (1778–1867), deciphered Egyptian hieroglyphics, thereby opening a new door to the past.

Another door was opened by Henry C. Rawlinson (1810–95). Rawlinson studied the Indian and Persian vernaculars while a soldier in the service of the East India Company and later as a major on duty in Persia. While in Persia in 1837, he had himself lowered by block and tackle down a high cliff at Behistun so that he could copy some cuneiform inscriptions. These were written in three languages, Old Persian, Akkadian, and Elamite. Rawlinson was able to decipher and interpret the Old Persian text by 1846. The Elamite and Akkadian texts were more difficult, but these, too, had been mostly deciphered by scholars by 1857.

Between 1843 and 1846, Paul Émile Botta excavated the Assyrian palace of Sargon II, finding huge sculptures, impressive relief work, and inscriptions. In 1845 Austin Henry Layard began digging at Nineveh, where the palace of Sennacherib yielded piles of cuneiform tablets.

Similarly dramatic discoveries had meanwhile been made in the New World. In 1839 John Lloyd Stephens, an American author, lawyer, and traveler, accompanied by Frederick Catherwood, an artist, made their way through the jungles of Honduras, Guatemala, and Yucatán, coming upon one amazing Maya ruin after another, most of them overgrown with tropical vegetation. The Maya buildings, with their elaborate baroque façades, were drawn with great exactness and skill by Catherwood. His drawings and Stephens' descriptions astonished the literate world, as did the reports of Botta and Layard from Mesopotamia.

During the following decades, there was much speculation and argument about the possibility of contact between the Old World and the New in pre-Columbian times. Did the American Indians build up their own civilization independently, or had there been communication with ancient Egypt or Southeast Asia? The Egyptians had pyramids; so did the Maya. Pottery, weaving, and metallurgy were found in both hemispheres. Were these similarities due to independent invention (parallelism) or to

Maya bas relief
(drawn from a
plaster cast).

diffusion, the spreading of a culture trait from one society to another?

During the early part of the 20th century, a school of pan-Egyptian diffusionism developed in England, favoring the view that most aspects of high civilization in the New World had their origins in Egypt. This view was rejected by most American anthropologists, who have generally considered the American Indian cultures to have been largely autochthonous, the products of independent cultural evolution. Even today, however, the problem is not altogether settled, and there is a minority group which stresses the likelihood of past contacts across the Pacific from Southeast Asia.

One unfortunate aspect of the early excavations of advanced centers of civilization was the way in which the discoveries were exploited. Statues, bas reliefs, jewelry—all were carted and shipped off to Europe or the United States. Local natives, realizing the value of such artifacts, began to do their own digging and selling to collectors. One person who realized the dangers of these tendencies was a Frenchman, August Manette, who excavated in Egypt. Although he did send many of his finds to the Louvre, Manette believed that Egypt should try to preserve its own antiquities. Through his efforts an Egyptian National Museum and a National Antiquities Service were established in 1859.

William Flinders Petrie, an Englishman, was one of Manette's successors in Egypt. In various ways, his work marked an advance over that of previous excavators. Petrie was not so concerned about making spectacular finds, and he was more methodical in his excavation procedures, note taking, and publication. He was interested in sequence dating, establishing a chronology based on stratification and typology of artifacts such as pottery. Petrie discovered that pottery like that found in one of his Egyptian sites also turned up in a Mycenaean Greek assemblage. This not only provided evidence of trade but helped to date both cultures.

The excavator of the Mycenaean material was a German businessman, Heinrich Schliemann. Schliemann was a self-made merchant who worked his way from poverty to riches. He acquired American citizenship after he went to California in 1850. When he retired from business, from 1868 on, Schliemann devoted himself to the study of Homeric sites, thus achieving an outlet for his lifelong interest in the epics of Homer. He set out to find the site of Troy and found it in 1869 at Hissarlik in Anatolia, where he dug through several levels to unearth a treasure hoard of diadems, brooches, plates, bracelets, and other precious things. Later he was given permission to excavate at Mycenae in Greece, where, again, he found, among other things, a cache of gold and silver vessels, ornamental weapons, and gold death masks.

But it was not just the treasure that was important; Schliemann had shown that an earlier civilization lay behind that of classical Greece. Layard, Botta, and Schliemann had uncovered hitherto unknown centers of Bronze Age civilization. Beginning in 1899, Arthur Evans carried this search into the past a step further by excavating at Knossos in Crete and bringing to light the elegant civilization of the ancient Minoans. Another formerly unknown civilization was revealed by John Marshall in his archaeological work in the Indus Valley between 1922 and 1927. Still older than either the Cretan or Indus Valley civilizations was that of Sumer. Although excavations in Sumer began in the 19th century, the most revealing finds were made by Charles Leonard Woolley in the late 1920's.

Thus, gradually, archaeologists opened up more and more forgotten centers of early civilization.

At the same time, men were learning more about the still earlier periods which lay behind these civilizations. There were no written records for this vast extent of past time; whatever could be learned about it would have to come from the examination of archaeological sites and the study of artifacts. The term *prehistory* is a relatively new one, coined in 1857. It was popularized by John Lubbock in a book called *Prehistoric Times* (1865), in which a distinction was made between two subdivisions of the Stone Age: Palaeolithic (Old Stone Age) and Neolithic (New Stone Age). Lubbock knew that during the Palaeolithic there were animals living in Europe which later became extinct, such as the mammoth, cave bear, and woolly rhinoceros. He also knew that there were characteristic differences in the making of Palaeolithic and Neolithic stone tools.

An interest in European prehistory was spurred by the discovery and excavation of well-preserved Swiss Lake Dwelling settlements during the 1850's and 1860's. Some of these were Neolithic, while others dated from the Bronze and Iron Ages. Stratification helped to establish culture sequences. Meanwhile, excavations were also being made in Palaeolithic cave sites, particularly in the Dordogne region of France, where several sites became famous for their yields of skulls, skeletons, and artifacts, giving names to particular periods or types of early man: Le Moustier, La Madeleine, Aurignac, Cro-Magnon, and others.

In 1879 impressive Palaeolithic cave paintings were discovered at Altamira, in Spain, although their authenticity was generally doubted for many years. In the following decades, much Upper Palaeolithic art in bone, ivory, and clay was discovered and also more examples of cave painting, the most dramatic discovery being the marvelous prehistoric paintings found in 1940 at Lascaux Cave near Montignac, France.

Jacquetta Hawkes dates the beginning of modern archaeology at 1918.[2] Any such date must be somewhat arbitrary, but it is true that since World War I, archaeological research has become much more professional and sophisticated in method.

Gordon R. Willey states that a new kind of archaeology has come into being in the United States since 1950. This involves an interest in the comparative study of cultural processes, including settlement patterns, and the mutual influence of technological, social, and ideological aspects of culture.[3]

Modern archaeology is certainly more sophisticated than it was a generation ago. It now draws upon a host of sister disciplines, including geology, paleontology, botany, zoology, chemistry, and physics. Some of the methods used by modern archaeologists in their research will be discussed in the following chapter.

Three successful works of popularization can be recommended: C. W. Ceram, *Gods, Graves and Scholars: The Story of Archaeology*, trans. from the German by E. B. Garside (New York: Alfred A. Knopf, 1951); Geoffrey Bibby, *The Testimony of the Spade* (New York: Alfred A. Knopf, 1956); and Glyn Daniel, *The Idea of Prehistory* (Baltimore: Penguin Books, 1964).

Suggestions for further reading

A two-volume work which presents much of the history of archaeological research in the form of short selections by archaeologists describing their own excavations and which contains an introduction by the editor offering a survey of the history of archaeology is: Jacquetta Hawkes (ed.), *The World of the Past* (New York: Alfred A. Knopf, 1963).

See also Walter W. Taylor, *A Study of Archaeology*, American Anthropological Association, Memoir No. 69, 1948.

---

[2] Jacquetta Hawkes (ed.), *The World of the Past* (New York: Alfred A. Knopf, 1963), Vol. I, p. 84.

[3] Gordon R. Willey, "One Hundred Years of American Archaeology," in J. O. Brew (ed.), *One Hundred Years of Anthropology* (Cambridge, Mass.: Harvard University Press, 1968), pp. 29–53.

Chapter 15

Methods of archaeology

In their efforts to learn what they can about man's past cultures, archaeologists face such problems as the selection of sites for excavation, excavation procedures, methods of dating their finds, and the interpretation of the evidence.

Selection of a site

How does an archaeologist decide upon a particular site? How does he know where to dig? Sometimes the site is obvious, as in the case of the imposing Maya ruins which John Lloyd Stephens encountered in the jungles of Mexico and Guatemala in 1840. The ancient cities of Mesopotamia were also not hard to find, being built up on several layers of preceding habitations and debris and rising up like mounds from the level plain.

Barrows, mounds, and megalithic structures, like those of England, are also obvious features, as are kitchen middens—huge piles of shellfish—like those accumulated by Mesolithic peoples along the shores of northern Europe. Since early hunting-gathering people often lived in rock shelters or caves, their dirt floors have often been excavated in search of their remains. Sometimes archaeological material is revealed accidentally through erosion or through workmen blasting or digging in construction sites, quarries, or mines, making highways, or laying pipes.

The presence of house sites may sometimes be inferred by the presence of vegetation. If buried walls of brick or stone lie beneath a field, the plants growing above them are apt to be shorter than the surrounding crops, and they may ripen sooner and be lighter in color because of the relative lack of nutrients available to the roots. The outlines of house foundations may therefore be seen. If there are buried garbage dumps, pits, or ditches, on the other hand, their greater moisture produces more flourishing plants. In the survey of an area, an archaeologist looks for such telltale contrasts in vegetation.

The outlines of banks and ditches may sometimes best be seen in early morning or late afternoon, when the sun is low on the horizon, throwing shadows which bring out contours not usually seen.

Similarly, sites are sometimes best detected from the air. Features which are not noticed by a person walking through a field may be clearly evident from an airplane. For this reason, air reconnaissance has been used in some archaeological surveys. O. G. S. Crawford, a leader in this type of site detection, illustrated the principle involved by publishing together two photographs of a carpet. One was a cat's-eye view, seen close to the carpet; the other was a man's-eye view from above. The pattern of the carpet is immediately apparent to the man, but since the cat is so close to the fibres of the carpet, it cannot see the overall design.

The streets and gardens of Eski Baghdad were first noticed from the air, during World War I, by a British colonel who was taking photographs for military purposes. He wrote that the city was well planned

. . . with wide main streets or boulevards, from which wide roads branched off. . . . Had I not been in possession of these air-photographs the city would probably have been merely shown [on the map] by meaningless low mounds scattered here and there, for much of the detail was not recognizable on the ground, but was well shown up in the photographs, as the slight difference in the color of the soil came out with marked effect on the sensitive film, and the larger properties of the nobles and rich merchants could be plainly made out along the banks of the Tigris.[1]

The colonel could also see the outline of a series of detached forts which would not have been noticed on the ground; also the outline of an ancient irrigation system.

Pre-Columbian ridged fields covering large areas have been detected from the air in eastern Bolivia, western Ecuador, northern Colombia, and coastal Surinam in Dutch Guiana. From the ground one might not suspect the existence of such extensive man-made earthworks, but they are clearly seen from the air.

Sites are sometimes detected by surface finds. Bits of pottery may be strewn over a field, and an archaeologist may decide to dig a test pit or trench there, to see if the area deserves further exploration.

One way of helping to determine the precise place for excavation is *electrical resistivity*. When an electric current is run through the earth between two electrodes, the amount of resistance is measured on a meter.

---

[1] O. G. S. Crawford, "Archaeology from the Air," from O. G. S. Crawford and Alexander Keiller, *Wessex from the Air* (Oxford: The Clarendon Press, 1928) quoted in Jacquetta Hawkes (ed.), *The World of the Past* (New York: Alfred A. Knopf, 1963), Vol. I, p. 131.

Water is a good conductor of electricity; hence, if the soil is damp, there will be less resistance than in the case of dry soil or stone or brick foundations which have airspaces. Successive readings of resistance over a grid thus indicate the possible presence or absence of buried house foundations or other solid structures.

Another technique for the same purpose is *magnetic location,* in which a proton magnetometer is used like a wartime mine detector, to discover the presence of underground iron objects. Magnetometers may also locate kilns, furnaces, ovens, hearths, pits, ditches, and solid structures such as walls or tombs.

Probes have sometimes been used in archaeological surveys, especially to locate walls and pits.

A method used in connection with unexplored Etruscan tombs has been to drill a hole in the top of the tomb and to lower a flash-gun camera to take photographs of the inside. When the pictures are developed, the archaeologist can decide whether he wants to excavate the tomb.

Thus there are various methods which help the archaeologist to decide where to dig. Of course, there are different types of sites: *living sites,* where people lived; *butchering sites,* where animals were cut up; *workshop sites,* or "floors," where tools were made; *quarry sites,* where flint or minerals were extracted; *ceremonial sites;* and *burial sites,* such as graves and tombs.

Social and cultural inferences

Different kinds of information may be derived from these different kinds of sites. From a *living site* one may be able to make a rough assessment of the size of a settlement's population on the basis of the number and size of the dwellings and the general size of the settlement. If there is an adjacent cemetery, the number of burials may also provide clues, although one would have to determine how long the cemetery had been in use and estimate the characteristic life-span. Of course, one could not be sure that all the people who lived in that community were buried there, but at least a rough approximation of the population could be made.

From a living site one may also determine the basis of subsistence, whether hunting-gathering or agriculture. Animal bones and plant remains may be examined. There may be storage rooms, silos, or storage pits for grain. The impressions of grain on clay bricks or pottery are sometimes as clear evidence as the grains themselves. But ancient plant remains are often preserved, both in very dry environments, as in Peru and the American Southwest, and also in damp peat bogs, as in Scandinavia. Direct evidence of what some people have eaten has come from the intestines of corpses preserved in peat bogs in northern Europe and also from coprolites, human feces, found in dry caves. Analyses of coprolites may not only tell what was eaten but how the food was prepared. Botanists can identify plant remains, including pollen, and can also distinguish between wild and domesticated plants. Tools used in food preparation, such as metates, manos, cooking pots, and butcher knives, also give evidence of the kinds of foods eaten.

A living site may give some evidence of the nature of social organization. There may be evidence of planned settlement—large communal dwellings, a grid layout of streets, and walls enclosing the settlement—or else small, dispersed units may indicate a more atomistic social order. A living site may also provide evidence of class stratification, implied by striking differences in the size of dwellings or by the concentration of valued objects, such as jade, in limited areas. Implications of trade are suggested by objects, such as sea shells or obsidian, which must have come from considerable distances.

Butchering sites yield less information than living sites, but they may give evidence of communal hunting, as in a late prehistoric site in Montana where buffalo were stampeded over a cliff. Large numbers of the animals were killed at one time but were butchered in such a way as to get the maximum amount of meat, all of which was dried or made into pemmican at the site itself, for no parts of the carcases were taken away.[2] The butchering site at Torralba also gave evidence of communal hunting (see page 108).

Workshop sites and quarry sites yield information about technology, the making of tools. Ceremonial sites give an indication of the importance of religion in the life of the people. If there are representations of deities, some ideas may be gleaned about the kinds of gods worshiped. There may be archaeological evidence of sacrifice or of the existence of a priesthood. Burial sites not only yield skeletal material but very often grave goods as well, and indications of relative status may be deduced from the kinds of such associated material. They may testify to the existence of class stratification. Collective burials, as in the Neolithic passage graves of Europe may indicate the importance of lineages or clans.

Archaeologists have sometimes made use of computers to help them analyze their material statistically. The range, mean, and standard deviation in size of certain classes of artifacts may be determined. The relative incidence of types of tools in different settlements of a population may give clues to seasonal variations in subsistence or else may indicate different kinds of activities associated with different kinds of sites, such as living sites on the one hand and butchering sites on the other.

After a site has been chosen for excavation, the usual procedure is to stake it out in a grid plan, with the area divided into numbered squares.   **Excavation procedures**

----

[2] Thomas F. Kehoe and Alice B. Kehoe, "Observations on the Butchering Technique at a Prehistoric Bison Kill in Montana," *American Antiquity*, Vol. 25 (1960), pp. 420–23.

Before excavation a scale map is made of the area. A fixed point, known as the *datum* point, is established on or near the site, marked by an object of steel, cement, or other durable material. This is the reference point for the excavations. If work is done on the site in later years, it can be determined where the earlier excavations were made. A grid may be dispensed with if a structure such as a house with different rooms is being excavated. The rooms may then become convenient units rather than grid squares.

Preliminary test pits or trenches may be dug first. As the excavation proceeds, photographs are taken from different vantage points. When an artifact is uncovered, its position is recorded in its particular square and also in depth; it is numbered, cataloged, and listed in a register. Objects are placed in strong paper or cloth bags, labeled with identifying numbers.

Sites are often stratified. Objects found in lower strata are generally older than those nearer the surface, although this stratification may be disturbed and sometimes reversed. For example, the former inhabitants may have dug a large hole and piled up the dirt from it nearby. Animal burrowings, frost heaving, and other natural forces may cause disturbances in strata.

Objects found together presumably come from the same time period, although there may be exceptions, as in the preservation of heirlooms. It is necessary to have records of the spatial location of all the material found, if one is to make an adequate interpretation of the remains.

Excavation at
Cahokia, Illinois.

The associated material found in a site, known as an archaeological *assemblage,* consists of *artifacts,* which are man-made objects; *features,* which are man-made but which are usually not removed from the site, such as storage pits; and objects which are not made by man, such as animal bones, plant seeds, shells, and ashes.

Animal bones and remains of plants and pollen are preserved for analysis by specialists to determine the types of animals and plants collected or domesticated. These remains may also help to date the site. If the dig is in an area suitable for the application of tree ring analysis, logs or beams are preserved. These may require special treatment to prevent decay and decomposition. Bits of charcoal are also collected for dating purposes, as will be explained later. Shells found in the site may give an indication of climatic conditions. It may be determined if they are of local origin or brought or traded from a distance. The sources of pieces of stone or metal may also be deduced, as well as techniques of manufacture of artifacts made from stone, bone, metal, or other materials. Casts and molds are sometimes made of valuable objects, particularly perishable ones, and tracings or rubbings may be made of rock carvings or of bas reliefs if they are present, as has been done in the Camonica Valley in Italy and in Maya sites in Guatemala.

Field methods in archaeology have become progressively more painstaking and detailed. This is partly because of recent advances in dating methods, which have shown the value of preserving and analyzing organic materials, pollen, logs, and other objects which formerly received little attention. But the great care taken with excavations nowadays is also due to the realization that a site can properly be excavated only once, for to excavate a site is to destroy it.

Archaeologists do not only dig; they sometimes dive under water, or have professional divers do it for them. Ancient Roman wine jars and marble statues have been brought up from wrecked ships at the bottom of the Mediterranean. Maya incense burners have been recovered from the bottom of Lake Amatitlán, Guatemala. It is a common human practice to throw garbage into a lake or stream, where refuse piles may accumulate, often containing objects in a good state of preservation. Sacrifices to the water have been made in different parts of the world. Reindeer hunters in northern Europe, around 17,000 years ago, used to throw a whole reindeer, weighted with a heavy stone, into a lake, perhaps as a thank-offering or bribe to the spirits. The Maya of Yucatán tossed human sacrificial victims into deep wells, and also bowls, vases, earrings, beads, and other valuable offerings. Submerged villages or camp sites and shipwrecks may be explored by underwater archaeology, which involves a host of specialized techniques and equipment.

It is interesting to note that even the grid system used in archaeological excavations on land has been employed in underwater archaeology. At

Yassi Ada, off the southwestern coast of Turkey, a scaffolding of pipe and angle iron was set up over a submerged shipwreck. The position of objects within the grid could thus be accurately plotted. Underwater "vacuum cleaners" removed dirt, and underwater photographs were taken during the process of uncovering the wreck. This turned out to be an old Roman ship, dated from its cache of gold coins at between A.D. 610 and 641, during the reign of the emperor Heraclius.[3]

Dating techniques

The most valuable and widely used system of dating is radioactive carbon dating, but it is less precise than some other techniques which have a more restricted range. Let us start with two examples of the latter sort, *dendrochronology* and *varve analysis,* both of which give "absolute" or chronological dates.

Dendrochronology

A tree adds a new growth ring each year. By counting the annual layers one can find out just how old the tree was when it was cut down. Thus, some redwood trees in northern California are known to be hundreds of years old. The rings on a tree are sometimes thick and sometimes thin, depending upon the amount of rainfall during the year. When plenty of moisture is available, they are wide; in times of drought they are narrow. Since all the trees within a particular area are affected by the same weather conditions, their tree ring sequences show the same patterns. Let us say that we have three thin layers, then a fat one, then two thin ones, then three fat ones, and so on. By comparing the tree ring sequences of many trees in a particular area, a master chart may be drawn up to show the characteristic tree ring sequence for that area. This chart can be extended far back in time, as progressively older trees are found whose later tree ring sequences overlap those of younger trees.

The technique of dendrochronology has been mainly used in the southwestern area of the United States, where a master chart of tree ring sequences goes back almost to the time of Christ. If a Pueblo ruin is excavated in Arizona, let us say, a cross section of a beam is analyzed to see how its tree ring sequences fit into the master chart. In this way, it is possible to say in which year the beam was cut, which may also give the year in which the Pueblo structure was built. There is a minor catch, however; for the beam might have been used in an earlier house and later transferred to the Pueblo structures; it might have been added to the

---

[3] For interesting illustrations of this deep-sea archaeological operation, see George F. Bass, "Underwater Archaeology: Key to History's Warehouse," *National Geographic,* Vol. 124, No. 1 (July, 1963), pp. 138–56. See also George F. Bass, *Archaeology under Water* (New York: Frederick A. Praeger, 1966).

house some time after it was built. Despite such ambiguities, tree ring analysis has been very helpful in dating sites in the American southwest.

Dendrochronology cannot be applied to all kinds of trees or in all kinds of environments. Apparently it will not work in New Zealand, and it could not be used in areas where there is little annual variation in rainfall. However, tree ring analysis has been practiced with some success in England, Germany, Norway, Turkey, Egypt, and various parts of the United States, including Alaska.

Varve analysis

Varves are annual layers of sediment deposited by ice sheets in glacial lakes. During the summer thaw, melting glacial ice runs down into the lake, carrying sediments, the coarser of which sink to the bottom of the lake. When winter comes, the lake freezes over, and the melting stops. During the winter the finer sediment gradually sinks down and settles on top of the coarser silt at the bottom of the lake. When the melting process resumes in the following summer, another annual layer is deposited with first a band of coarse sediment, later followed by one of finer sediment.

Varves vary in thickness from less than half an inch to over 15 inches, depending upon the warmth and length of the summer period. This is reminiscent of the annual layers of trees. Although varve analysis is much older than dendrochronology, it is interesting that its originator, Baron Gerard de Geer, was struck by the parallel with tree rings. In a presidential address to the Eleventh Geological Congress in Stockholm, he said:

Already at my first field-work as a geologist, in 1878, I was struck by the regularity of these laminae, much reminding of the annual rings of the trees. The next year, therefore, I commenced, and during the following years pursued, detailed investigations and measurements of these laminae in different parts of Sweden.[4]

Counting varves gives a date in years for the period of the melting and retreat of the glaciers. In Sweden and Finland, dates have thus been determined going back to before 10,000 B.C. This is based on the assumption that each varve stands for a year, which may not always be true. Nevertheless, the method provides considerable accuracy for dating late Pleistocene and early recent times in northern Europe. Varve analysis has also been applied in the United States.

One limitation of the method in relation to archaeology is that human artifacts are not likely to be found in glacial lakes. Men did not camp right beside the glaciers. However, if one knows where the ice fields were

---

[4] Quoted in Geoffrey Bibby, *The Testimony of the Spade* (New York: Alfred A. Knopf, 1956), p. 185.

at any given time, one can form some idea of the possible range of the contemporary human settlements. Upper Palaeolithic and Mesolithic hunters in Europe used to follow the reindeer herds north in the summer months. This gives a clue to the archaeologist: ". . . knowing where the ice was, he knows where the reindeer were, for their habits have assuredly not changed overmuch; and, knowing where the reindeer were, he knows where man was at all times during the retreat of the ice."[5]

Radiocarbon dating

The most widely used archaeological dating technique is radiocarbon dating. This method is based on the discovery that all living things, both plants and animals, contain a radioactive carbon known as carbon 14. Plants absorb this carbon from the atmosphere. Animals acquire it by eating plants, or by eating animals that have eaten plants. The amount of ^{14}C normally present in a living plant or animal species is known. Although some disintegration of radioactive carbon may take place during the life of an organism, it is balanced by the intake of ^{14}C; so in a living organism the amount of radioactive carbon remains fairly constant. After death, however, no more ^{14}C is taken in, and disintegration of ^{14}C proceeds at a steady rate. Since the rate at which ^{14}C disintegrates is known, it is possible to date the time of death of some organic material by determining how much radioactive carbon remains in it. Charcoal is among the most suitable such material for analysis. Shells are less reliable. Carbon 14 dates derived from marine mollusks may have to be corrected by the addition of several hundred years, since shellfish take in carbonates from sea water.

The date yielded by the radioactive carbon method is not a definite specific date but one plus or minus a certain number of years, giving a standard deviation. Thus, instead of 15,300, the date would be given as 15,300 ± 300, which means that there is a 67 percent chance that the correct figure will fall between 15,000 and 15,600; it does not mean that the correct figure *must* fall between these two extremes.[6]

This technique was tried out by testing it with various objects whose ages were known through historical records or other sources, such as linen from the Dead Sea Scrolls, and wood from an Egyptian tomb known to be dated between 4,700 and 5,100 years ago. The radiocarbon dates met these tests very well. Since then the method has been applied to archaeological sites all over the world.

The method is not foolproof. Sometimes objects have been contami-

---

5 *Ibid.*, p. 188.
6 François Bordes, *The Old Stone Age*, trans. from the French by J. E. Anderson (New York: McGraw Hill Book Co., 1968), p. 19.

nated by recent radioactivity. Sometimes different laboratories have given quite different dates for materials taken from the same site. The reason for such apparent failures to give consistent dates is not always understood. Nevertheless, radioactive dating seems to be the most useful dating technique for the archaeologist. Unlike dedrochronology and varve analysis, it is applicable in all parts of the world. When first developed, ^{14}C dating could be tried only with objects dating back about 30,000 years, but now, through new methods, its range has been extended to about 60,000 years.

Potassium-argon dating

Potassium-argon dating follows similar principles. In this case, a radioactive form of potassium decays at a known rate to form argon. The ages of some rocks can be dated by measuring the potassium-argon ratios. One advantage of this technique is that it can be used to date older sites than those within the range of ^{14}C dating. But most archaeological sites cannot be dated by the potassium-argon method. It is mainly useful for sites dating to 500,000 years or more ago, and it is applicable only to rocks or sediments rich in potassium, such as volcanic ash. The main achievement of the method has been the assignment of an age of 1,750,000 years to *Zinjanthropus*, the *"Paranthropus"* found by Leakey at Olduvai Gorge.

Pollen analysis

Although very small, the pollen released from flowering plants is quite durable under certain conditions. Pollen trapped in peat bogs is almost indestructable. Pollen grains are also well preserved for long periods of time in lake mud, alpine and desert soils, and in glacial ice, where the action of bacteria is restricted. By analyzing the pollen found in a stratum of peat, one can find out what kinds of trees and other plants were growing about at the time of its deposition. By similarly analyzing earlier strata of peat at the site, one can see what changes took place in the local flora from one period to another. In this way, pollen analysts have reconstructed the stages of forestation in Europe after the retreat of the glaciers. It appears that birch forests first appeared, followed by pine and later by mixed oak forests.

Pollen analysis is not only, or even primarily, useful as a dating technique. It also provides a picture of the ecological conditions to which man had to adjust at different times in the past. The ratio of tree pollen to other kinds of pollen, for example, gives an indication of forest density. Pollen analysis can even find evidence for agricultural activities and forest clearing by man, as in the case of some European Neolithic sites, where slash and burn horticulture was practiced. James Deetz writes:

Pollen "profiles" made up by identifying the pollen from layer to layer in sites in the area, show this sequence clearly. The lowermost levels have pollen of forest trees, followed at times by a thin layer of charcoal representing the burning of a plot in the vicinity. Atop this charcoal layer is found the pollen of domesticated plants, and finally the pollen of wild grasses, showing the abandonment of the plot and its reversion to grass cover.[7]

Pollen analysis may be combined with radiocarbon dating when a section of peat is dated by the ^{14}C method. It has thus proven to be a very useful technique, particularly in the study of European prehistory.

Associated fauna

When animal bones are found in a site, they may provide clues to chronology, particularly in the case of extinct animals, the date of whose disappearance is approximately known. Different kinds of animals flourish in warm and cold periods. During warmer periods there were animals like elephants and hippopotami in Europe; during cold periods of glacial advance there were reindeer and cave bears.[8] Associated faunal remains may therefore help to date a human occupation or butchering site. Small animals may be particularly useful for clues to climatic conditions, for rodents, birds, and especially mollusks, are very sensitive to changes in climate.

Other methods

Fluorine analysis was briefly described in Chapter 10. This method provides relative dates for bone materials, indicating whether a particular bone in a deposit is of the same age, more recent, or older than another.

Typological classification of artifacts may also help to date sites. Ceramic sequences serve as an example. In areas where pottery has been in use for a long period of time, there will be different ways of making pottery, different decorative techniques and styles characteristic of different periods. In the absence of stratigraphy, there may be no way of knowing the sequence of development of these styles, but sometimes it can be inferred on logical grounds in a process known as *seriation*. William Flinders Petrie, the great Egyptologist, made a relative dating sequence of Egyptian tombs on the basis of changes in the form of the pots found in them. Early pots, he concluded, had handles which gradually became smaller over the years, until finally there was nothing but a painted line

---

[7] James Deetz, *Invitation to Archaeology* (New York: Natural History Press, 1967), p. 71.

[8] But animal forms may persist in the face of seemingly unfavorable climatic changes. The hippopotamus, a "tropical" animal, survived in Italy until near the end of the Mousterian period (Bordes, *op. cit.*, p. 18).

in the place where the handle had formerly been. Tombs with pottery of the latter type were judged to be later than those which had pots with handles. A relative dating sequence like this can sometimes be tied in with absolute dating to give a more definite chronological order. Let us say that a particular Pueblo site in Arizona has been dated through tree ring analysis or ^{14}C. The pottery found at the site can thus be approximately dated, and subsequent finds of such pottery at other sites can then be cross-dated, falling into the same period.

Cross-dating may also be done with such trade objects as coins or axes. For example, Minoan sites have been dated through the presence of Egyptian trade items (see page 158).

Many other dating techniques could be mentioned.[9] The ones here reviewed, however, are those most commonly employed. An archaeologist can, of course, use a combination of these techniques, perhaps two or three or more. If the different methods yield similar dates, he can feel more confident of the results.

A good statement of methods used in archaeology may be found in James B. Griffin, "The Study of Early Cultures" in Harry L. Shapiro (ed.), *Man, Culture and Society* (New York: Oxford University Press, 1960), pp. 22–48, and in James Deetz, *Introduction to Archaeology* (New York: Natural History Press, 1967). A more extensive treatment is available in Frank Hole and Robert F. Heizer, *An Introduction to Prehistoric Archaeology* (2nd ed.; New York: Holt, Rinehart, & Winston, 1969). A still more exhaustive survey, useful mainly for professional archaeologists, is Don Brothwell and Eric Higgs (eds.), *Science in Archaeology: A Comprehensive Survey of Progress and Research* (New York: Basic Books, Publishers, 1963).

For dating methods, see Kenneth P. Oakley, *Frameworks for Dating Fossil Man* (Chicago: Aldine Publishing Co., 1961). For some aspects of the analysis of prehistoric sites, see Creighton Gabel, *Analysis of Prehistoric Economic Patterns* (New York: Holt, Rinehart & Winston, 1967). See also Bruce C. Trigger, *Beyond History: The Methods of Prehistory* (New York: Holt, Rinehart & Winston, 1968), and Gordon R. Willey and Philip Phillips, *Method and Theory in American Archaeology* (Chicago: University of Chicago Press, 1958).

Suggestions for further reading

---

[9] See the massive compendium edited by Don Brothwell and Eric Higgs, with a Foreword by Grahame Clark, *Science in Archaeology: A Comprehensive Survey of Progress and Research* (New York: Basic Books, Publishers, 1963).

Early prehistory

VII

Chapter 16

The Lower and
Middle Palaeolithic

From the time when our ancestors first began to use stone tools over 2 million years ago, down to about 8,000 B.C., man lived by hunting and gathering. Although there have been exceptions in areas richly supplied with game, this form of subsistence generally entails a nomadic or semi-nomadic way of life. If the game in a particular area is hunted out, the hunters must move elsewhere to where animals may be found. If they depend upon herding animals such as bison or reindeer, the hunters must follow the herds. The nomadic nature of a hunting-gathering way of life helps to account for the great dispersal of man from the Lower Pleistocene period on. This early dispersal was, of course, a gradual process, made on foot; but before the end of the Pleistocene epoch, man had spread over most of the Old World and moved into the New. He had not yet settled in the Pacific Islands, since that depended upon the development of navigation, the first clear evidences of which date from early postglacial times. Entrance into the New World was probably made via a land bridge in the Bering Straits, across which many animals made their way back and forth in Pleistocene times.

Subdivisions of prehistory

Since the period of prehistory is immensely long, some way must be found to subdivide it, so that developmental stages may be traced and placed in sequence. As was noted in Chapter 14, an early effort to create some order in this field was Christian Thomsen's distinction of three phases: a Stone Age, a Bronze Age, and an Iron Age. Based upon the materials used for making cutting tools, these phases not only represent progressive increases in man's control over nature but also reflect an in-

A stag hunt. Cave
painting, Spain.

creasing specialization, division of labor, and growing complexity of social
structure.

The Stone Age has been subdivided into Lower, Middle, and Upper
Palaeolithic (or Old Stone Age); Mesolithic (Middle Stone Age); and Neolithic (New Stone Age). We know that cultural advance was more rapid in
the Near East than elsewhere; so while a Neolithic or even Bronze Age
economy was in operation in the Near East, northern Europe had a Mesolithic way of life.

The fact that the foregoing scheme of cultural stages is tied to Europe
and cannot be applied very well in other regions, such as the New World,
has led to its rejection by some prehistorians. Nevertheless, it continues
to be used by most archaeologists. Since the prehistory of Europe has

been studied longer and is better known than that of most other regions, this conservatism is understandable. Until a new generally accepted scheme for dividing the stages of prehistory comes along, we might as well go along with the old one. This text, therefore, will follow the traditional system.

With the foregoing qualifications kept in mind, the following approximate dates based partly on radiocarbon dating may be given, with the focus being on Western Europe. It is hard to say when the Middle Palaeolithic "begins," but its "end" can be placed around 32,000 B.C. We then have 32,000–11,000 for the Upper Palaeolithic and 11,000–5,000 for the European Mesolithic.

The Neolithic period begins earlier in the Near East than in Europe, from around 8,000 to 3,500 B.C.

Much of what we know about the early cultures is based on the analysis of stone tools. This focus on stonework is an unavoidable overemphasis. Of course, man did not use only stone for cutting tools in the Stone Age; he must also have used bone, horn, wood, and other materials. In Chapter 8 on the australopithecines, some evidence was presented to show that *Australopithecus* probably used animal bones for clubbing and stabbing. Men also worked bone in the Middle Palaeolithic period. More use was made of bone, horn, ivory, and antler in the Upper Palaeolithic. The engraving and cutting tools of the Upper Palaeolithic made it possible to work more successfully in bone, horn, ivory, and antler.

Wood was used for spears as far back as the Lower Palaeolithic. The early spears were not headed with stone projectile points; instead the tips were sometimes hardened in fire. A spear found at Clacton in Essex, England, dates from the Middle Pleistocene. Another, which comes from a site in North Germany, is dated at least 80,000 years ago. A fire-hardened spear at Lehringen, 8 feet long, was found between the ribs of an extinct form of elephant. Worked wood fragments have been recovered in the early Palaeolithic site at Torralba, Spain. Digging sticks and a club dated by radiocarbon as 57,000 years old, have been found at a site in northern Rhodesia. Finds like these are rare, since wood usually disintegrates. Stone, however, is indestructable. Much of our knowledge about the Palaeolithic period, therefore, has to do with the development of man's stone technology.

Lower Palaeolithic stone technology

It is not always easy to determine whether a particular piece of stone was deliberately fashioned by man. Early man made much use of flint, which fractures easily when given a blow. But stone can be flaked by natural agencies, by rapid changes in temperature, by frost, glacial action, and other causes. However, a close examination of the stone may reveal whether man-made blows dislodged the flake. As a leading authority on this subject has written:

Plaster casts of
choppers used by
Peking Man.

. . . the surface of a fracture due to a sharp external blow appears clean-cut,
and shows a definite bulb of percussion with faint radial fissures and ripples
originating at a point on the edge of the flake or flake-scar.[1]

The earliest stone tools showing deliberate flaking were choppers, pebble tools with a jagged cutting edge formed by striking off a few flakes.
Choppers were the most common tools found in Bed I in Olduvai Gorge;
they have come to be known as Oldowan tools. Such tools, sometimes
flaked on both sides or in two directions, (and thus clearly not shaped by
geological accident), have been found from the Cape in South Africa, to
the Transvaal, Kenya, Morocco, Algeria, and Abyssinia. There were
hominids early in the Pleistocene using Oldowan choppers in most parts of
Africa before stone tools first appeared in Europe. Simple choppers were
used by Peking man and have been found in many parts of eastern Asia,
including China, Burma, Indonesia, and India. Some early European sites
have also yielded tools similar to the Oldowan and Peking choppers, notably Clacton-on-Sea, Swanscombe, Vértesszöllös, near Menton in southern France, and a couple of sites in Romania.

In Africa the Oldowan chopper gradually gave rise to a more advanced
tool, the hand axe. A slow transition of this sort appears in Beds II to IV
at Olduvai Gorge. Does this mean that Olduvai Gorge was the place
where this technological advance first occurred? Not necessarily. It seems
likely, however, that the hand axe did originate in Africa and spread from
that continent to other parts of the Old World. It is possible that hand axes
developed from choppers in various regions, but this development apparently did not take place in eastern Asia.

A hand axe is a pear-shaped core tool made of some stone, like flint,
which fractures easily. Here we must distinguish between *core* and

---

[1] Kenneth P. Oakley, *Man the Tool-maker* (Chicago: University of Chicago Press,
Phoenix Books, 1964), p. 17.

Some Lower
Palaeolithic
hand axes.

flake tools. Suppose you grasp a rough piece of flint and give it a blow on the top or side with another stone. If you keep banging away at it effectively enough, you will knock off some flakes or slivers of stone. If you can dislodge these flakes so as to shape the original piece of stone into the kind of tool you want, you end up with a *core* tool, so called because it consists of the core of the stone which has been trimmed.

It might happen that one of the flakes struck off from the core has a sharp cutting edge. It might make a good knife or scraper. If you use it as a tool, you have a *flake* tool. Both core and flake tools were used in the Lower Palaeolithic. The hand axe, also known as a core-biface (because trimmed on both sides), and as a *coup de poing* from the French "blow of the fist," was the characteristic tool of the Lower Palaeolithic. In the Upper Palaeolithic, the hand axe ceased to be used. The Palaeolithic is marked by a gradual increase in the number and kinds of flake tools, which became particularly prominent in the Upper Palaeolithic.

Hand axes were fashioned so as to have a continuous cutting edge all around the bottom part. They were not hafted to handles but held in the hand. They may have been all-purpose tools, used for cutting, banging, scraping, and digging. The hand axe had a wide distribution throughout Africa, Western Europe, and India. The appearance of hand axes was very stable throughout this vast area, so that one found in Madras looks just like one that comes from South Africa or France.

In Africa hand axes have been found in association with skeletal remains of *Homo erectus*. It seems likely that the use of this tool spread northward into Europe during the Lower Pleistocene and eastward to India. But the hand axe did not extend into China and other parts of

Upper Palaeolithic tools (left to right): burin or graver; blade; borer or drill; blade core, from which blades are struck off; blade with sharp cutting edge.

eastern Asia, where the chopper remained the characteristic stone tool of the Lower Palaeolithic.[2]

The distribution of the hand axe in Europe is rather puzzling. It is found in Spain, Italy, England, and France, but not east of the Rhine.

Early hand axes have been called Abbevillian (formerly Chellean) from Abbeville, a site in France where such tools were found. More expertly made Lower Palaeolithic hand axes of a later period are called Acheulean, after the French site of St. Acheul.

Acheulean hand axes have straighter, less irregular cutting edges. Kenneth P. Oakley writes:

. . . in the Acheulean stages man had acquired such good mastery over stone that the form of the biface is indistinguishable whether it be made in lava, dolerite, ironstone, or quartzite. Even the fineness of craftsmanship was scarcely affected by the type of rock.[3]

During the Acheulean period a new technique, called Levalloisian, was developed for making flake tools. This involved preparing a "striking platform" at the top of a core before dislodging flakes. Flakes detached from such specially prepared "striking platforms" were larger and more symmetrical than flakes knocked off in the hit-or-miss fashion of earlier times.

---

[2] Hand axes did, however, appear in Java, perhaps as an independent invention, according to François Bordes (*The Old Stone Age* [New York: World University Library, 1968], pp. 81, 136, 139).

[3] Kenneth P. Oakley, *Frameworks for Dating Fossil Man* (Chicago: Aldine Publishing Co., 1964), p. 179.

With this invention, flake tools became more important, and there was more control over their production.

The Levalloisian technique was widely used in Africa, Western Europe, the Near East, and India, but like the hand axe it did not spread as far east as China in Middle Pleistocene times. The invention may, however, have been independently arrived at in several different areas where man habitually worked flint. It may, for example, have been developed independently in Africa and Europe. Flakes made in the Levalloisian manner also appear in Hopewell sites in ancient North America, again probably due to independent invention.

The Acheulean period in Europe was very long, extending from the second to the close of the third interglacial stage. During this time some hominids used fire in Europe (Vértesszöllös) and in China (Choukoutien), but there is no evidence of the use of fire in Africa until the latter part of the Acheulean period. Through most of the Lower Palaeolithic, man camped in open stations, beside rivers and lakes, hunting both small game and large animals, such as the elephants at Torralba and Ambrona in Spain or the rhinoceros and other animals at Choukoutien.

The Middle Palaeolithic

The term *Middle Palaeolithic* is a bit vague and does not represent a cultural stage differing sharply from the preceding one. In material culture, there is also much continuity in the succeeding Upper Palaeolithic, but the latter represents a much richer culture in many ways. The term *Middle Palaeolithic* has the drawback that it is mainly applicable to Western Europe and has not been extended to some other areas, such as India, eastern Asia, and Africa south of the Sahara. Nevertheless, the traditional usage will again be followed here.

The Mousterian industry, associated with Neandertal man, falls in the Middle Palaeolithic period in Western Europe, dating from about 80,000 to 32,000 B.C. During this period, the Levallois flaking tradition continues. Although hand axes are still found, their numbers decline, and the main emphasis is on flake tools. The first known projectile points, evidently used on hand-thrown spears, appear at a site at Ehringdorf, Germany, near the edge of the northern Eurasiatic plains, which man was now beginning to occupy.

Some use was made in Mousterian times of bone, but only in a rudimentary way in contrast to the Upper Palaeolithic, when bone tools become prominent.

During parts of the Middle Palaeolithic period, glaciers moved down across northern Europe, and the weather became extremely cold. Such animals as reindeer and cave bears replaced fauna adapted to warm weather conditions. Neandertal man at least had the use of fire, and he found some protection in caves. It seems likely that he wore animal skins as clothing, to judge from the abundance of scrapers among his tools.

Although the stone tools were well made, the culture of Neandertal man was still quite primitive. He seems to have lacked aesthetic inclinations, for there is no evidence of art, ornaments, or decorative design. Moreover, some Neandertalers were cannibals, as suggested by the skeletal remains at Krapina, Yugoslavia, and Monte Circeo, Italy.

Implications of religious beliefs

At the same time, Neandertalers were the first people known to bury the dead. They did not always do so—sometimes their bones, mixed up with those of animals, appear in disorder in the backs of caves. But sometimes graves were dug in the dirt floors of their caves. The limbs were often flexed, perhaps to save space, although there may have been other reasons for this practice. The legs must have been tightly bound before the corpse had a chance to stiffen. In these burials we see the beginnings of a practice which became more elaborate in later periods—the placing of grave goods with the dead. At Le Moustier in the Dordogne region of France, a youth was buried with his head resting on a pile of flint fragments, with the charred and split bones of wild cattle around him and a fist axe near his hand. In a burial at La Chapelle aux Saints, also in the Dordogne, were a number of shells, some Mousterian flints, and various animal bones. At Mt. Carmel some large animal jawbones were included in the burial. At Teshik-Tash in Uzbekistan, a child's corpse was surrounded by six pairs of goats' horns, whose points were pushed into the ground.

Where grave goods are buried with the dead among present-day peoples, the practice is usually associated with the idea of an afterlife and with the notion that the spirit of the dead person will use the object in the other world. Neandertal man may have had such ideas, which are certainly very old, to judge by their universality among primitive peoples. To be sure, there may be other explanations for these burial practices.

There are, however, other implications of religious beliefs held by Neandertal man in the collections of bear skulls found in his caves. The mere preservation of skulls need not suggest anything religious, but in some cases special attention was given to their placement. In one cave, five bear skulls were found in niches in the cave wall. The skulls of several cave bears in a group have been found surrounded by built-up stone walls, with some skulls having little stones placed around them, while others were set out on slabs.

All this suggests some kind of bear cult, like that practiced until quite recently by the Chippewa and other northerly American Indians. After a Chippewa hunter had killed a bear, he used to cut off the head, which was then decorated with beads and ribbons, (in the period after contact with Europeans). Some tobacco was placed before its nose. The hunter would then make a little speech, apologizing to the bear for having had to kill it. Bear skulls were preserved and hung up on trees, so that dogs and wolves could not get at them. Bear ceremonialism of this and related kinds had a wide circumpolar distribution—from the Great Lakes to the northwest coast of North America in the New World and from the Ainu of northern Japan through various Siberian tribes, such as the Ostyaks and the Orotchi, to the Finns and Lapps of Scandinavia. So wide a distribution of this trait, associated as it was with other apparently very early circumpolar traits, suggests great age. It is possible, therefore, that some aspects of this bear ceremonialism go back to Middle Palaeolithic times.

Careful burials with grave goods and the evidence for bear cults provide the earliest signs of human religious practices and beliefs. Further evidence of early religious and magical practices soon appear in abundance in the next stage of human cultural development, the Upper Palaeolithic.

Suggestions for further reading

Some good works which deal with the stone technology of early man are Kenneth P. Oakley, *Man the Tool-Maker* (Chicago: University of Chicago Press, Phoenix Books, 1964); S. A. Semenov, *Prehistoric Technology*, trans. from the Russian by M. W. Thompson (New York: Barnes & Noble, 1964); Robert J. Braidwood, *Prehistoric Men* (7th ed.; Glenview, Ill.: Scott, Foresman & Co., 1967); and François Bordes, trans. from the French by J. E. Anderson, *The Old Stone Age* (New York: McGraw-Hill Book Co., 1968).

Grahame Clark and Stuart Piggott, *Prehistoric Societies* (New York: Alfred A. Knopf, 1965) is highly recommended. For a survey of Palaeolithic cultures, see J. M. Coles and E. S. Higgs, *The Archaeology of Early Man* (New York: Frederick A. Praeger, 1969).

Chapter 17

The Upper Palaeolithic
and Mesolithic

When the glaciers began to retreat in Europe during the last inter-glacial period 50,000 years ago, they left behind a relatively treeless tundra, across which blew loess, the yellowish brown dust deposited by the glaciers. In warmer, moister weather, loess is gradually converted into loam. During the warm summer months, grasses and other vegetation sprang from this soil, providing admirable grazing grounds for the four-footed herbiverous ungulates which flourished in Europe at this time. Wild horses, reindeer, mammoth, bison, rhinoceroses, and other animals moved across the open plains, providing splendid opportunities for human hunters.

Around 30,000 years ago, *Homo sapiens sapiens* appeared, man of modern physical type, represented by such early examples as Cro-Magnon man. These men were like ourselves, but more ruggedly built. Their skeletal remains are much more numerous than those of their predecessors, suggesting that a steady population increase was taking place at this time due partly to the abundance of game. But we must also credit man's ingenuity in devising new hunting tools, for this was a period which saw many cultural innovations, despite the fact that the Upper Palaeolithic covered only a fraction of the whole Palaeolithic period.

Upper Palaeolithic inventions

One of the new inventions was the spear-thrower or throwing-board. Spears had been in use for a long time before this, but the new device gave them greater impetus. Instead of being thrown directly by hand, the spear was now propelled from a grooved board, gripped near the front end. The butt of the shaft was held by a projection at the back of the board. With a twist of the wrist, a spearsman could now send a shaft through the air with much greater force than with the unaided arm. This invention is probably earlier than that of the bow and arrow. The throwing-board was used by early American Indians, the Eskimos, and the Australian aborigines. The widespread use by hunting peoples of different continents suggests great age. The Aztec name for spear-thrower, *atlatl*, is sometimes used for this device in anthropological literature.[1]

The bow and arrow was in use in Egypt in Upper Palaeolithic times. In Europe it is known to have been in use in the later Mesolithic period but was probably also used in the Upper Palaeolithic. One bit of early evidence is a collection of about 100 wooden arrows found near Hamburg, dated at about 10,500 years ago. What look like representations of feathered arrows (although they may have been darts) appear in the cave paintings of Lascaux.

Harpoons with detachable heads were used by Upper Palaeolithic hunters, as they have been used by Eskimos. Eskimos harpoon seals and other sea mammals, and we think of harpooning as a technique for killing whales and seals. Bibby believes that the earliest use of harpoons was against land animals such as reindeer, although they may also have been used for spearing fish. Some former reindeer hunters who settled along the fjords of central Norway around 7,000 B.C. are believed to have been the first to transfer the harpooning technique to the killing of sea mammals.[2] Leroi-Gourhan, on the other hand, thinks that Upper Palaeolithic harpoons were used for spearing fish, and he believes that the weapon was not thrown but held in the hand.[3]

It may be noted that these various hunting devices—throwing-board, bow and arrow, and harpoon—are not only ingenious, far from obvious, inventions but they also required a good deal of training and practice to be effective. Moreover, they are all composite tools consisting of different parts, often of different materials. Instead of having fire-hardened tips, spears and harpoons now had separate heads made of antler, bone, ivory, and flint. The harpoon consisted of three parts: head, shaft, and line. The bow consisted of wood and sinew.

---

[1] Although most archaeologists seem to accept Upper Palaeolithic hooked rods as being spear-throwers, a leading French authority, André Leroi-Gourhan seems uncertain about it: ". . . nothing prevents us from regarding the 'hooked rods' as 'spear-throwers'; on the other hand there is no clear archaeological evidence that they were used as such" (André Leroi-Gourhan, *Treasures of Prehistoric Art* [New York: Harry N. Abrams, 1967], p. 63).

[2] Geoffrey Bibby, *The Testimony of the Spade* (New York: Alfred A. Knopf, 1956), pp. 166–67.

[3] Leroi-Gourhan, *op cit.*, p. 59.

The characteristic stone tools of the Upper Palaeolithic were blades and burins. A blade is a sharp-edged flake with long parallel sides. It is made from a carefully prepared core of flint or obsidian, from which the flakes are knocked off. A burin is a chisellike stone tool used as a graver. Blades were used as knives and scrapers. Burins were used for working bone, antler, ivory, and wood. At least, that is what archaeologists have assumed on the basis of their forms. When we speak about knives, scrapers, and borers, we cannot always be sure that the men who made these tools used them as we assume.

Recently, European investigators have been making microscopic analyses of wear patterns, striations on stone tools, in order to get a better idea of their possible functions. Some striations run parallel with the sides of a blade, for example, while others are at right angles. By analyzing the type of wear, one may deduce whether the tool was apt to have been used for cutting, scraping, or piercing.

It has been assumed that some of the Upper Palaeolithic stone tools were used for making bone tools. At any rate, more use was now made of materials other than stone. Bone was used for chisels, gouges, and arrow straighteners. The presence of bone needles and ivory pins suggests that skin clothing was worn. Various materials were used for decoration. Necklaces have been found in Upper Palaeolithic burials made of shells, fish vertebrae, deer teeth, and pieces of bone and ivory.

Decorative art

Decorations and animal figures were often engraved on the shafts of spear-throwers, shaft-straighteners, and other objects. Some of this artwork is quite beautiful.

An implement of bone or horn, looking somewhat like a monkey wrench is called a pierced staff. Such "staffs" are often decorated, particularly with the figures of horses. Since much artistic elaboration had been devoted to these objects, it was formerly thought that they were scepters or *bâtons de commandement,* as they were called. More recently it has been decided that they were thong-stroppers or shaft-straighteners, similar to objects used by Eskimos and Indians for straightening arrows and spears.

Other decorated tools included bone spatulas, half-rounded horn rods, and objects (perhaps pendants) evidently meant to be suspended, since they had holes for the insertion of cords.

The men of the Upper Palaeolithic are the first artists whose work has been preserved. There are no remains of art from the Lower and Middle Palaeolithic periods. One might expect that the first known artwork of early man would be rather crude, but the art of the Upper Palaeolithic is not at all crude; it is vigorous and well executed. This art was produced in various media: clay sculpture, engraving in antler and ivory, and paintings on the walls of caves. The major subject matter of the representational art consisted of the animals hunted by Upper Palaeolithic man, such as reindeer and deer, mammoths, wild horses and cows, bison, and rhinoceroses.

Cave paintings

The most impressive of Upper Palaeolithic artworks are the cave paintings of Spain and southern France, where walls were covered with the forms of animals, some small, some as large as 20 feet in length. These were painted with mineral oxide pigments, the main colors being black, red, and yellow. At Lascaux Cave, large bulls were painted, outlined in black, but there were also filled-in, shaded figures with more subtle colors such as lavender and mauve. Blue and green do not appear, although it is possible that the artists used such colors of organic origin which have since disintegrated. The colors which remain are still fresh and clear.

The pigments seem to have sometimes been used solid as pastels, sometimes mixed with water or grease. They were applied directly with the fingers, smeared on with pads of moss or lichen, or applied with some kind of brush. In some cases, it looks as though the paint may have been blown through a bone tube, for some of the animals have vague, fuzzy outlines, reminiscent of Chinese wash drawings. Hollow bones filled with ocher have been found in the caves. Shoulder blades of large animals have also been found, stained with color, as well as naturally hollowed stones containing pigments. These were probably mortars in which mineral oxides were crushed and ground.

Cave painting of bison, Altamira, Spain.

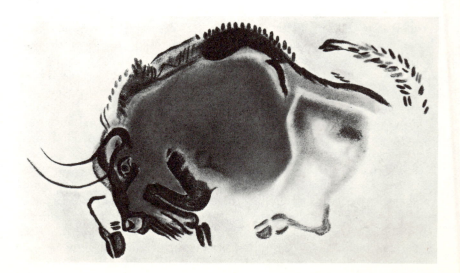

The animals are not depicted in settings or landscape; plants are seldom shown. Earlier observers were struck by the seeming absence of composition. For example, a later animal figure is sometimes superimposed over an earlier one. But there is some degree of composition, as in some of the groupings at Lascaux.

The animals are drawn with skill, showing good anatomical observation. There is no doubt about which animals were meant to be shown. However, the drawings are not always complete. Legs and belly lines were sometimes left out. Sometimes natural features of the rock were utilized in the painting, so that an outward bulge of rock, for example, was turned into a horse's flank.

Human figures are seldom shown in the cave art. When they appear, they are sometimes stick figures, lacking the close observation and accuracy of the animal drawings. When men are depicted, they often wear animal masks or have animal heads.

Some of the large animal figures, such as the bulls of Lascaux, 13 and 16 feet long, must have involved a lot of work and perhaps the cooperation of several men. Some figures on the ceilings of caves suggest that scaffolding was erected. So these must have been serious projects involving some group planning and cooperation.

Why did Upper Palaeolithic men make the numerous animal paintings? We do not know for certain. A commonly accepted explanation has been that the paintings had magico-religious functions and were designed to increase the number of game animals or to win control over them. It was pointed out that the main motive cannot have been aesthetic; it was not a question of art for art's sake. This is suggested by the fact that many of the paintings are found in deep recesses, in pitch darkness, a long way from the entrance. Some cave art at Niaux in the Dordogne is over two thirds of a mile from the mouth of the cave. Sometimes, in order to reach the paintings, one has to crawl through narrow tunnels. The difficulty of access, remoteness, and darkness are testimony to the serious, religious nature of cave art.

We can only speculate about why men explored these dark caves, so far from daylight, and why they painted on the rocky walls. It seems likely that men first made paintings and engravings near the mouths of caves and later moved into more remote recesses. The earlier paintings might conceivably have been a kind of decoration to brighten up the home, if men lived at the cave entrances; but the later paintings cannot have had such a function.

Figures of bison, horses, and mammoths sometimes show darts or arrows sticking in them. Some animals painted on rather soft rock are pitted with holes. It has been inferred that spears were violently thrown at these paintings. A cave at Montespan has 20 clay animals which seem to have been similarly speared. This is reminiscent of the old and widespread magical practice of sticking pins into a doll which represents an enemy. By making a representation of something one gets control over it; by damaging it, one wounds the object or person it represents. Thus, by painting animals the Palaeolithic hunters might have thought that they were getting control over them; by spearing them they ensured their later slaughter.

On the other hand, the number of depictions of wounded animals is small, amounting to fewer than 10 percent. As we shall see, André Leroi-Gourhan, who made this statistical assessment, has given other reasons for doubting the hunting-magic interpretation.

Another proposition of the hunting-magic view is that the hunters not only magically killed their game but magically increased it by depicting female animals as pregnant.

The human female figurines of the Upper Palaeolithic, rather oddly named "Venuses," also often have a pregnant appearance; at any rate, the secondary sexual characteristics are exaggerated: broad hips, large breasts and abdomen, but spindly arms and stunted legs. No facial features are shown, although the hairdo may be indicated. It seems unlikely that Upper Palaeolithic women actually looked like that, but perhaps it was an ideal type or expressed a wish for fertility as in the "pregnant" animals painted in the caves.

Leroi-Gourhan is not convinced that the fat-looking animals on the cave walls are meant to be pregnant; it is often impossible to say whether they are male or female animals. Maybe they are simply fat.

The hunting-magic hypothesis seems reasonable, but there are other possible ways of interpreting Upper Palaeolithic cave art. A recent line of inquiry has been pursued by Annette Laming-Emperaire and André Leroi-Gourhan. They have made statistical analyses of the different kinds of animals painted and the locations of the paintings on the cave walls. Their findings suggest that certain animals had a symbolic significance for the artists.

Not all animals known to the Palaeolithic hunters were painted on the cave walls. The number of species depicted is smaller than that known to have existed at the time. In Leroi-Gourhan's analysis of 2,188 animal figures from 66 caves and rock shelters, the following species are the most common: 610 horses, 510 bison, 205 mammoths, 176 ibexes, 137 "oxen," 135 hinds, 112 stags, 84 reindeer, 36 bears, 29 lions, and 16 rhinoceroses.

These animals tend to appear in particular parts of caves; they are not distributed at random. Some species tend to be found in the central portions of caves: 91 percent of bison, 92 percent of "oxen," 86 percent of horses, and 58 percent of mammoths. Remaining species have a percentage of less than 10.

Stags and ibexes are found at the entrances and backs of caves. Twelve percent of the horses are found with the stags and ibexes. Stags, ibexes, and horses seem to have been associated symbolically, for these form the overwhelming majority of animals depicted on spears, harpoons, spear-throwers, and handles of pierced staffs. Partly because of their association with men's weapons, Leroi-Gourhan classifies stags, ibexes, and horses as "male" animals, while the bison, "oxen," and hinds are classified as "female." Human female figures are often found in the center along with the large herbivores, while male figures are found at the backs of caves or on the peripheries of a central composition.

One difficulty with this male-female classification is that the horse is called a male "framing" animal, like the stag and ibex, and yet 86 percent of the horses are found in the center. On the other hand, they are usually smaller than the wild cattle, which are sometimes huge in comparison. While peripheral animals may appear in the center, bison and "oxen" are not found in peripheral zones.

Various signs or symbols commonly appear in the caves, such as dots, strokes, ovals, and triangles. Although a dubious Freudian projection may be involved here, Leroi-Gourhan has divided these into male and female signs. Dots, strokes, and barbed signs are held to be male, while enclosed signs, such as ovals, triangles, and rectangles are considered female. It is consistent with Leroi-Gourhan's analysis that male signs usually occur at entrances and backs of caves, although sometimes also in the center, while female signs, like bison and "oxen," do not occur at entrances and backs of caves but are concentrated in the center, where they are matched with male signs.

While some of this analysis may be doubtful, the work of Annette Laming-Emperaire and André Leroi-Gourhan has brought to light a hitherto unsuspected order and pattern which applies to many caves and rock shelters. There is evidently more sophistication and symbolism in Upper Palaeolithic art than was formerly believed. Leroi-Gourhan writes:

> What constituted for Palaeolithic men the special heart and core of the caves is clearly the panels in the central part, dominated by animals from the female category and female signs, supplemented by animals from the male category and male signs. The entrance to the sanctuary, usually a narrow part of the cave, is decorated with male symbols, either animals or signs; the back of the cave, often a narrow tunnel, is decorated with the same signs, reinforced by horned men and the rarer animals (cave lion or rhinoceros).[4]

Even if this symbolism be granted, we still do not know the exact purpose of Upper Palaeolithic cave art. Some effort to control or increase the supply of game is still a possibility. On the other hand, the caves may have been settings for initiation ceremonies, rites of passage for boys entering manhood. Most of the footprints found in the caves seem to be those of

---

[4] Leroi-Gourhan, *op. cit.*, p. 144.

youths or boys. The dark caves would, of course, have been an awesome setting for an initiation, and we can imagine the effect it may have had when lighted torches suddenly revealed the procession of animal figures on the cave walls.

When we focus on the possible religious and magical functions of Upper Palaeolithic art, we should not forget its aesthetic aspects. If one draws an animal to spear, control, or increase it, one need not draw it well. But the Upper Palaeolithic artists often drew with great skill. This suggests that aesthetic satisfaction accompanied the magico-religious motivation, whatever that may have been. The engraved antler rods, for example, seem to be purely decorative and beautifully done. Art had evidently become an important value for human beings by Upper Palaeolithic times.

Upper Palaeolithic cultures

The foregoing description of the Upper Palaeolithic has been cast in general terms, but it should not be supposed that Upper Palaeolithic culture was uniform, everywhere the same. As in later periods, there was much cultural variation. The area best known, because first studied, is that of Western Europe, which also happens to be the region of the most impressive cave art. But Upper Palaeolithic cultures extended eastward to Siberia and China, and cave paintings, similar to those of the Dordogne, have been found in the south Ural district of Russia.

One of the earlier and more widespread Upper Palaeolithic cultures was the *Aurignacian,* whose stone technology was characterized by an abundance of flake scrapers and burins, or gravers. Much use was made of bone in such tools as split-base bone points, detachable heads for shafts, pins, awls, chisels, gouges, and arrow-straighteners. Aurignacian industries have been found over a wide area from Afghanistan and Iraq through the Near East to France, Germany, and Spain. Their appearance in Europe seems abrupt, as though a fully equipped culture had moved in from elsewhere. It has been thought that the Aurignacian culture originated in Asia rather than Europe. Radiocarbon dates indicate that it flourished in western Asia by around 35,000 B.C. The distribution of Aurignacian split-base bone points in Bulgaria, Hungary, and other parts of the Balkans suggests that the westward route of this culture may have passed through the Balkans and central Europe.[5]

The Aurignacians were cave dwellers, and the earliest cave paintings in Western Europe, including the older ones at Lascaux, are attributed to them.

---

[5] Grahame Clark and Stuart Piggott, *Prehistoric Societies* (New York: Alfred A. Knopf, 1965), p. 70. For a different interpretation, see Jacquetta Hawkes, *Prehistory; History of Mankind; Cultural and Scientific Development* (New York: Mentor, in cooperation with UNESCO, 1963), Vol. 1, Part 1, p. 139.

Another early widespread Upper Palaeolithic culture was the *Gravettian,* ranging from south Russia to Spain, but centering mainly in central and eastern Europe. Gravettian tools included flint points and knife blades, which are absent from Aurignacian technology. The Gravettians in central and eastern Europe and in south Russia were mammoth hunters, and they made use of mammoth ivory for weapons, implements such as spoons, necklaces, and pins, and artwork. Shovels or scoops were made of mammoth ribs. Mammoth bones seem also to have been used as fuel.

The Gravettians were skilled artists. In Czechoslovakia they made figurines of animals in clay, which were fired like pottery: mammoths, cave bears, bison, horses, rhinoceroses, and other animals. Figurines were also carved from bone, ivory, limestone, and steatite. It was the Gravettians who made the "Venus" figurines, found in Upper Palaeolithic sites from Russia to France. They also made elaborate decorative carvings in ivory and antler with meanders, chevrons, and other patterns. Cave paintings of mammoths, cave bears, and horses in Russia resemble those of southern France.

In parts of Europe where caves were available the Gravettians occupied them, as did the Aurignacians; but in the Russian plains they seem to have built dwellings. It is hard to reconstruct such shelters, but they may have been skin tents with poles, the corners being held down by stones and mammoth bones. Burials were more elaborate than they had been in the Middle Palaeolithic periods. Corpses, with knees flexed, were sprinkled with red ocher and sometimes sheltered by large stones or bones.

In the caves and rock shelters of Western Europe, Gravettian industries overlie Aurignacian ones. Radiocarbon dates for this area assign a period of from 32,300 B.C. $\pm$ 675 to 28,850 $\pm$ 250 for the Aurignacian and from 26,200 $\pm$ 225 to 20,830 $\pm$ 140 for the Gravettian.[6]

Later than the Aurignacian and Gravettian, the *Solutrean* culture existed in France around 18,000 B.C. Solutrean industries have also been found in Hungary and Spain. They are mainly characterized by what are called laurel leaf and willow leaf blades, beautifully fashioned by pressure flaking. The workmanship devoted to these blades far exceeds utilitarian needs and gives further evidence of the strength of aesthetic values in man of the Upper Palaeolithic period.

The culmination of Upper Palaeolithic culture came in the *Magdalenian* period, dated by radiocarbon in France between 15,240 $\pm$ 140 and 9700 $\pm$ 200. Magdalenian industries have also been found in Hungary, Germany, and Spain. This was the period of the finest polychrome cave paintings and incised work on bone and antler. The range of tools was elaborate: harpoons with barbed heads, spear-throwers, eyed needles,

---

[6] Grahame Clark, *World Prehistory: A New Outline* (Cambridge, England: The University Press, 1969), p. 66.

burins, scrapers, and other characteristic Upper Palaeolithic tools, with a new, increased emphasis on the use of bone and antler.

The Mesolithic   About 12,000 years ago, with the withdrawal of the ice sheets from Europe, changes in climate and vegetation began to take place which brought about some modifications in man's culture. The weather became warmer. Forests began to appear, first birch, then pine, and later mixed oak forests. As the open plains of Upper Palaeolithic times were gradually replaced by woods, the fauna necessarily changed. The herds of four-footed grazing animals, such as the buffalos, wild horses and cattle, began to disappear; the mammoths were gone, and reindeer made their way up to the north. At the same time, animal figures vanished from the walls of caves. The Azilians, a Mesolithic people occupied the same caves as the Magdalenians but left no cave paintings. They had a more abstract kind of art, painting pebbles with mysterious symbols, the significance of which is still unknown. The general culture of the Azilians, however, seems to have been less vigorous than that of their predecessors. A decline appears to have set in. Man now had to find new sources of food, new ways of adapting to a rapidly changing world.

One important new development in the Mesolithic period, from around 11,000 to 5,000 B.C. in Europe,[7] was the increased attention given to fish and seafood. Mesolithic settlements in northern Europe were found along the coast from England to Russia. (The coasts in those days did not follow the same outlines as the seacoast today, for the North Sea area was mostly dry and the Baltic was a lake.) The northerly coastal culture has been called *Maglemosian,* from a Danish phrase meaning "big bog," for remains of this culture have been found in swampy areas near lakes and streams. The Maglemosians had various devices for catching fish: hook, line, and sinker; spears or harpoons; and seine nets. Men of the Upper Palaeolithic ate fish too, but this source of food seems to have become much more important in Mesolithic times, as the fishhooks and other implements suggest. Dugout canoes were invented at this time; animal skins were also used for boats, stretched over a framework, like the water craft of the Eskimos.

Particularly toward the end of the Mesolithic period, the northern Europeans ate shellfish and left discarded shells in large heaps known as kitchen middens. Seals, which then were found in coastal waters, were also killed.

Inland, Mesolithic men hunted forest animals which had replaced the fauna of Upper Palaeolithic times—aurochs, moose, deer and elk, beavers, wild pigs, and other animals. They used bows and arrows, remains of

---

[7] In parts of England and Scandinavia, Mesolithic cultures persisted until around 2500 B.C. or later.

which have been found preserved in bogs. Their bows were notched at both ends for the bowstrings. Arrow heads were microliths, small stone points, held in place by resin. Spears were used, with heads of bone or antler.

One consequence of the growth of forests was an increased use of wood. Now, for the first time, axes of stone, bone, or antler were hafted to handles. Crude but apparently effective axes and adzes were used for chopping down trees, making dugout canoes, paddles, and perhaps house constructions. Wooden runners found in peat bogs show that sleds were used in wintertime.

Suggestions for further reading

Grahame Clark and Stuart Piggott, *Prehistoric Societies* (New York: Alfred A. Knopf, 1965), is again recommended. Chester S. Chard's *Man in Prehistory* (New York: McGraw-Hill Book Co., 1969), presents a good world survey.

For its analysis of Upper Palaeolithic cave art, see André Leroi-Gourhan, *Treasures of Prehistoric Art* (New York: Harry N. Abrams, 1967), a beautifully produced, understandably expensive publication.

Geoffrey Bibby, *The Testimony of The Spade* (New York: Alfred A. Knopf, 1956), is well written and interesting, particularly on the Mesolithic period.

See also Jacquetta Hawkes, *Prehistory; History of Mankind; Cultural and Scientific Development* (New York: Mentor, in cooperation with UNESCO, 1963), Vol. I, Part 1; François Bordes, *The Old Stone Age*, trans. from the French by J. E. Anderson (New York: McGraw-Hill Book Co., 1968); and J. M. Coles and E. S. Higgs, *The Archaeology of Early Man* (New York: Frederick A. Praeger, 1969).

Chapter 18

The Neolithic in the Old World

The Neolithic period in the Near East, between 8000 and 3500 B.C., saw the most crucial transformation in man's way of life. Up to this point man had been a hunter and collector, living on game and fish, wild fruits, nuts, and vegetables. As shown by the enormous dispersal of man over the world's surface by Neolithic times, this hunting-gathering way of life involved a nomadic or seminomadic existence.

This does not mean that hunters were always on the move. The Indians of the northwest coast of North America lived in an area rich in fish, sea mammals, and other food resources, and they were able to live in permanent villages consisting of large plank-walled houses. The Ainu of northern Japan also had permanent settlements, as did some of the hunting-gathering tribes of California.

The hunters of the present day live in the less favored marginal regions of the world, but in Palaeolithic times they occupied all the best available terrain, and no doubt many of them were largely sedentary, or moved about within a circumscribed area. Like present-day hunting people, they probably occupied different areas at different times of the year, depending upon the ripening of fruits or plants in particular patches of land or the seasonal movements of animals.

The major transformation of the Neolithic period was the domestication of plants and animals, which made permanent village life more feasible. Although the Neolithic period was relatively short, this did not happen all at once. Long after farming was first begun, hunting must have continued to be the main source of subsistence, with horticulture only a sideline. Even after farming became a major source of food, seminomadic conditions persisted when soil resources were depleted, forcing a shift to new quarters. For example, a Neolithic settlement in the Rhineland consisting of 21 households is estimated to have been occupied seven times during a 450–year period. Sites like this were inhabited for about 10 years and then abandoned to give the soil time to regenerate itself. Nevertheless, the potentiality for permanent settlement based on food production was established in the Neolithic period.

The domestication of plants seems to have developed in more than one center. Besides the Near Eastern or southwestern Asiatic center, there was also a center of plant domestication in Southeast Asia, possibly one in western Africa and probably more than one in the New World. Perhaps "center" is not the right word. We must conceive of plant domestication as a very gradual process engaged in to greater or less extent by many hunting-gathering peoples in these different regions. Plants may be said to be domesticated when their seeds, roots, or shoots are planted by human beings who keep them from one season to the next for this purpose. Plant domestication may facilitate certain kinds of mutations, for example in the direction of the retention of seeds. In the wild state, such mutations would not be favored by natural selection. Some cultivated plants are characterized by gigantism in certain organs. Human beings have sometimes found such alterations useful and, either consciously or unconsciously, have preserved and encouraged their development. Man has also transferred plants to regions outside of the areas where they originally flourished with often interesting results. Hans Helbaek gives an example of the shift from cultivation of plants in the uplands of Iraq to the Mesopotamian plains:

Domestication of plants

In the beginning man had domesticated the wild Emmer and the wild two-row barley of the northern mountains and he also took up the cultivation of the wild flax. Presumably during the fifth millennium farmers migrated into the river plain in the south with its fertile alluvial soil, and there they eventually developed irrigation agriculture. The forcible change of environment led by mutation to the transformation of the two-row barley into the six-row form, and Emmer and flax attained a higher state of efficiency.[1]

The domestication of plants and animals in the Near East must have occurred in regions where wild forms of these plants and animals were found. The wild ancestors of wheat and barley grew in upland regions in altitudes of 750–1,000 meters above sea level. Some of these wild prototypes still grow in the uplands of Iraq.

Two types of wheat were grown in the Neolithic period: einkorn and emmer. Wild forms of einkorn range from the Balkans to western Iran. Emmer was found in northern Mesopotamia, eastern Turkey, Iraq, Syria,

---

[1] Hans Helbaek, "Palaeo-Ethnobotany" in Don Brothwell and Eric Higgs (eds.), *Science in Archaeology: A Comprehensive Survey of Progress and Research* (New York: Basic Books, Publishers, 1963), p. 184.

Palestine, and Jordan. Barley occurred in the same area, although wild barley has a wider range, from central Asia to the Atlantic. However, early farming was not based on barley alone but on a combination of barley and wheat.

It seems likely that such crops were collected by hunting-gathering peoples who gradually depended more and more on this source of food and began to plant their seeds and cultivate them, pulling up weeds and driving away birds and foraging animals.

How were these cereals first prepared for food? Carleton S. Coon believes that porridge of some kind preceded the making of bread, which required a communal oven. Porridge is easier to prepare than bread and is eaten throughout the Middle East. A maize porridge was eaten by the Indians of South and Central America. The California Indians, who gathered wild seeds, also made porridge. Paul C. Mangelsdorf believes that the earliest cereals were popped or parched, and that bread making came later.

Jonathan D. Sauer has a radically different view. He has argued that the purpose of early plant domestication was to produce not food but beer. Sauer points out that the yields of primitive grain crops must have been quite poor and their harvesting hardly worth the trouble. But if thirst rather than hunger was the motive, this activity becomes more understandable.[2]

But the domestication of plants may have had various motivations in different times and places. Carl O. Sauer, for example, has argued that Mesolithic fishing people in Southeast Asia learned to propagate roots and cuttings in order to increase the plants that they used for fish poison, net fibers, and bark cloth.

Early farming was a form of simple horticulture; its principal tool was probably the digging stick. More advanced horticultural societies had hoes and made use of terracing and techniques of fertilization. At a still more advanced level, that of agriculture, Old World farmers had animal-drawn plows and dug irrigation channels to fertilize their fields.

Domestication of animals

Animals are domesticated when they can breed successfully while being dependent on human beings. Men had to have rather assured control over their environment and food supply to forego killing off such animals. The most important animals to be domesticated by Neolithic man—sheep, goats, cattle, and pigs—inhabited the same upland regions of the Near East where wild barley and wheat were found. Sheep seem to have been

---

[2] A debate on this subject in which the views of Coon, Mangelsdorf, Sauer and others were presented, appeared in *American Anthropologist*, Vol. 55 (1953), pp. 515–26 under the title "Symposium: Did Man Once Live by Beer Alone?" Most of the contributors favored the view that production of chewable food in some form, rather than beer, was the original motive.

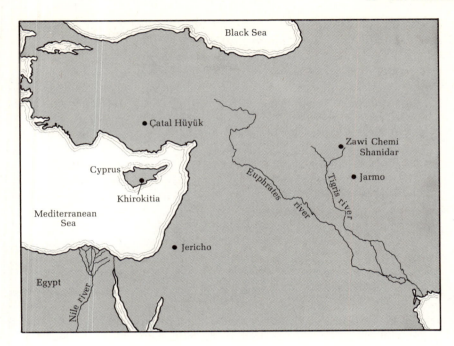

An outline map showing location of early Neolithic sites.

the first animals to be domesticated in this region, being kept at Zawi Chemi at Shanidar, Iraq, as far back as around 8900 B.C. and appearing also in the early levels of excavations at Jarmo and Jericho. The domestication of sheep and other animals may have developed independently in several places in Asia Minor and in Europe, for the idea of domesticating seems to have spread faster than the domesticated animals themselves. Both in the Baltic area and in Iraq there are gradual transitions from wild to domesticated forms of pigs. Similarly, cattle apparently developed from wild aurochs both on the southern shore of the Bosphorus and in Schleswig-Holstein.[3]

The dog is often stated to have been man's first domesticated animal and to have joined forces with man during the Mesolithic period in northern Europe, although the evidence for this is not strong. The antiquity of the dog's domestication is suggested by the fact that dogs were used for hunting and other purposes in different continents, Africa, Australia, and North and South America. But dogs seem to have been domesticated later than sheep, goats, and pigs in the Near East.

Cattle were also domesticated later than sheep and goats, perhaps

---

[3] Wolf Herre, "The Science and History of Domesticated Animals," in Brothwell and Higgs (eds.), *op. cit.*, p. 242.

because they were larger and less tractable. The first evidence for their domestication dates from around 8500 years ago.

The horse appears not to have been domesticated until Bronze Age times. About 2500 B.C. horses were hitched to wheeled vehicles in the Near East. Horse-drawn chariots revolutionized warfare and made possible the invasion and conquest of Egypt by the Hyksos. Horseback riding, which led to still other developments in warfare and in pastoral economy, does not seem to have been common until about 3,500 years ago, when it was practiced in the Eurasian steppes.

The most likely purpose of most animal domestication was to keep a ready supply of meat around. At any rate, sheep were not domesticated for their wool, since wild forms have little of it; wool developed in the course of domestication. Similarly, cows were not domesticated for their milk, since wild forms do not produce much milk.

Advantages of village life

It has been pointed out that sedentary village life is possible at a hunting-gathering level and that agriculture does not preclude some nomadism. However, a consequence of food production was greater stability in the long run. Sedentary village life has several advantages over a nomadic way of life. Nomadism imposes a hardship on the old and sick. Young children have to be carried, along with the worldly goods of the hunters. The Eskimos solved the problem by inventing the dogsled. Nevertheless, old Eskimo men and women often asked their relatives to kill them when they felt unable to keep up on the march. Or they might be left behind with some provisions, perhaps to survive, perhaps not. The Sirionó of eastern Bolivia, who are mainly hunting-gathering people, although they also practice some slash-and-burn horticulture, similarly abandon old, infirm persons when they break camp. This is not done by all nomadic peoples, but such practices demonstrate the difficulties involved. Newborn babies were often killed by the Eskimo, some Australian aboriginal tribes, and other nomadic hunters, not because they were hard-hearted people—quite the contrary—but because they already had too many children or because conditions were such that they could not adequately feed them and bring them up. Village life did not do away with such problems, but it did provide for better care for the old, the very young, and the sick.

Agriculture also facilitated the preservation of food. Grain could now be stored for the future. Hunters have no special problem if their region is rich in game, but if it is not, and if they have no techniques for salting, drying, or preserving meat, they are out of luck. Perhaps the Eskimos were fortunate to live in a natural icebox in winter; their food could be cached out of reach of dogs and wolves for later consumption. The Blackfoot and other Indian tribes of the Plains pounded dried lean meat, sometimes mixed with berries and bone marrow, to make pemmican, which they stored in buffalo skin containers. Although hunting peoples such as these devised various ways of preserving meat, it is a common practice for hunters to divide their game right after the kill and eat it within a short time. Then the hunters must be off again for more. The addition of easily stored grain to man's diet added to his security.

It must be due to reasons such as these that the Neolithic period saw a population explosion. Skeletal remains from Neolithic burial sites greatly outnumber those of preceding periods, despite the relatively short duration of the Neolithic.

We need not assume from the foregoing contrast of nomadism and village life that hunters are necessarily more anxious about food supplies or less well fed than village farmers. A conference of anthropologists who had worked with present-day hunting-gathering groups was held at the University of Chicago in 1966. Their findings were presented in a published volume.[4] One of their conclusions was that meat generally plays a minor role in the diet of such peoples, constituting from 20 to 40 percent. Vegetable foods, fish, and shellfish make up the bulk of the diet. (Exceptions occur among peoples such as the Eskimo who lack vegetable foods.) Even though they live in poorly favored marginal regions, the hunting-gathering peoples of the present day do not seem to suffer from food shortages. They know where available roots, berries, or nuts are apt to be found and usually do not have much anxiety about where their next meal is coming from. Two or three hours of work may suffice to provide the day's food. (Again, there are exceptions, as among Eskimos or northern Algonquians, especially in wintertime.)

Hunting-gathering peoples often live longer than one might expect. In a Bushman group numbering 466, there were 46 persons over 60 years of age.[5] The ways of life of hunting-gathering peoples of the present day who live in the most ill-favored parts of the world cannot be representative of the pre-Neolithic hunting-gathering life. The Old World hunters lived in much more favorable environments, and they must have been better fed than the hunters of today.

Still, when all this is acknowledged, the settled life of Neolithic times must nevertheless have had distinct advantages. This is clearly indicated by the enormous population increase and by the burst of new inventions characteristic of the period.

Housing

When sedentary life was made possible, people could begin to give more attention to their dwellings, building more substantial houses than hunting-gathering peoples are usually apt to do. The material used de-

---

[4] Richard B. Lee and Irven De Vore (eds.), *Man the Hunter* (Chicago: Aldine Publishing Co., 1968).

[5] *Ibid.*, p. 36.

pended on what was locally available and the climatic conditions. In the Near East, for example, at the Turkish site of Çatal Hüyük, which is described in more detail later, houses were often made of rectangular sundried mud bricks, reeds, and plaster. There was little use of stone at Çatal Hüyük, for it is not found locally in the alluvial plain. The houses were closely huddled together, perhaps for defense. Çatal Hüyük rather resembles a Southwest American Indian pueblo, including the feature that entrance to a house was made by ladder from the roof.

The houses of Khirokitia in Cyprus were large, domed circular dwellings, like beehives, with stone foundations and mud brick walls. Entrance was through wooden framed doors sunk slightly below ground level. Some of these houses had a second story resting on square limestone pillars.

It is understandable that in the wooded regions of Europe much of the Neolithic housing was made of wood. The Danubian farmers built long houses with gabled roofs. Somewhat similar wooden structures were built by the Swiss lake dwellers.

At Skara Brae in the Orkney Islands, trees to provide wood did not flourish because of the strong winds which sweep over the islands. The islanders hollowed out a settlement in the sand dunes made largely of stone with a roofing of whalebone rafters. There were narrow entrances only 4 feet high with stone doors. The houses were furnished with stone beds, softened with heather and skins, and had stone "dressers" with shelves. These houses were connected by roofed alleyways, forming a tightly knit community.

Since the houses of Skara Brae were built of stone and were later covered by sand dunes, they have been remarkably well preserved. They give an impression of coziness and seem more "advanced" than one might expect of such a marginal Neolithic community. Neolithic homes in more favored regions such as Çatal Hüyük were even more comfortable.

Stonework

The term *Neolithic*, or *New Stone*, refers to the fact that the stone tools used during this period were different from those found in the Palaeolithic. Neolithic tools included ground stone axes and adzes, hafted to handles. Similar tools were used in Mesolithic Europe. Axes and adzes made possible the carpentry involved in the construction of Danubian longhouses, doors, beds, and other furniture. Such tools could be made of granular stone instead of flint and were fashioned by rubbing and grinding. This is a more laborious, time-consuming process than flaking, but the resulting tool is more durable and effective. Axes and adzes were sometimes drilled to provide for a shaft or handle. In early Neolithic times, this was probably done with a bow drill, drilling from both sides. Querns, rubbing stones, mortars, and pestles are common Neolithic tools used for preparing cereals.

In some Near Eastern sites, such as Jericho, Jarmo, and Khirokitia, polished stone bowls were made.

Flake tools continued to be used, however, and the chipping technique was not abandoned. Arrowheads, scrapers, and sickles were still made of flint.

Weaving was a by-product of the domestication of plants and animals, utilizing the fibers of plants such as flax or of animals such as sheep wool. The making of basketry and matting must have preceded weaving; it is sometimes hard to distinguish between them in archaeological remains. Woven textiles, characterized by being made from spun or twisted threads, depend upon some spinning technique. An old and widespread device for this purpose is the spindle, a thin rod usually made of wood, equipped with a weighted whorl of wood or clay. Some twisted fiber is fastened to the spindle, which is then dropped toward the ground, rotating, while the spinner draws out the thread and adds more fiber.

Weaving

Weaving can be done without a loom in a way similar to the making of woven baskets, but finger weaving is a slow process. The invention of a loom in the Neolithic period greatly facilitated the making of textiles. Woven garments thenceforth supplemented or replaced animal skins for clothing. There is abundant evidence of woven clothing at Çatal Hüyük, where fur and animal skins (especially leopard skins), were also worn. Neolithic Egyptian graves have yielded textiles. The material most often occurring in early Neolithic sites is flax. Domestication of cotton evidently came later, first attested to in the Indus Valley civilization of the third millenium B.C.

Pottery is not always found in Neolithic sites. It is absent, for example, from the lower strata of excavations at Jarmo and Jericho. It occurs in some nonagricultural sites. Some of the oldest-dated pottery, estimated at about 12,600 years ago, comes from Kyushu in southern Japan, before agriculture was introduced.

Pottery

Some nomadic hunting-gathering peoples, such as the Bushmen and the Eskimo, have pottery. Generally, however, pottery is inappropriate for such people, being rather heavy, bulky, and breakable, and skin or basketry containers are more suitable. With settled village life, however, pottery can be very useful. Large jars can then be used to store grain; dishes, mugs, cooking pots, and other vessels can be made. Thus pottery is usually found in abundance in later Neolithic sites.

The properties of clay were known to men before the Neolithic period. Clay figurines, sometimes fired, were made by Upper Palaeolithic hunters. Clay generally requires some treatment before it can be worked. If it is too dry, water must be added. If it is too sticky, it may be tempered by adding grit, sand, shell, or other material. Such tempering also helps to prevent cracking when the vessel is fired. Clay is usually mixed and kneaded before working, to ensure uniform texture or composition.

Neolithic pottery was not made on the potter's wheel but was built up of coils or strips of clay, one above the other. Making a large pot in this manner may take two or three days. The clay must always be kept at an appropriate degree of dampness, not too wet and not too dry.

Firing involves exposing the vessel to heat long enough (above 500°C.) to drive out its water content. This was first done in open fires, but later kilns or ovens were built for the purpose.

Since pottery is porous, water kept in a jar may seep through. Glazing was invented in the Near East to give the ware a smooth, waterproof finish.

The earliest Neolithic pottery was not decorated, but in the late Neolithic period, vessels were painted in southern Turkey. Red-on-cream ware is dated at around 5500 B.C. Finely made dark burnished ware comes from Çatal Hüyük. Pots of various sizes and shapes, including anthropomorphic types, and painted with various designs, including imitations of basketry, have been found at Hacilar in southern Turkey, dated at around 5200 B.C. The practice of painting pottery extended from Iran to the Balkans in the sixth millennium B.C.

Trade

It used to be thought that there was little trade in Neolithic times, since each community was apt to be self-sufficient—able to meet its own needs for food, clothing, and other necessities. Whatever trade was engaged in was apt to concern only luxuries, nonessentials.[6] This was probably true of many Neolithic settlements, but not of Çatal Hüyük, where most of the raw materials used, apart from clay, reeds, and wood, seem not to have been available locally. Timber had to be brought from the hills, obsidian from volcanoes, marble from western Anatolia, stalactites from caves in the Taurus Mountains, and shells from the Mediterranean. This was evidently a society depending heavily on trade from many different sources. Çatal Hüyük seems also to have been characterized by considerable specialization and division of labor. In these respects Çatal Hüyük anticipated the stage of civilization. Perhaps the dividing line between the Neolithic and Bronze Age civilization is more uncertain, and traceable to an earlier period, than was formerly believed.

"World view" of Neolithic farmers

Can anything be said of how life appeared to the men of Neolithic times, of what values and attitudes they shared? It may seem too speculative to raise such a question, for we are dealing with a period before the appearance of written records, and one can only make deductions of doubtful validity. Nevertheless, the question seems worth trying to answer, for the Neolithic was an important transition point for humanity

---

[6] V. Gordon Childe, *Man Makes Himself* (New York: Mentor Books, 1953), p. 74.

from a hunting-gathering way of life to one based on agriculture and the domestication of animals. The changes in man's patterns of subsistence must have involved the adoption of quite different daily routines and the cultivation of virtues different from those of hunting-gathering peoples.

We are probably safe in saying that patience and perseverance were necessary Neolithic virtues. This is not to say that hunters and gatherers did not also have these qualities. The hunter stalking his prey, the Eskimo waiting by the blowhole of a seal, must also maintain great patience and perseverance. But the technological developments of the Neolithic surely enhanced such tendencies. It takes more time and patience to make a ground stone adze than a flake tool; many days, many stages go into the making of a textile garment or a clay vessel. Neolithic man learned to adopt a routine way of life involving a round of chores. While the hunter lives more in the present, the farmer must think ahead and sow seeds to be harvested in a later season.

Hunter and farmer focus their attention on different things. The hunter is alert to spoor and tracks, slight disturbances in the soil; he must know the characteristics of different kinds of wild animals. The farmer is more concerned about the sun, rainfall, and the changes of seasons. Although this chapter deals with the Neolithic in the Old World, an illustration may be drawn from the New. The quite individualistic religion of hunting-gathering northern Indians such as the Ojibwa (Chippewa) focused on health, so vital to a hunter, while the more collective religion of the agricultural Hopi, with its cycle of calendrical ceremonies, focused on rainfall and fertility of the fields. One may say that the farmer learns to think in calendrical seasonal terms and to study the movements of the sun, moon, and stars for clues to the proper times for planting, harvesting, and other stages in the agricultural cycle.

Despite all his hard work, the farmer cannot count on success. Drought, frost, hail, windstorms, floods, locusts, fire, and other acts of nature may ruin his crop. He has to wait for the seeds to grow and must depend on the gods for conditions favorable to growth. He repeats practices that have worked before. Conservatism and patience seem to be encouraged by such a life, and perhaps also a mystical attitude toward nature, the Earth Mother, and other deities on whom the farmer depends.

At the same time, Neolithic man had reason to develop a growing self-confidence. Childe has suggested that the making of pottery reacted on human thought:

The lump of clay was perfectly plastic; man could mold it as he would. In making a tool of stone or bone he was always limited by the shape and size of the original material; he could only take bits away from it. No such limitations restrict the activity of the potter.[7]

---

[7] Childe, *op. cit.*, p. 79.

Clay and pottery thus became symbols of the process of creation.

Neolithic community life involved much group cooperation. This may be true of hunters, too, as in the case of animal drives or surrounds such as the communal buffalo hunt of the North American plains. But Neolithic community cooperation seems to have been more sustained. This is suggested by the relatively ambitious architecture at such settlements as Khirokitia and Çatal Hüyük and perhaps even more by the late Neolithic megalithic cults of Europe, described later, in which enormous stones were sometimes moved over great distances.

A symbolic expression of the collective tendency in Neolithic times is the pattern of group burial associated with megalithic passage graves (see pp. 211–12). Here we see something new, not previously attested to in the European archaeological record. Lineage, clan, and community had evidently become strong focuses of loyalty and solidarity. Such sentiments no doubt had existed before, but they seem to have received a special emphasis in Neolithic times.

If we may speculate further, the domestication of animals must also have involved a change in man's attitude toward living things. Although still ultimately exploitative in his relation to animals, man now adopted a nurturant attitude as well, being responsible for the well-being of his flocks and herds. The cow and bull, largest of the domesticated beasts, became deified in some areas, as at Çatal Hüyük. The cow is still a sacred animal in India today, survival of a cult which probably antedated the Indus Valley civilization. In some parts of the Old World, the cow became symbolically associated with a mother goddess.

The maternal emphasis which we find in Neolithic religion is prefigured in the "Venuses" of Upper Palaeolithic times; we have already noted an association between the female principle and buffalo and "oxen" in Upper Palaeolithic cave art. But the new way of life based on the domestication of plants and animals must have further emphasized the maternal principle. We see an expression of this in the European megalithic cults; it appears as well in some of the ancient legends of the Old World, such as the Greek tale of Ceres and Persephone.

Some writers have hypothesized that women were the first agriculturists and the first potters. This cannot be proven, although it is quite possible. In any case, a "maternal," nurturant attitude toward the soil and toward domesticated animals seems to have entered into the way of life and "world view" of Neolithic man. While this, of course, is speculation, there is much in the archaeological record which could be cited in its support.[8]

---

[8] See G. Rachel Levy, *Religious Conceptions of the Stone Age and Their Influence upon European Thought* (New York: Harper Torchbooks, 1948, 1963).

Natufian culture

Around 8500 B.C. there were some people with a Mesolithic culture called *Natufian* living in various parts of Palestine. They were hunters who usually lived in the mouths of caves. Their stone technology included blades, burins, microliths, grinding and polishing stones, net weights, and hammer stones; they used bone for making skewers, needles, awls, harpoons, and fishhooks. Microliths constituted about 80 percent of their chipped-flint work. These people do not seem to have domesticated animals, but there is some evidence of harvesting in their flint blades, mounted on bone handles. Surviving examples of these implements have a sheen which seems to have been acquired by reaping. Moreover, well-made stone pestles and mortars suggest the preparation of plant food. The plants that were harvested may not have been domesticated, but the existence of the pestles and mortars seems to be evidence of incipient agriculture.

There are also evidences of population growth and extended occupation of particular sites. One Natufian cemetery had 87 burials, another more than 700. Walls and paved platforms were sometimes built, and at one site, circular stone houses were constructed with plastered bell-shaped pits.

Some early agricultural settlements

Jarmo

An early settlement, dated at around 6750 B.C., has been found at Jarmo in the hilly regions of northern Iraq. It contains definite indications of early agriculture. Carbonized kernels of wheat (emmer) and barley have been recovered, the barley being of a two-row variety in contrast to present-day six-row cultivated barley. Dogs, goats, and perhaps sheep were domesticated.

Jarmo was a small village with about 150 persons occupying about 25 houses. These were mud huts containing rectangular rooms with matted floors. Later homes had ovens and chimneys.

Microliths made up about 40 percent of the flint stonework; there were also knives and sickle blades. Querns, rubbing stones, and mortars and pestles, as well as ground stone axes and adzes, were found. The many tools made of obsidian, a volcanic glass, suggest that trade was practiced, for the nearest source of obsidian was about 200 miles away. Decorative seashells uncovered at Jarmo must have come from the Persian Gulf. The lower levels at Jarmo contain no pottery, but finely made stone vessels were found in all levels. Only about 5 percent of the animal bones in the site at Jarmo belonged to wild species, indicating that farming and animal husbandry were taking precedence over hunting.

Over 5,000 fragments of clay animal and human figurines have been found at Jarmo. Perhaps they served some magico-religious function.

Jericho

One of the earliest known towns in the world is Jericho. It was situated in a fertile oasis region, north of the Dead Sea. The lowest level, dated by carbon 14 at around 7800 B.C., was occupied by people with a Natufian culture. The presence of bowls, querns for grinding grain, and reaping knives again imply agricultural practices, although hunting is also attested by the presence of gazelle bones. The remains of goats were also found, and it may be that these were domesticated.

A Neolithic settlement gradually developed at Jericho. The inhabitants first built round huts of clay or wattle and daub construction. Later they constructed a huge stone tower and massive walls for defense, over 6 feet thick. The tower still stands, 21 feet high. The earlier levels at Jericho, like those at Jarmo, contain no pottery. There is no direct evidence of grain cultivation, but it seems likely that the townsfolk were agriculturists, judging from the size of the settlement, which covered 8 acres at around 6800 B.C. A population of perhaps 2,000 could not have lived on hunting and the gathering of wild grain. The tower and defense walls suggest the existence of some central political organization. In keeping with this, it is not unlikely that irrigation was practiced, although there is no archaeological evidence for it. The oasis must have been an attractive, fertile area which had to be defended against outsiders.

It is possible that the early inhabitants of Jericho were, in fact, overpowered by invaders, for there is a rather marked change of culture between the levels designated Pre-Pottery Neolithic A and Pre-Pottery Neolithic B. The stone tools, querns, and mortars of the two cultures are different, and so is their architecture. Perhaps, because of unknown calamities, the site was abandoned by the first inhabitants and later reoccupied by newcomers. The latter, at any rate, built houses of a new architectural plan, made of bricks which were quite different in shape from those of the A people. The rooms were large and rectilinear. The houses were built around courtyards, where the cooking was done. The floors were covered with lime plaster. Some of the buildings seem to have been shrines or temples, one containing a niche in which a carefully worked stone was placed.

Many skeletons, often dismembered, were found below the floors of the dwellings. A group of seven skulls had the features of the deceased restored in plaster, with inlaid cowrie shells for eyes. Judging from their appearance, these people were lightly built, with fine-boned, narrow skulls.

As at Jarmo, there is evidence of trade: some obsidian which may have

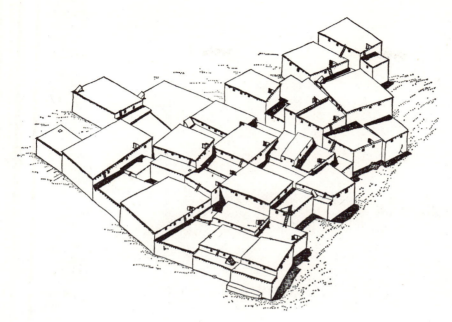

Schematic reconstruction of a section of Level VI at Çatal Hüyük.

come from Anatolia, turquoise from the Sinai Peninsula, and cowrie shells, perhaps from the Mediterranean.

Çatal Hüyük

A remarkably sophisticated Neolithic settlement, dating from around 6500 to 5700 B.C., has been found at Çatal Hüyük on the plateau of Anatolia in Turkey. The settlement covered 32 acres. The people here raised crops (barley, wheat, peas) and had sheep and cattle. Pottery was made. The plastered, mud brick houses were laid out in a rather orderly manner, rectangular in shape and grouped around courtyards. Some of the houses, which may have been shrines or temples, contain the earliest murals to have been found on man-made walls.

A large bull, 6 feet long, rather reminiscent of the big bulls at Lascaux Cave, covers one of the walls. It is surrounded by very small human figures. (Many pairs of bull horns, some set in plaster, have also been found at Çatal Hüyük, suggesting the existence of a cult of the bull, like that which developed later at Crete.) Deer are also depicted in the murals together with human hunters holding bows. The most impressive of the murals shows about a dozen men grouped in three rows performing a dance. Some hold bows, one beats a drum, and some are jumping. This is a lively scene, well executed. These paintings were applied with a brush

Reconstruction of
a Neolithic village
(Denmark)

on white plaster, the colors including red, pink, mauve, black, and yellow. There are also wall paintings of giant vultures attacking human bodies. This may imply a practice of exposure of corpses to vultures, as is done by the present-day Parsis of India. The defleshed bones were assembled for secondary burial beneath the floors of the houses.

Handicrafts were varied, including, among other things, beautifully made wooden bowls and boxes, basketry, pins, knives, and obsidian mirrors.

There is a good deal of sculpture, including many seated goddesses, sometimes depicted giving birth. They tend to be rather fat, like Upper Palaeolithic "Venuses." Similar statuettes came from other Neolithic sites in the Near East, including Hacilar and Jarmo.

Khirokitia

A slightly later Neolithic settlement has been uncovered at Khirokitia in southern Cyprus, dated by radiocarbon at around 5500 B.C. It may have contained as many as a thousand houses, which, as mentioned earlier, were round structures of stone and mud brick with high-domed roofs and often contained a second story in part of the home. Several thousand people may have lived in this community. Judging from its size and from the presence of sickle blades and querns, it is likely that agriculture was practiced at Khirokitia, although there are no preserved remains of grain. Sheep and goats seem to have been domesticated and perhaps pigs as well. Pottery was evidently tried and given up at an early stage, and stone bowls and dishes were used instead. Still later, pottery was reintroduced. The practice of weaving is indicated by the presence of spindle whorls.

Suggestions for further reading

Some of the readings suggested at the end of the preceding chapter can be recommended for this chapter's material as well, notably the works by Clark and Piggott, Chard, and Hawkes. The following are also recommended.

V. Gordon Childe, *Man Makes Himself* (New York: Mentor Books, 1936, 1951).

Ralph Linton, *The Tree of Culture* (New York: Alfred A. Knopf, 1955), especially Chapters 13–18.

James Mellaart, "Roots in the Soil," in Stuart Piggott (ed.), *The Dawn of Civilization: The First World Survey of Human Cultures in Early Times* (New York: McGraw-Hill Book Co., 1961), pp. 41–64.

James Mellaart, *Çatal Hüyük: A Neolithic Town in Anatolia* (New York: McGraw-Hill Book Co., 1967). This is a well-illustrated report of an important site.

G. Rachel Levy, *Religious Conceptions of the Stone Age and Their Influence upon European Thought* (New York: Harper Torchbooks, 1948, 1963). Much of this work is of an imaginative, speculative nature, and may be vulnerable to critical objections, but it assembles much valuable information.

On technology, see R. F. G. Spier, *From the Hand of Man: Primitive and Preindustrial Technologies* (Boston: Houghton Mifflin Co., 1970).

Chapter 19

Diffusion of the Neolithic

Already by 5500 B.C. we find large, complex Neolithic communities across the water, some distance from the coast of Asia Minor. Khirokitia, as we have seen, had a population of thousands. Neolithic communities soon appeared in Crete, Sicily, Malta, and southern Europe. This diffusion must have proceeded by sea. Overland routes through the Balkans of "Danubian" peasant cultures have also been traced. While southern and eastern Europe was being influenced by the introduction of farming and animal husbandry, Mesolithic hunting-gathering cultures continued to exist in northern and western Europe until around 2500 B.C.

Westward diffusion of Neolithic traits

There were Neolithic communities in eastern Europe by the sixth millennium, in central Europe by the fifth, and in England by the fourth millennium B.C.

Meanwhile, Neolithic cultures also spread across North Africa. In climate and in culture, the African Mediterranean coast resembled that of Europe. Racially too there was much similarity. The Berbers, ancient peoples of North Africa, are Caucasoids. Some of their more isolated groups in the Atlas Mountains have retained an essentially Neolithic way of life down to recent times.

Much of North Africa today, particularly the deserts of Libya and the great Sahara Desert, is bleak and inhospitable. But before 2000 B.C., the land was well watered. This is indicated by the presence of bones of many animals which could not live there now: giraffe, hippopotamus, elephant, antelope, and others. (Ancient isolated trees still survive in soil where seeds no longer grow, and stunted crocodiles inhabit desert pools which they could not have reached by waddling overland.)

Neolithic pastoralists once lived in the Tassili Plateau in the central

Sahara in Algeria, where they painted beautiful frescoes on rock walls. The first settlers brought sheep and goats; a later wave had herds of cattle, which are depicted with realism and elegance on the rock. Also shown are scenes of men hunting rhinoceros and hippopotamus, girls of Ethiopian type with sugarloaf hair style and white robes, and a woman with a row of pots, cooking food.

Paintings of a later period show Egyptian influence: stiff but graceful stylized figures of bird-headed goddesses. There are even drawings of horse-drawn chariots in the last phase at Tassili, when dessication had already begun to set in.

The human figures show varieties of racial types, both Mediterranean Caucasoids and Negroes from the south. It is possible that the population density here was greater than anywhere else in the world at that time. Carbon 14 analyses of charcoal from Tassili hearths give dates ranging from 3500 to 2500 B.C., but the total span of human activity in this region must have been much longer.

Megalithic cults

One feature of the Neolithic and Bronze Age cultures of Europe was the diffusion of megalithic (large-stone) cults. By now man had learned how to move and set up large, sometimes enormous stones. This must have involved the cooperation of many persons. Food resources were evidently plentiful enough to divert time from the food quest to this difficult work.

The simplest megalithic structure is the *menhir,* a single standing stone. Sometimes a row of menhirs is formed in an orderly line; this is called an *alignment,* many of which are found in Brittany, some extending for a mile in length. Sometimes menhirs are arranged in a circle or horseshoe formation, as in Avebury and Stonehenge in England and at Hagar Qim in Malta. Sometimes menhirs are shaped to form a long communal grave, known as a *passage grave.*

European passage graves have many common features. Passage graves imply some kind of ancestor worship and are associated with a mother goddess cult. This cult evidently diffused by sea, for passage graves are found near the coasts of Spain, Brittany, Ireland, and Denmark.

An early site of this kind in southern Spain, dated at before 2800 B.C. is Los Millares, a strongly fortified colony whose architecture closely resembled that of contemporary eastern Mediterranean towns. The Los Millares passage graves, in which hundreds of persons were buried, were evidently used as chapels as well as tombs. A short corbel-roofed passage led to a circular chamber lined with large stone slabs. This plan later appears in northern European sites together with female figurines showing consistent stylistic peculiarities, such as owllike eyes and herringbone patterns. A particularly impressive site of this sort is New Grange near the

Boyne River in Ireland. Thus the diffusion of a complex of religious beliefs and practices—collective burial, ancestor worship, and a mother goddess cult—seems to have spread by sea from the eastern Mediterranean to Spain, the British Isles, France, and Scandinavia.

The most famous megalithic structure is Stonehenge on the Salisbury plain in England, dating back nearly 4,000 years. The bluestone menhirs which make up one of the concentric circles must have been transported from the Prescelly Mountains of Wales, which are 130 miles away as the crow flies. But, of course, their transportation could not have followed a straight course. The stones are believed to have been moved largely by sea on raft floats and overland by a system of rollers, altogether over a distance of 240 miles. Eighty or more of these bluestones weighed up to 5 tons each.

Even larger and heavier are the sarsen stones which form the most imposing segments at Stonehenge. Large stone lintels were somehow hoisted up and laid across some of the pairs of menhirs. The sarsens, which average 30 tons, were moved from 20 miles away. One estimate of the work involved in setting up this awesome structure is that it must have required about 1.5 million man-days of physical labor, to say nothing of the planning and brainwork involved.

The purpose of this enormous effort has long been a subject of speculation. An astronomer, Gerald S. Hawkins, has offered the most probable explanation: that Stonehenge served as a kind of astronomical observatory, providing sighting points for sunrise at the longest and shortest days

Stonehenge.

of the year and also for midpoints at the times of equinoxes. The arrangement of the stones also made possible prediction of eclipses of the moon. The structure of Stonehenge is so perfectly adapted for such observations that it would be hard to consider its layout a matter of chance. Stonehenge must have been conceived, designed, and set up by men who had learned a good deal about the orderly movements of the sun and moon.

Some authorities find it so hard to credit the "barbarians" of that time with such sophisticated astronomical knowledge—far in advance of contemporary Egypt and Mesopotamia—that they have rejected the Hawkins interpretation. But it seems hard to do so. Rather, we should probably revise our assumptions about the men of prehistoric times who seem to have been often capable of remarkable inventions, deductions, and discoveries. We need not assume that the builders of Stonehenge were purely rational in their motives. Religion was probably mixed up with their science; very likely the sun and moon were their gods. But it must have been reassuring for the people of Stonehenge to know that their gods were so reliable and that it was possible to predict to the day when the solstices would come and the moon fall under eclipse.[1]

Passage grave
near Carnac.

---

[1] See Gerald S. Hawkins, in collaboration with John B. White, *Stonehenge Decoded* (New York: Doubleday & Co., 1965).

Adaptations to different environments

As Neolithic ways of life spread, the early farmers encountered environments which sometimes differed greatly from those of the Near East or the Mediterranean coasts to which they had been accustomed. Dwellers on the edge of the Eurasiatic steppes found the latter suitable for grazing herds but not for agriculture. Central Europe was covered with deciduous forests which had to be cleared to permit farming. Special adaptations were required to meet each new ecological setting, which affected such matters as population density and the possibilities for political organization.

Swidden cultivation

The solution in central Europe was the adoption of "swidden cultivation," or "slash-and-burn" agriculture or horticulture. This process involves clearing a patch of land by burning, planting crops and tending them for a year or more, and then abandoning the plot so that its fertility may be renewed. New plots are opened up in the same way; earlier ones, once abandoned, may be reopened once their fertility is restored. This kind of cultivation must have developed independently in many forested regions. It is still widely practiced in different parts of the world today among tribal groups in India, the Congo, the Amazon, and Oceania and among peasants in Mexico and Southeast Asia.

Swidden cultivation is usually done on a small scale, often with plots of an acre or less. Plow and draft animals are seldom used, and the tools are of a simple sort, such as axes, hoes, and digging sticks. The population density in societies practicing this type of cultivation tends to be low; settlements are small, seldom with more than 250 persons. This type of agriculture or horticulture does not encourage political unification, although it may occur.

Pastoralism

Pastoralism is a way of life which developed in semiarid grasslands, deserts, and steppes, in which dependence on animal husbandry became the main basis of the economy and plant cultivation of lesser or little importance. We see the development of pastoralism reflected in the Tassili rock paintings. In post-Neolithic times, pastoral tribes ranged across the Asiatic steppes from Hungary to Manchuria.

Different kinds of animals have been herded by pastoralists in different parts of the Old World: reindeer by the Lapps of northern Europe, cattle in Africa, camels in Arabia and the Sahara Desert, and herds of mixed composition in many areas.

Pastoralists often engage in some agriculture as a sideline. This is true, for example, of the Marri Baluch of Baluchistan, among whom there are

groups which may temporarily abandon farming if their herds grow large
enough. Pehrson writes:

Once the herd reaches about one hundred animals, its value is so great that
other considerations become secondary compared with the welfare of the herd,
and unless very favorably situated the camp then breaks loose from its village
nucleus, migrating widely in search of pasture and water.[2]

The migrations of pastoral tribes, however, are not usually erratic and
random. Nomads often follow traditional routes in cycles which may require several years to complete. Or else an annual cycle, known as trans-
humance, may be observed, which involves having different winter and
summer camps. Thus pastoralists in the western part of the Indian subcontinent drive their herds up to the mountains in summer, down to the
plains in winter. Cattle herders in the upper Nile valley have different
grazing grounds in dry and wet seasons.

Cattle-herding pastoralists often engage in fighting and raiding. This
has been noted for various African cattle-raising groups and for such peoples as the ancient Aryans.

The Neolithic food-producing economy spread eastward as well as
toward the west, laying the groundwork for the later development of
civilization in India and China.

**The Neolithic
in southern,
eastern, and
central Asia**

India

The Indus Valley civilization cannot have sprung from nothing, but its
Neolithic antecedents have not yet been uncovered, although some early
sites in Baluchistan, dated by carbon 14 at around 3500–3100 B.C., suggest that the originators of that civilization may have come from the west.
Early farming communities were widespread in India.

Two such settlements in Andhra State in southern India have been
given a radiocarbon date of 2100 B.C. (4120 ± 150). These were contemporary with, but geographically far distant from, the Indus Valley civilization.

In northwestern India, we find the same crops and domesticated animals that occur in the Near East, together with pottery, weaving,
adzes for carpentry, and other aspects of the Neolithic complex. An interesting parallel with Europe is the appearance of abundant megalithic constructions in southern India in Neolithic and later times, including menhirs, dolmens, and rock cut tombs. Group burials have been found,
suggesting the importance of lineage or clan groupings in those times.

---

[2] Robert N. Pehrson, *The Social Organization of the Marri Baluch* (New York:
Viking Fund Publications in Anthropology, No. 43, 1966), p. 14.

The pattern of megalithic construction later spread to Indonesia, Melanesia, and the Philippines.

China

The Chinese Neolithic is better documented than that of India. The use of wheat and barley must have diffused eastward from southwest Asia, moving along the southern edge of the steppes. But the grain that became most popular in northern China was millet, which may have been domesticated locally. Cattle were also introduced, although the Chinese never took to drinking milk.

Neolithic settlements developed in a region in North China where three great rivers come together, the Huangho, Fenho, and Weishui, and where three modern Chinese provinces adjoin: Honan, Shansi, and Shensi. In these three provinces, an early Neolithic culture, which has been named Yangshao, flourished. To the east and northeast, was another Neolithic culture named Lungshan, which was formerly thought to have been contemporary with Yangshao. More recently, it has been shown that in some settlements proto-Lungshan assemblages overlie Yangshao remains and that Lungshan culture evidently derived from Yangshao, although neither has yet been accurately dated. Stratigraphically, Yangshao sites lie above Palaeolithic and Mesolithic strata but beneath Lungshan remains.

The following are some of the characteristic traits of the Chinese Neolithic: cultivation of millet and rice; domestication of pigs, cattle, sheep, dogs, and chickens; construction of stamped earth and wattle-and-daub structures; domestication of silkworms and possible loom weaving of silk and hemp; cord marked pottery and ceremonial ware; use of jade; and scapulimancy (divination by means of cracks in shoulder blades).[3]

An extensively excavated Yangshao settlement is Pan-p'o-ts'un in Shensi Province. Here millet was the staple crop. Only dogs and pigs seem to have been domesticated; deer hunting evidently provided the bulk of the meat consumed. Most of the dwellings were round or oblong semi-subterranean houses with thatched roofs. Clay was used to make cupboards, benches, and ovens. In the center of the village was a plaza with a large communal structure, around which the smaller houses were ranged in a circle, with the doors facing the center. North of the dwelling area was a village cemetery. Six pottery kilns have been found on the outskirts. Most of the ware was coarse household pottery, but finer painted vessels used for funerary purposes were buried with the dead. The potter's wheel does not seem to have been used.

The planned layout of Pan-p'o-ts'un, the communal building and the

---

[3] Kwang-chih Chang, *The Archaeology of Ancient China* (New Haven, Conn.: Yale University Press, 1963), p. 55.

common cemetery, suggest a consciousness of community, perhaps along clan or lineage lines. The Chinese ancestor cult may have its origin in this early period, although there is more definite evidence of such a cult in the later Lungshan stage. This tightly knit community seems to have been largely self-sufficient, but there is evidence of trade in the remains of sea-shells and stone materials, such as jade, from distant regions.

Settlements of the Lungshan stage were spread out over a much wider area than the earlier Yangshao. The house construction was similar to that at Pan-p'o-ts'un, but the villages were larger and more permanent, occupied over longer periods of time. It has been inferred that the Yangshao people practiced slash-and-burn horticulture and had to shift their settlements occasionally, but by Lungshan times agricultural methods had improved, perhaps with the adoption of irrigation, fallowing, use of fertilizers or other practices. Yangshao villages had no defensive works and little evidence of fighting equipment, but Lungshan villages had permanent walls of stamped earth, indicating a need for fortification. All this suggests population increase, movement of farming peoples to new areas, and increased conflicts between communities.

There is some evidence of craft specialization. The potter's wheel was now in use. Since some of the black ceramics, characteristic of the Lungshan culture, were finely made, pottery may have become a specialized craft. Some settlements also produced fine work in jade. There is more evidence of status differentiation than in the more egalitarian Yangshao settlements, as seen in distinctions in burial practices and the concentration of jade artifacts at isolated spots in one site. Scapulimancy was practiced, and there is now evidence of an ancestor cult.[4]

Although it shared some of the same domesticated plants, animals, and other features as the Southwest Asiatic Neolithic, the Chinese Neolithic seems to have had a characteristic Chinese style from early times.

The Southeast Asiatic Neolithic

Ralph Linton has argued that a food-producing culture based on root and fruit crops and rice cultivation must have originated somewhere in Southeast Asia, independently of the Southwest Asiatic (or Near Eastern) Neolithic, and diffused eastward to the islands of the Pacific and westward to Madagascar. Since the archaeological record in Southeast Asia is meager, Linton's reconstruction of this culture was based on marginal survivals. He pointed out that when a culture complex has been diffused over a wide area, older forms tend to survive in marginal and isolated regions long after they have died out in the original center of diffusion. The carriers of the hypothesized early Neolithic culture were speakers of

---

[4] *Ibid.*, pp. 92–93.

Malayo-Polynesian languages, which have their center in southeastern Asia and Indonesia. Culture patterns found in the now widespread Malayo-Polynesian societies should therefore give clues to the original Southeast Asiatic culture stratum from which they were derived. This is an ingenious, though speculative, approach to historical reconstruction. Let us see how Linton describes the posited Southeast Asiatic Neolithic culture complex.

The economy, he claims, was based on root and fruit crops, "supplemented in inland hill regions by unirrigated rice raised by the cutting and burning method."[5] Pigs, chickens, and dogs, were domesticated. Instead of pottery being used, food was boiled in sections of bamboo or baked in earth ovens. Instead of loom weaving, clothing was made from bark cloth or matting. Cutting tools were made of bamboo rather than stone. (Since bamboo figured so prominently in the technology, and since it is perishable, the archaeological remains in the area are often scanty.) The bow and arrow was not important; instead, slings were used.

The basic house type was a rectangular structure with a gabled roof and a floor elevated on posts or an earth platform. Seaworthy canoes were in use. Political organization was weak, and there was no governmental unit larger than the village, which was normally an endogamous unit. In contrast to the more restrictive sexual mores of the Southwest Asiatic Neolithic region, premarital sexual relationships among adolescents were encouraged by the institution of "dormitories" for boys and girls and by traditions of sexual permissiveness. Ancestral cults were important in religion.

In the Southwest Asiatic Neolithic, by contrast, wheat and barley were the principal crops; cattle, sheep, and goats were the main domesticated animals, and pottery and weaving were practiced. In contrast with custom in the Southeast Asiatic center, the virginity of unmarried girls was highly prized and premarital promiscuity disapproved.

Linton's reconstruction of a Southeast Asiatic Neolithic complex has neither been demonstrated as valid nor has it been disproven. Just where and when this complex originated is not known. Yet Linton's suggestion seems very plausible.

Evidence has been presented which indicates that agriculture may have started in Southeast Asia earlier than in the Near East. Wilhelm G. Solheim of the University of Hawaii, director of an archaeological team in Thailand, has announced that cultivated plant seeds of peas, beans, cucumbers, and water chestnuts found in a cave in Thailand have been dated by radioactive carbon at 11,700 years ago. There is also evidence that rice was cultivated in Thailand prior to 3500 B.C., before it was grown in either India or China.

---

[5] Ralph Linton, *The Tree of Culture* (New York: Alfred A. Knopf, 1955), p. 174.

Occupation of the steppes

The vast steppes of central Asia were sparsely inhabited in Neolithic times and did not become important highways for East-West cultural diffusion until the pattern of horseback riding developed. Some sedentary agriculturalists lived along the fringes of the steppes. In the Ukraine, remains of what has been called the Tripolye culture (circa 3000–1700 B.C.) have been uncovered. This differs from later cultures of the steppes in not being nomadic. The Tripolyans lived in wattle-and-daub huts arranged in a circle. They raised wheat, barley, and millet, and bred horses, cattle, goats, sheep, and pigs. There is no evidence that a plow was used. The largest Tripolyan village excavated so far had as many as 200 houses grouped in five concentric circles. But farming without metal plowshares is difficult in such terrain, and villages of this sort were exposed to attacks by nomads, which increased after horse riding became widely practiced.

Suggestions for further reading

Once again, see Clark and Piggott, especially Chapters 9–11. On Tassili, see Henri Lhote, *The Search for the Tassili Frescoes: The Story of the Prehistoric Rock-Paintings of the Sahara,* trans. from the French by Alan Houghton Brodrick (New York: E. P. Dutton & Co., 1959). Handsomely illustrated. See also Henri Lhote, "The Fertile Sahara," in Edward Bacon (ed.), *Vanished Civilizations of the Ancient World* (New York: McGraw-Hill Book Co., 1963), pp. 11–32. On the megalithic cults: Gale Sieveking, "The Migration of the Megaliths," *ibid.,* pp. 299–322.

For a fascinating encounter between astonomy and archaeology, see Gerald S. Hawkins, in collaboration with John B. White, *Stonehenge Decoded* (New York: Doubleday & Co., 1965). On early India: Stuart Piggott, *Prehistoric India to 1000 B.C.* (Harmondsworth, Middlesex: Penguin Books, 1950). See also Ralph Linton *The Tree of Culture* (New York: Alfred A. Knopf, 1955), especially Chapters 13–18. On early China: Kwang-chih Chang, *The Archaeology of Ancient China* (New Haven, Conn.: Yale University Press, 1963); William Watson, "A Cycle of Cathay," in Stuart Piggott (ed.), *The Dawn of Civilization: The First World Survey of Human Cultures in Early Times* (New York: McGraw-Hill Book Co., 1961), pp. 253–76. On pastoral nomads: E. D. Phillips, "The Royal Hordes: The Nomad People of the Steppes," *ibid,* pp. 301–28. Also recommended: Marshall D. Sahlins, *Tribesmen* (Englewood Cliffs, N.J.: Prentice-Hall, 1968).

Civilization in
the Old World

Chapter 20

The development of civilization in the Old World

We have seen that some Neolithic communities such as Jericho, Çatal Hüyük, and Khirokitia, developed some rather sophisticated culture traits and by the late Neolithic period had formed towns with sizable populations. Pottery was being made; in Çatal Hüyük and probably elsewhere fresco paintings were executed. These communities were moving in the direction of what has vaguely been called "civilization." Perhaps they could be said to have already reached that level, but that would depend on one's definition of the term.

Criteria of civilization

Civilization has sometimes been equated with urbanism or city life, though with the added implication of a more polished way of life—"civil," "urbane" behavior, in contrast with the roughness and naïveté of rural yokels.

A difficulty with using city life as a criterion for civilization is that it is hard to determine at just what point a town becomes a city. During the pre-Dynastic period and much of its early history, Egypt seems to have been a country of villages and market towns with no cities except for temporary capitals. John A. Wilson writes that "Probably one would have to come far down into history—possibly down to the Eighteenth Egyptian Dynasty before one could be sure of a city in the modern sense."[1] Crete, also, did not represent a true city culture.

The presence of a writing system has also been suggested as the dis-

---

[1] John A. Wilson, *The Culture of Ancient Egypt* (Chicago: University of Chicago Press, 1951), p. 34.

tinguishing mark of civilization. It is true that Sumer, Egypt, the Indus Valley, and Crete all had writing systems in the Bronze Age period, but the pre-Columbian Incas of Peru possessed no writing, although they did have city life, metallurgy, and other features commonly associated with civilization.

Since the advanced cultures of the Old World developed in what has been called the Bronze Age, between around 3500 and 1500 B.C., it is tempting to use bronze metallurgy as an indicator of civilization; but such metallurgy was unknown to the Aztecs of Mexico, although they knew how to work copper and gold.

Another yardstick for civilization is the presence of a state, a ruling governmental body. A state and city life seem to be related. In a tribal society, kinship units provide agencies for social control; but in a city many men are strangers, and informal social sanctions are harder to apply. A superordinate governmental agency becomes necessary, if social order is to be maintained.

We need not insist on a single criterion for the level of "civilization." In addition to those already cited, some other common features of civilizations may be mentioned: the building of monumental constructions with mass labor, class stratification, division of labor and craft specialization, development of trade and communications, the development of warfare, and advances in knowledge in such fields as mathematics, astronomy, and calendrical calculations. These topics, among others, will be elaborated upon further in this chapter.

Courses toward civilization have probably differed greatly in different regions. Yet there have often been striking parallels in such cultural advances, so that the civilizations of Mexico and Peru, although largely independent in their development, not only showed many similarities to one another, but both resembled in many respects the Bronze Age civilizations of the Old World. In a later chapter, we shall trace the development of culture in the New World. The present chapter concerns the Old World Bronze Age civilizations.

One important precondition of civilization is the productivity of agriculture, which makes large concentrations of population possible. Some new inventions facilitated increased agricultural production.

Agricultural productivity

New farming techniques

One was the invention of the ox-drawn plow, which was used in Mesopotamia by 3000 B.C. The ox-drawn plow appears in Egypt and the Indus Valley at about the same time, perhaps due to diffusion of the idea from Mesopotamia. With a plow drawn by oxen, man could put a much greater area of land under cultivation than before, with less time and effort involved.

Oxen also pulled carts with solid wooden wheels in Bronze Age centers and were sometimes used for trampling grain as a form of winnowing.

Another aid to agriculture was the use of metal sickles for reaping, which were in evidence by 3000 B.C. Another was the pick ax, a prominent tool in Sumer, where a seeder plow which dropped seeds into newly plowed land through a kind of funnel was also developed.

Large granaries have been found in the remains of Old World centers of civilization, which show that a sizable surplus of grain could be stored. These granaries provide direct evidence of the enhanced productivity of agriculture in the Bronze Age.

Irrigation

Still another contribution in this direction was the development of irrigation. It may be noted that the civilizations of Mesopotamia, Egypt, and the Indus Valley all developed in rather dry regions through which rivers run.[2]

In Mesopotamia, there are the Tigris and Euphrates rivers; in Egypt, the Nile; and in the Indus Valley, in what is now West Pakistan, there are the Indus River and its tributaries. The dryness of the climate in these regions would naturally encourage the development of irrigation networks to tap the river waters. In northern China, where the Bronze Age Shang dynasty civilization developed, the climate has been described as semi-arid. Here, too, irrigation was resorted to on a large scale.

The earliest of these civilizations dependent upon irrigation developed in Mesopotamia, a flat treeless plain, where irrigation had to be employed if farm communities were to survive. But only one of the two great rivers in this region lent itself well to irrigation. The Tigris had too deep a bed to be easily tapped by canals. The Euphrates, however, had a high bed and was flanked by banks which rose high above the surrounding plains. The high level of this river made it well suited for irrigation.

The first settlements beside the Euphrates must have had relatively simple canals, but as the riverside communities expanded, an increasingly complex irrigation network developed with various smaller channels leading off from the larger ones and reaching fields progressively further away from the river. This system of irrigation greatly enhanced the productivity of agriculture and made it possible for the Mesopotamian farmer to harvest two crops a year. He was no longer dependent on rainfall as the upland Neolithic farmers had been, or as were the swidden

---

[2] The Indus Valley, however, is thought to have been more fertile and better watered at the time of Harappa and Mohenjo-daro than it is at present.

agriculturalists of central Europe. His settlement was also more permanent; the Mesopotamian farmer no longer had to move his village or his fields from time to time.

An irrigation network requires some centralized supervision to prevent the outbreak of quarrels over access to the water. This may have been one of the reasons for the development of political organization in the early city states of Sumer. Moreover, large cooperative undertakings were required to build, maintain, clean, and repair the canals, and to combat the danger of floods to which Mesopotamia was subject. Such efforts had to have some direction, and this may have been one of the functions of the nascent city government.   **Social control**

Monumental constructions and mass labor

In each of the earliest centers of Old World civilization, one finds massive structures which must have required the organization and direction of large work gangs. In Egypt there are the pyramids, in Mesopotamia the ziggurats, and in the Indus Valley cities the large mounds or citadels, as they have been called. The purpose and significance of these great structures differed in the respective societies, but they all attest to the ability of a centralized power to exact hard labor from large numbers of men. Some authorities have argued that this labor need not have been particularly burdensome and that it may have been done in small doses during spare times after the harvest. Be that as it may, these huge constructions embody many man-hours of work. Herodotus was told that 100,000 men worked on the Great Pyramid. Even if we grant this to be an exaggeration,[3] it is clear that a great labor force was required. About 2.3 million stones went into the making of the Great Pyramid (completed about 2600 B.C.) with an average weight of 2.5 tons, although some weigh 15 tons, and there are also some granite slabs which weigh nearly 50 tons.

The ziggurats of Mesopotamia and the mounds of the Indus Valley cities were made of piles of sundried brick; so they are less awesome constructions, as far as their logistics is concerned. Yet they are impressive structures too. The ziggurat at Ur was 68 feet high, topped with a shrine to the moon god. It could be seen 15 miles away across the flat plain. A ziggurat at Uruk has been estimated to have required a full-time labor force of 1,500 men working for five years. The walled citadel at Mohenjo-daro in the Indus Valley was up to 50 feet high and contained several public buildings. Here again a large labor force under the supervision of overseers must be assumed.

It may be that collective work on the irrigation canals provided the

---

[3] A recent estimate is that only about 4,000 men were employed at a time.

Egyptian pyramid
and sphinx.

model for later large-scale enterprises. The needs of defense were involved in some cases, glorification of the state or its religion in others. Palaces and royal tombs were built to honor kings or pharaohs and to emphasize their power and wealth.

Class stratification: slavery

There is archaeological evidence to show that such societies had class stratification. There are considerable differences, for example, in the size of Indus Valley homes, some being large, with many rooms, while there are also cramped rows of what have been called workingmen's quarters. Sumerian cities also had class stratification. Kramer states that the population consisted of four categories: nobles, commoners, clients, and slaves. Nobles owned large estates; the poor lived in humble quarters.[4]

A similar situation appears at the later 14th century B.C. Egyptian site of Tell el-Amarna, where there were royal palaces, lavish homes of court nobility, well-appointed middle-class dwellings, and also the cramped quarters of the poor.

[4] Samuel Noah Kramer, *The Sumerians: Their History, Culture, and Character* (Chicago: University of Chicago Press, 1963), pp. 77, 89.

Ur, with the ziggurat in the background.

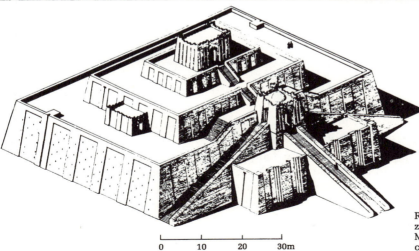

0   10   20   30m

Reconstruction of ziggurat at Ur, Mesopotamia, c. 2000 B.C.

Slavery was a recognized institution in both Egypt and Sumer. Some Egyptian rulers from the 15th century B.C. on brought large numbers of Asiatic captives back from their wars. Many were employed in quarries and mines; others became house slaves.

There were special laws in Mesopotamia regarding the treatment of slaves. The latter were usually captured prisoners of war, but in Mesopotamia one might also became a slave through failure to pay debts, or one might sell a wife or child into slavery to avoid bankruptcy. But freemen who became slaves in this way could be ransomed and freed, and their period of slavery was meant to be temporary, limited by law to three years. It can be seen from this that slavery in Mesopotamia was a somewhat different institution from slavery in the United States before the end of the Civil War, where slavery was usually a lifelong inherited condition associated with a particular racial group.

Division of labor

The early civilizations of Mesopotamia, Egypt, and the Indus Valley were characterized by the development of a division of labor. During the preceding Neolithic period, there seems to have been relatively little division of labor. Men did the hunting and worked in the fields, while women wove cloth and made pottery. There was relatively little craft specialization and trade, except in some communities like Çatal Hüyük.

In the new centers of civilization a growing division of labor was made possible by the heightened productivity of agriculture, which ensured a grain surplus and thus allowed some segments of the population to engage in specialized nonagricultural tasks. It was no longer necessary for all able-bodied workers to till the fields. New technological advances also spurred the division of labor.

Metallurgy

One of the new specialists was the metallurgist, whose complex craft involved technical knowledge, which was often kept secret. The smelting of ores under high temperatures, the preparation of casts, hammering, and annealing all required extensive training. The smith was widely regarded as a kind of miracle worker, skilled in magic; it was to his own interest to maintain this reputation.

The making of bronze tools was an important development in what has come to be known as the Bronze Age. Bronze is an alloy of copper and tin which is harder than copper alone. Mineral resources of copper and tin are not usually found together. It has been suggested, therefore, that man learned to work copper before he made bronze tools and that a Copper Age should be interposed between the Neolithic and the Bronze Age.

This seems logical, but in practice it is difficult to draw a line at any point between these metalworking periods.[5]

The introduction of copper and bronze was a gradual process. Stone continued to be used for cutting tools long after the discovery of metallurgy. Metal objects were scarce and valuable at first and were traded over great distances. It is noteworthy that Egypt, Mesopotamia, and the Indus Valley had to import copper, as well as most other metals. Metallurgy can hardly have originated in any of these regions. It seems likely that it first began in eastern Anatolia, in part of the hilly region extending eastward from the Black Sea area which contained the richest mineral deposits in the Old World.

Once introduced, metal tools showed various advantages over those of stone. Metallurgy allows a greater variety of sizes and shapes, limited only by the size and shape of the mold into which the molten metal is poured, while in the case of stone, the tool's size and shape are considerably determined by the original dimensions of the stone from which it is fashioned. Metal tools, moreover, are durable and have a good cutting edge. If a bronze knife breaks, it can be melted down again and a new tool fashioned; but if a stone tool breaks, it generally has to be discarded. The utility of metal is shown by the types of early tools that were used in the Bronze Age: chisels, knives, and saws for carpentry work, and bronze tweezers and cutting tools for the metallurgist. Since the metallurgist's craft was so mysterious and highly specialized, he ranked high among the artisans of the early civilizations.

Pottery

Another new specialist was the potter. It is probable that in the preceding Neolithic period the womenfolk of a particular household usually made their own pots and jars, building up the walls by hand with strips or coils of clay. In the Bronze Age, however, there were professional potters who exchanged their wares for other goods.

This specialized trade resulted from yet another technological innovation: the potter's wheel, which first appeared in Mesopotamia in the fourth millennium B.C. In this technique, the potter centers a damp lump of clay on a horizontal revolving wheel which may be rotated either by hand or

---

[5] A suggestion similar to that of a Copper Age is the interposition of a "Chalcolithic" period between the Neolithic and the Bronze Age. This would refer to a period when copper was known but reserved for small objects like pins, while most tools continued to be made of stone. A "Chalcolithic" period, if recognized, could be regarded as a terminal phase of the Neolithic period. Usually the term *Bronze Age* is used for the period here under review, when advanced cultures appeared in the Near East and adjacent regions. This terminology will be followed in the present account.

by pumping a foot pedal. He forms a rim of clay by holding his hands steadily together on the circumference of the clay lump and quickly raises up the sidewalls as the wheel revolves.

Mastery of the potter's wheel is not easy; training and practice are required to learn this art. But once he has acquired the knack, a potter can produce pottery vessels on the wheel much more quickly than by the old coil strip method. Moreover, wheel-made ware is more finished in appearance, being more perfectly round and smooth.

Other specialties

With the development of writing systems, the scribe appeared, having knowledge and training which gave him relatively high status. This is reflected in an Egyptian text dating from perhaps the 11th Dynasty (late third millennium B.C.) in which a father urges his son to study hard to enter this profession. The father contrasts the easy and prestigious work of the scribe with the demanding, unpleasant labors of the smith, stonemason, barber, and farmer.

We learn from this text that the barber was another specialist, one low in the hierarchy:

The barber shaves from morning till night; he never sits down except to meals. He hurries from house to house looking for business. He wears out his arms to fill his stomach, like bees eating their own honey.[6]

Weaving was a hereditary specialty in Mesopotamia, where guilds and workshops developed. Indeed, there were separate guilds for spinners, dyers, and fullers.

Other specialists referred to in early texts include brickmakers, carpenters, goldsmiths, and jewelers. Merchants were specialists of a kind, devoted to trade. Priests were also, of course, specialists. In Egypt there were various classifications of priests, whose services at the temple were complemented by other specialized personnel: singers, musicians, astrologers, interpreters of dreams.

. . . doorkeepers and guardian beadles of the sacred buildings, the less important personnel of the shops, bakers, butchers, florists, even their overseers, the offering bearers at whose long-syllabled intonations, twice a day, food is brought to the altars of the god; the sweeper, who erased all trace of footprints on the sand of the chapels; then all the squads of artists and architects, engravers, painters, sculptors, who repaired, constructed, decorated the religious buildings according to directions from the scribe of the House of Life. . . .[7]

---

[6] Quoted in Sir Leonard Woolley, *The Beginnings of Civilization: History of Mankind, Cultural and Scientific Development* (New York: Mentor Books, 1965), Vol. I, Part 2, p. 170.

[7] Serge Sauneron, *The Priests of Ancient Egypt*, trans. Anne Morrissett (New York: Grove Press, 1960), pp. 72–73.

Not only were there many kinds of specialists, some of a hereditary nature, but these occupations were often ranked high or low in relationship to others. Some, like the higher scribes and priests, had high status; others, like barbers and sweepers, ranked low. Here we see the development of class or caste differentiation.

Peasantry

We do not usually think of the peasant as a kind of specialist, but peasants are now coming to be seen as dependent on urban life, in which respect they differ from tribal groups which practice agriculture.

There were no peasants before the development of civilization. George M. Foster has written:

When settled rural peoples subject to the jural control of outsiders exchange a part of what they produce for items they cannot themselves make, in a market setting transcending local transactions, then they are peasants. We see peasants as a peripheral but essential part of civilization, producing the food that makes urban life possible, supporting (and subject to) the specialized classes of political and religious rulers and the other members of the educated elite.[8]

Does the peasant way of life bring about a particular "style of life" or world view? Some writers have thought so. Robert Redfield found some common attitudes and values implicit in the literature about Greek, Polish, Chinese, Kurdish, and Guatemalan peasants. There is a practical utilitarian attitude toward nature combined with a religious view, a de-emphasis of emotion and a preference for security rather than adventure, a desire for children and for wealth.[9]

Foster has further described the peasant view of life as involving "The Image of Limited Good," meaning that peasants conceive of their world as one in which all the desired things of life exist in finite quantity, always in short supply. The peasant sees no way of increasing the total supply of goods. Therefore, a family can improve its position only at the expense of others. Foster sees peasants as exhibiting extreme caution and reserve, a reluctance to reveal true strength and position. There is an avoidance of display.[10]

Generalizations such as those made by Redfield and Foster may be

---

[8] George M. Foster, "Introduction: What Is a Peasant?" in Jack M. Potter, May N. Diaz, and George M. Foster (eds.), *Peasant Society: A Reader* (Boston: Little, Brown & Co., 1967), p. 6. See also the definition in Eric R. Wolf, *Peasants* (Englewood Cliffs, N.J.: Prentice-Hall, 1966), pp. 3–4.

[9] Robert Redfield, *The Primitive World and Its Transformations* (Ithaca, N.Y.: Cornell University Press, 1957), p. 39.

[10] George M. Foster, "Peasant Society and the Image of Limited Good," *American Anthropologist*, Vol. 67, No. 2 (April, 1965), pp. 293–315. See also the section, "Peasant Personalities," in Potter, Diaz, and Foster, *op. cit.*, pp. 296–375.

rather vague, and perhaps they do not apply to some particular peasant societies; but they do suggest that the peasant way of life encourages a different world view from those of—say—merchants or equestrian nomads; it emphasizes different attitudes and values. Thus we see the development of civilization as fostering differentiations in personality along with specialization and division of labor.

Trade and communication

Since Bronze Age specialists were now producing various kinds of goods, it is evident that trade was concomitantly increasing. Trade was both local and far-ranging. It has been mentioned that Mesopotamia, Egypt, and the Indus Valley all had to import copper and other metals from elsewhere. Egypt and Mesopotamia both imported wood, and Sumer and the Indus Valley imported stone. Since these were all commodities of basic importance, foreign trade was clearly a necessity. Improved means of transport had to be developed to meet such needs.

Although wheeled vehicles such as the ox cart existed, they were not suitable for long journeys, and there were few roads in Bronze Age times. The light, two-wheeled chariot drawn by asses or horses was geared to the uses of warfare rather than trade. It was not known to the Egyptians until the invasion of the Hyksos in 1730 B.C. Pack asses were mainly relied upon for overland transport, although camels were also used. Water transport, however, was much preferred in the valleys of the Nile and Tigris and Euphrates. Sailing ships also plied the Mediterranean, bringing luxury goods such as silver, lapis lazuli, and other precious stones, as well as oil, myrrh, and resin. Ships that carried such cargo over long distances had to be larger and more strongly built than the simpler craft of Neolithic times. The Bronze Age, then, saw various advances in communication—improvements in shipping and navigation, and the domestication of animals used in transportation, such as the donkey, camel, and horse.

Abundant evidence of contact between distant communities appears in the archaeological record. Seals made in the Indus Valley have turned up in Sumer, and Egyptian beads, palettes, and stone tools have been found in the Syrian port of Byblos. Texts are available of treaties made between the Egyptian Pharaoh and the King of the Hittites in the 15th century B.C. Despite much trade and communication, however, these different societies remained distinct in culture, each with its own writing system and its characteristic styles of art and architecture.

The Indus Valley seals found in Sumer probably belonged to a colony of merchants. Long-term mercantile representatives could be stationed in such centers to place orders and make purchases—a more effective system than having occasional caravans engage in trade at intervals, without any on-the-spot, advance negotiations. Some such colonies seem to have been established outside the walls of their host cities. They have been compared with the "factories" which the British East India Company set up in India in the 18th century.

An important early "international" port was Ugarit, also known as Ras Shamra, in northern Syria. In the second millennium B.C. there was a trading colony there from Crete, importing Minoan pottery. Trade goods from Mycenaean Greece and Cyprus passed through Ugarit. In this region we can see a blending of various art styles—Egyptian, Mesopotamian, and Greek.

Woolley has described a similar port of trade, Al Mina, situated less than a hundred miles north of Ugarit.[11] Here there were Cretan, Hittite, and Egyptian influences. Writing of Ugarit and Al Mina, another observer has suggested:

The geographic proximity and exposed strategic location of these eminently important trading centers must force us to the conclusion that during centuries of the second millennium Hittites and Egyptians were tacitly agreed to respect the neutrality and inviolability of each other's *epineion*.[12]

The original form of trade exchange in the early Bronze Age must have been barter, but in time a medium of exchange became established, first in grain and later in metal. As early as 2400 B.C., silver was a recognized medium of exchange in Mesopotamia, with a fixed ratio to grain, one *mina* of silver equaling 60 *gur* of grain in value. The development of such a standard further facilitated international trade. In Mesopotamia both internal and international trade ultimately became protected by legislation relating to rates of interest, debt, safe conduct for merchants in foreign countries, and related matters.

It should not be assumed that all these merchants were free agents concerned only with profits for themselves. Karl Polanyi has presented evidence that Babylonia in Hammurabi's time had a "marketless" economy, in which prices were fixed.[13]

In Egypt, where trade was dominated by the Pharaoh, merchants seem to have had even less freedom of action.

One by-product of the development of civilization was a steady increase in the scale of warfare. With larger concentrations of population, the **Warfare**

---

[11] Sir Leonard Woolley, *A Forgotten Kingdom* (Baltimore, Md.: Penguin Books, 1953).

[12] Robert B. Revere, " 'No Man's Coast': Ports of Trade in the Eastern Mediterranean," in Karl Polanyi, Conrad M. Arensberg, and Harry W. Pearson (eds.), *Trade and Market in the Early Empires: Economies in History and Theory* (New York: Free Press, 1957), p. 54.

[13] See Karl Polanyi, "Marketless Trading in Hammurabi's Time," in Polanyi, Arensberg, and Pearson, *op. cit.*, pp. 12–26; and A. L. Oppenheim, "A Bird's Eye View of Mesopotamian Economic History," *ibid.*, pp. 27–37.

number of persons involved in a siege increased. More men could be drawn into battle. The Bronze Age workers who were conscripted to build pyramids or ziggurats could also be conscripted to fight. Meanwhile, metal weapons—spears, swords, helmets, shields, and other accouterments—increased the efficiency of war.

The Sumerians seem to have been the first to organize drilled armies in which there were different types of soldiers—infantry, spearmen, and charioteers. These are depicted in the Royal Standard of Ur (circa 2700 B.C.). Most of the early fighting among the Sumerian city-states seems to have been over possession of water and land resources; later there was fighting for control of trade routes. The Royal Standard shows orderly phalanxes of helmeted footsoldiers and chariots with solid wheels drawn by onagers. To be effective the Sumerian phalanxes must have been

Section of Royal Standard of Ur.

drilled to act in unison. Phalanxes were named and had special insignia. No doubt efforts were made to establish *esprit de corps* in such units.

Drilled armies of increasing size became a common institution in Mesopotamia. Akkadian troops waged distant campaigns, with Sargon (2872–2817 B.C.) leading a standing army of 5,400 men.

Being protected by natural boundaries of desert and sea, Egypt was relatively well protected from outside attack, but around 1730 B.C. was invaded by the Hyksos, nomadic warriors who ruled the country until around 1570 B.C. The Hyksos had the advantage of a secret weapon unfamiliar to the Egyptians, the horse and chariot, which had long been in use in Mesopotamia. They also had a composite bow built up of layers of wood, sinew, and horn glued together, which was more effective than the bows used in Egypt. The Hyksos wore body armor and had new types of swords and daggers. All these factors gave them the upper hand over the almost naked and poorly armed Egyptians, from whom the Hyksos proceeded to exact tribute, while living apart in fortified camps.

After the Egyptians had acquired the use of the new military devices, they succeeded in driving out the Hyksos. Not content with that, a new imperial spirit developed in the ruling dynasty. Under Thutmose III (1490–1436 B.C.) Egyptian armies invaded Palestine and Syria. This resulted in changes in the composition of troops. Although conscription had been practiced formerly, the Egyptian farmers had always been needed on the land to produce their crops; but now a standing army was required in Syria. The problem was solved by forming foreign mercenary troops. In Syria, the Egyptian forces came up against the Hittites, who were said to have had 3,500 chariots at the battle of Carchemish, although this may have been an exaggeration. Thus warfare raged back and forth through the Near East with different nations rising and falling, Hittites, Assyrians, Persians, etc.

Suggestions for further reading

V. Gordon Childe's *Man Makes Himself* (New York: Mentor Books, 1951), makes good reading; it is the work of an archaeologist with a gift for analysis and clear exposition.

Sir Leonard Woolley, *The Beginnings of Civilization; History of Mankind: Cultural and Scientific Development* (New York: Mentor Books, 1965), Vol. I, Part 2. This is a learned, thick compendium of information, available as an inexpensive paperback.

Stuart Piggott (ed.), *The Dawn of Civilization: The First World Survey of Human Cultures in Early Times* (New York: McGraw-Hill Book Co., 1961). Many references have been made in these chapters to this excellent, beautifully illustrated collection of articles by authorities in the field.

For an attempt to analyze causal factors accounting for political centralization in "hydraulic societies," see Karl A. Wittfogel, *Oriental Despotism: A Comparative Study of Total Power* (New Haven: Yale University Press, 1957). For a concise analysis of peasant societies, see Eric R. Wolf, *Peasants* (Englewood Cliffs, N.J.: Prentice-Hall, 1966).

Chapter 21

Civilization in the Old World, *continued*

Writing

Advances in knowledge

The earliest Sumerian and Egyptian written texts date from the last quarter of the fourth millennium B.C. Since writing of quite different type appears in the two societies at about the same time, one conclusion could be that the invention of writing was made independently in both Mesopotamia and Egypt. Some authorities, however, hold that Mesopotamians were the first to develop a writing system and that the *idea* of writing, if not the specific system, spread from Sumer to Egypt. The people of the Indus Valley also had a distinctive writing system at the time in which they had trade relations with Sumer. Here again, it is possible that the idea of writing was derived from Mesopotamia. The Cretan writing systems, which date from the first half of the second millennium B.C. are also different from those of the other Bronze Age centers, and so is that of ancient China, dating from about the same period. It is known that various culture patterns diffused from Egypt to Crete and from the Near East to China; so the idea of writing may have diffused as well. At any rate, each of these Bronze Age centers had its own form of writing. Evidently, man's way of living had come to require some system of keeping records and transmitting information in relatively permanent form.

Writing at Sumer was done on clay tablets. The cuneiform (wedge-shaped) inscriptions were made by a stylus, often a reed, while the clay was still damp. The earliest clay tablets at Sumer contain lists of things stored at the temple and give the number of cows, sheep, and other items owned. From this concern for bookkeeping, it has been held, a writing system ultimately developed. In early Egyptian writing, however, the underlying need seems to have been the communication of orders and the recording of royal accomplishments. In ancient Mesopotamia, where merchants played an active role, most of the clay tablets are business contracts; in Egypt, on the other hand, writing mainly recorded the commands and achievements of Pharaoh and preserved valued spells and magical formulae. Large numbers of texts have been preserved in both Mesopotamia and Egypt. The Mesopotamians baked important clay tablet contracts; the firing process made them practically indestructable. But many unfired sundried clay tablets have also been unearthed in good condition, still legible. The Egyptians sometimes carved inscriptions in stone, which, of course, survived; but so did many writings on papyrus, the Egyptian paper made from the papyrus reed. Rolls of papyrus have often remained well preserved because of the dryness of the Egyptian climate.

Not all the ancient writing systems have been deciphered. Scholars can read Egyptian hieroglyphics, Mesopotamian cuneiform tablets, and the ancient Chinese script, but the Indus Valley writing remains largely indecipherable.[1] One of the Cretan writing systems known as Linear B, was decoded in 1952; its language proved to be Greek. Another Cretan script, Linear A, has not yet been deciphered.

The earliest writing systems are pictographic in character, consisting of a series of pictures or pictograms. The pictures stand for concepts, not specific sounds; so if they are clear enough, they may be understood by people speaking different languages. A weakness of such a system is that abstract ideas are hard to convey in this form of writing.

A later stage of writing is ideographic, in which the individual symbols are called ideograms. One symbol may stand for various things; a round disk is not only the sun but may also represent heat, light, day, and other concepts. When seen in context, the right meaning may be understood, just as we immediately know what is meant when we see a skull and crossbones on the label of a bottle. This system may express abstract ideas, but it may also lead to confusion. Should the picture of a foot be interpreted to mean foot, walking, standing, or what? One way of coping with such ambiguities was the insertion of classifying signs, indicating the category of objects to which the word belonged—birds, gods, or whatnot. Sumerian scribes placed such markers before or after the more ambiguous symbols; such signs are known as determinatives.

The oldest known Mesopotamian and Egyptian scripts are not purely ideographic, although they may have been so in earlier stages of their development. The first writings known already contain phonetic elements, and so are referred to as mixed or transitional—presumably on their way

---

[1] Some Finnish scholars of the Scandinavian Institute of Asian Studies centered in Copenhagen claim to have partially deciphered the Indus Valley script, but some other scholars have expressed skepticism about this. See Gerard Clausen and John Chadwick, "The Indus Script Deciphered?" *Antiquity,* Vol. 43 (1969), pp. 200–207; and T. Burrow, "Dravidian and the Decipherment of the Indus Script," *Antiquity,* Vol. 43 (1969), pp. 274–78.

to becoming phonetic scripts, although some of the early "transitional" scripts lasted for 3,000 years or more.

When concepts were hard to represent in pictograms, a phonetic principle might be employed. To express *I*, one might draw an eye; they sound alike. The Sumerian word *ti* meant both arrow and life. The latter more abstract term could be expressed by the picture of an arrow.

Phonetic writing, the last stage, may be either syllabic or alphabetic. The most important form in the development of the modern world has been alphabetic writing, in which letters represent single sounds. This is the most simplified, efficient writing system. The alphabet has between 22 and 26 signs, in contrast to about 460 Egyptian hieroglyphs, 600 Babylonian characters, and 400 in the Indus Valley script. Kroeber has drawn attention to the fact that the alphabet was invented only once. Although there are many alphabets in the world today which look quite different from one another, all are traceable to a single source, some Semitic people, perhaps the Phoenicians in southwestern Asia before 1000 B.C.[2]

Mathematics

Besides developing writing systems, the civilizations of the Bronze Age also increased knowledge of mathematics, although this advance was uneven. In Mesopotamia much was known about algebra, geometry, and arithmetic. (The Babylonians were familiar with the "Pythagorean theorem," with squares, cube roots, and multiplication tables.) But in Egypt there was relatively little knowledge of these subjects despite the very accurate calculations involved in the construction of the pyramids. The Egyptians had a decimal system of numeration, while the Mesopotamians had a sexagesimal system, with units of 60. This applied to weights, so that 180 grains made a shekel, 60 shekels equaled a *mina,* and 60 *mina* were a talent.

Both decimal and sexagesimal systems have influenced our modern ways of reckoning. The Mesopotamian system survives in our way of dividing the circle into 360 degrees, the hour into 60 minutes, and the minute into 60 seconds.

Astronomical and calendrical calculations

Many nonliterate peoples with a simple technology have some knowledge about the phases of the moon and the movements of the stars. We have already noted the extraordinary achievements made along these lines by the builders of Stonehenge.

---

[2] A. L. Kroeber, *Anthropology* (New York: Harcourt Brace & Co., 1948), p. 313, 514.

Some knowledge about the yearly cycle is useful to farmers who have
to plan ahead, sow seed at a propitious time, and harvest their crops at the
right moment. In the Bronze Age, astronomical and calendrical calculations were facilitated by the development of writing and mathematics,
which made it possible to keep records of astronomical phenomena, to
note the lengthening and shortening of days, and to record other cyclic
manifestations. Such calculations could be made by educated priests in
Egypt and Mesopotamia, who not only used the information for immediate agricultural purposes, but who also had to determine fixed dates for
the celebration of annual festivals, which generally had some relationship
to the agricultural cycle.

The astronomical knowledge of the time was mixed up with astrological notions about the influence of gods and planets on human life. Nevertheless, many accurate observations were made and recorded. Because
of their superiority in mathematics, the Babylonians had greater knowledge of astronomy than the Egyptians. They studied the risings and settings of the moon, and of Venus, and the lengths of day and night in
different seasons. The Babylonians do not seem to have developed any
scientific theory about these phenomena, but they did embark on a preliminary phase of scientific investigation: the systematic recording of
observations.

The Babylonians had a calendar of 12 lunar months of 29 or 30 days
each. The months were divided into four seven-day weeks with one or two
additional feast days thrown in. The Babylonian calendar was thus like
ours in some respects, although there was some awkwardness in the fact
that the lunar calendar did not jibe with the yearly solar one, and hence
it was necessary to insert an intercalary month now and then to reestab-
lish uniformity.

The ancient Egyptian calendar was the forerunner of the one in use
today, since their year consisted of 365 days with 12 months of 30 days
plus 5 additional days. This was the time usually involved from one
inundation of the Nile to the next. The year was divided into three seasons
of four months each. The early Egyptians did not insert an intercalary
day every four years as we do today; so their calendar, like that of the
ancient Mesopotamians, became more inaccurate with time. Egyptians of
a later period, however, found a fixed astronomical peg for their calendar
in the heliacal rising of Sirius, which used to occur just before the annual
flooding of the Nile. It was the Egyptians who first broke up the day into
24 hours, dividing day and night into 12 segments each. They invented a
water clock which remained the best timing device until the medieval
European invention of the mechanical clock.

Our knowledge of the religions of Old World Bronze Age civilizations **Religion**
is uneven. No structures clearly identifiable as temples have been found

in either Crete or the Indus Valley; there is no collection of texts to tell us about the religious concepts held in either of these centers of civilization. On the other hand, large temples have been excavated in both Mesopotamia and Egypt, and both areas have yielded many religious texts. Even so, we cannot always tell from the archaeological remains what religious beliefs and practices were associated with them. Oppenheim has written that even today we do not know why the Mesopotamian temple towers were built or what they were for.[3] There seems to have been no uniformity in the various religions of this period, although many peoples, such as the Sumerians, held beliefs in an Earth Mother goddess, a Sky Father god, and deities of the Moon, Thunder, and other manifestations of nature.

Local gods and their occasional expansion

Each Sumerian city state was held to be under the protection of one of the gods just mentioned. The gods were believed to meet in council to debate matters, a belief which has been thought to imply a relatively democratic society in ancient Sumer. There was a presiding deity, Anu, the sky god, whose voice carried the most authority. While Sumerians recognized the power of all the gods, foremost respect was given to the deity of the city-state where one lived. Such a god might be elevated in power if his city-state successfully subjugated others and might then receive a wider worship.

Similar processes took place in Egypt. Worship was not given to one god only, to the exclusion of others. The god Ptah, although known elsewhere, was given special worship at Memphis. While Memphis remained an unimportant town, Ptah was only a run-of-the-mill deity as far as non-Memphis Egyptians were concerned, but after the pharaohs of the First Dynasty chose Memphis for their capital, Ptah became a god to be reckoned with, and Egyptian mythology was revised to accord with his new status.

Rê was the chief god of the Nile Valley. The local deity of Thebes, home of the 12th Dynasty pharaohs, was Amon-Rê, one of Rê's manifestations. With the advance of Pharaoh's armies into Syria in the 15th century B.C. the range of Amon-Rê's influence correspondingly increased. Tribute sent back to Thebes spurred rebuilding of the god's temples and brought about a sharp rise in the political and economic power of his priests.

Influence of the priesthood

Although Egyptian and Sumerian religions differed considerably in content, both saw a great expansion of the priesthood and the development of huge temple complexes in the Bronze Age. In both areas temples

---

[3] A. Leo Oppenheim, *Ancient Mesopotamia: Portrait of a Dead Civilization* (Chicago: University of Chicago Press, 1964), p. 172.

owned land. It has been estimated that at one point temple lands amounted to about one fifth of all Egypt. The temples of Sumer were not only places of worship but also elaborate centers of production, with workshops for weavers, tailors, sculptors, goldsmiths, carpenters, and other specialists. The temples also provided formal education (although there were private secular schools as well in Sumer), and the priests formed the principal group of educated men, often skilled in writing, mathematics, and medicine, as well as in ritual. Some of the Egyptian priests were similarly learned.

Egyptian priests were considered to be servants of a particular god, whose statue stood in the most secret and sacred of a complex of rooms in a temple compound. This sanctuary was not for the multitude. Before entering it the priest had to purify himself by bathing; he was not allowed to wear wool, but wore mainly linen clothing, and his head and body had to be shaven, free of hair. One of the functions of the priests was to change the god's clothing, putting on a clean set of garments for him. The priest also set out food for the deity. On certain occasions the god was taken out of his temple and carried through the streets, where he could be worshipped by the common people.

It has been estimated that the average temple sanctuary had a permanent staff of between 10 and 25 priests, but there were hundreds at the temple of Amon at Karnak.

Egyptian priests were ranked, with some having great power, sometimes to the extent of posing a challenge to the authority of the central government. In the 14th century B.C., deliberate attempts were made by the pharaoh to bypass and weaken the priesthood. Amenhotep IV (also known as Akhenaton) established the cult of Aton as a state religion, and worship of the old Egyptian gods was forbidden; but this move was not successful in the long run, and the priests regained their functions and influence after his death.

Like the Egyptian temple, the temple of late Mesopotamian times (Babylonia, Assyria) was the house of a god, represented by a statue which his soul was believed to inhabit. Unlike some of the Egyptian gods, which were depicted with bird or animal heads, the Mesopotamian deities were almost always represented as purely human in appearance. Mesopotamian priests clothed and fed their gods, as did the Egyptian priests, and as priests do in parts of South India today. At Uruk a god was given two meals a day, one in the morning when the temple was opened, and one at night before the doors of the sanctuary were closed. The offerings to the Mesopotamian god were taken to the king to eat. Other food, including animals to be slaughtered, was divided among the temple personnel. While the god was having his meal, his statue was surrounded by linen curtains so that he could eat in privacy.[4]

---

[4] Oppenheim, *op. cit.,* pp. 183–98.

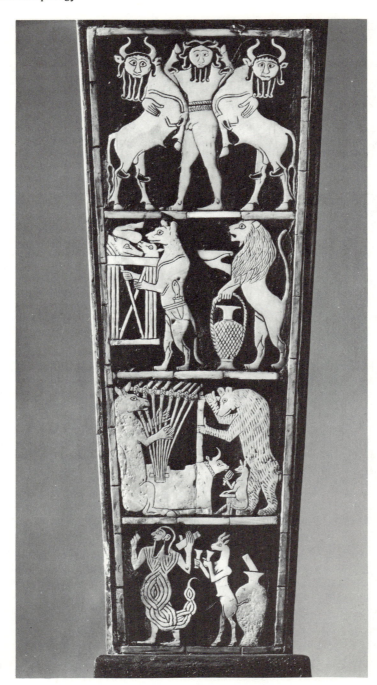

Decorative plaque
made of shell on
lapis lazuli
depicting mythical
episodes, found in
the Royal Tombs at
Ur.

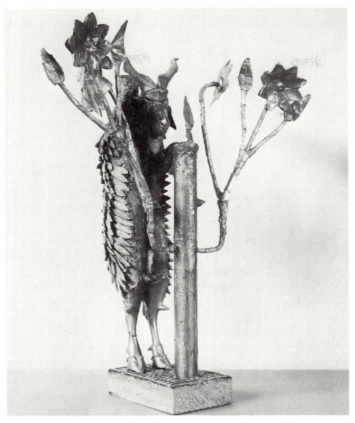

Figurine of a goat made of wood overlaid with gold, silver, shell, and lapis lazuli, found in the Royal Tombs at Ur.

As in the case of the Egyptian deities, the Mesopotamian gods were taken out of the temple on special occasions and carried through the streets, where the common people could see them.

Cults of the dead

With the appearance of class differentiation and the accumulation of wealth on the part of kings, royalty, and nobility, we find elaborate cults of the dead in some of the Bronze Age civilizations. Tombs were stocked with lavish equipment for the afterlife. In some cases, attendants accompanied their ruler at his death to serve him in the afterworld.

An orderly retinue of 74 followers, unearthed in the Royal Tombs at Ur (circa 2500 B.C.) by Leonard Woolley, included soldiers, musicians, menservants, and maidservants. The men had stood in the tomb beside four-wheeled chariots drawn by oxen. The oxen were killed; their drivers, and all the other attendants were also put to death in some way, probably by drinking poison. Then the grave shaft was filled in. Many beautifully made objects were found in the tomb: a gold helmet, harps and lyres, a gaming board, silver tumblers, and a goat statuette made of gold, silver, and lapis lazuli. The queen, who seems to have been buried later than her husband and his attendants, wore an elaborate headdress and masses of jewelry.

Similar finds have been made in the Old Kingdom of Egypt dating from around 3000 B.C. A First Dynasty princess was buried with her servants, each having the special tools of his or her trade. A later Middle Kingdom official was buried in the Sudan with more than a hundred slaughtered servants. In the Shang dynasty of China (circa 1523–1028 B.C.), we find similar human sacrifices with royal burials. These practices can hardly have been popular with the victims or their relatives; perhaps it is understandable that they were ultimately discontinued in each of these regions.

In Egypt, from the Middle Kingdom on, tombs were supplied with figurines called *ushebtis,* which were expected to work in place of the dead man if the gods required him to labor in the fields or do some other burdensome task. Some tombs had hundreds or thousands of *ushebtis.* The dead man's spirit (*Ba*) was thought to remain with his mummified body but was believed able to leave it, especially at night. The private tombs of important, wealthy persons around 2400 B.C. were decorated with wall paintings showing peasants at work in the fields, driving herds and flocks, dancing, and playing games. This provided a setting in which the deceased could continue to enjoy the pleasures of this world. Food was also left with the dead, and provisions were made to have food offerings brought to the tomb on periodic festival occasions. This was done by a man's heirs in the Old Kingdom. Later it was customary to set aside a portion of the deceased's estate to pay priests to do the job. In this way a man prepared for "perpetual care" after death.

Despite all these orderly arrangements, there seems to have been a good deal of uncertainty about the afterworld and its possible dangers. The dead were equipped with spells and texts to vanquish threatening figures in the beyond. It was also believed that the dead had to appear before an assembly of gods who were judges. Here we find indications of belief in reward and punishment in the afterworld. A protestation of innocence is ascribed to a dead man in *Book of the Dead* as follows:

I have not done evil in the place of truth. I knew no wrong. I did no evil thing. . . . I did not do that which the god abominates. I did not repeat evil of a servant to his master. I allowed no one to hunger. I caused no one to weep. I did not murder. I did not command to murder. I caused no man's misery. I did not diminish food in the temples. I did not decrease the offerings of the gods. I did not take away the food offerings of the dead. . . . I did not commit adultery.[5]

---

[5] *Book of the Dead,* Chapter 125, quoted in James Henry Breasted, *Develop-*

Among other sins which the dead man denies having committed are taking milk from children and diverting irrigation water from the fields of others to his own.

The Sumerians also believed in an afterworld judgment; the sun god and moon god judged the dead.

Beliefs of this kind are not universal, nor is religion always so concerned with ethical matters. The involvement of ethics in religion seems to have been particularly associated with the urban life of advanced civilizations (see pages 265–67).

Suggestions for further reading

For a brief survey of writing systems, see David Diringer, *Writing* (New York: Frederick A. Praeger, 1962).

A very interesting account of cuneiform writing and related topics is available in Edward Chiera, *They Wrote on Clay: The Babylonian Tablets Speak Today* (Chicago: The University of Chicago Press, 1938).

There are chapters on writing, mathematics, the sciences, and religion in Sir Leonard Woolley's *The Beginnings of Civilization,* cited at the end of the preceding chapter. See especially Chapters 6 to 8.

For references on Egypt, Sumer, Harappa, and Shang China, see the Suggestions for Further Reading at the end of Chapter 22.

---

ment of Religion and Thought in Ancient Egypt (New York: Harper & Bros., 1959 [1912]), pp. 299–300.

Four centers of Old World civilization

In the preceding chapter, some general attributes of civilization were discussed. But the centers of Old World civilization were not all alike. While patterns may have diffused from one region to another, each society maintained its own culture and style of life. The languages and writing systems of Sumer, Harappa, Egypt, Crete, and China were all different from one another. Egyptian architecture was not like that of Mesopotamia or Crete, despite the communication between these centers. Greeks visited Egypt, but they did not borrow or imitate the pylon, pyramid, or obelisk, nor did they start to mummify the dead. Some of these centers of civilization were ahead of their contemporaries in some respects, behind in others. The metal work and handicrafts of the Indus Valley cities were not as good as those of Sumer, but their city planning and concern with sanitation were far in advance. Egyptian knowledge of medicine was superior to that of Mesopotamia, but the Mesopotamians were ahead in mathematics and astronomy. The advance of civilization was thus not uniform. Besides, the significance of a particular invention may have differed from one society to another. We have noted that the earliest use of writing in Mesopotamia was in connection with bookkeeping, while in Egypt it was used for the transmission of orders and the recording of royal achievements.

Some anthropologists, for example, Julian Steward, have focused on regularities in cultural evolution and have drawn attention to similarities in the evolution of culture in different parts of the world. But while the search for laws and regularities is one of anthropology's most important concerns, another approach also has its value: to see a particular culture as a configuration which may be unique in some respects. In this way, Ruth Benedict contrasted the culture of the Pueblo Indians of the Southwest with other American Indian cultures, while Henri Frankfort showed how Egyptian culture differed from that of Sumer in its dominant institutions and values.

In this chapter, we shall briefly examine four centers of Old World civilization with the focus on what was especially characteristic of each.

The names Mesopotamia, Sumer, and Babylonia have appeared a number of times in the preceding two chapters. The reader may have assumed that these are interchangeable terms; sometimes this is so, but sometimes it is not. Mesopotamia refers to a geographical region, the area of the Tigris and Euphrates rivers. Sumer was the land where the Sumerian civilization developed in the lower half of Mesopotamia, an area of approximately 10,000 square miles, "roughly identical with modern Iraq from north of Baghdad to the Persian Gulf."[1] The history of Sumer may be said to end and that of Babylonia to begin at about 1750 B.C., when Hammurabi conquered Sumer and established a larger Mesopotamian kingdom, stretching from the Persian Gulf to the Habur River, far to the northwest of Babylon.

Sumer

In the third millennium B.C., Sumer was made up of about a dozen walled city-states. Some of the most important ones (Eridu, Ur, Larsa, and Uruk) were in sight of one another without being separated by any natural boundaries. Since they were expanding land-hungry settlements, it is not surprising that warfare was endemic in Sumer. The appearance of a cluster of cities not far from one another presents a picture quite different from that of the Indus Valley, where the two main cities were nearly 400 miles apart, and also from Egypt, where city life developed more slowly.

The city-states of Sumer did not come into being all at once. It is now believed that the first settlers in this area were not Sumerians, for the names of the most important cities—Eridu, Ur, Larsa, Isin, Adab, Kullab, Lagash, Nippur, Kish—are not of Sumerian origin. The rivers must also have been named by people of a different linguistic stock. Moreover, many words used by Sumerians—words for farmer, herdsman, fisherman, plow, furrow, palm, date, metalworker, smith, carpenter, basketmaker, weaver, leatherworker, potter, mason and perhaps merchant—also seem to be of non-Sumerian origin.[2]

We do not know who these earlier settlers were or how they were supplanted by the Sumerians, but it is evident that they, rather than the

---

[1] Samuel Noah Kramer, *The Sumerians: Their History, Culture, and Character* (Chicago: University of Chicago Press, 1963), p. 3.

[2] *Ibid.*, pp. 40–41.

Sumerians, were the first civilizing force in the area. They have come to be known as the Ubaid people, after the site of Tell al-Ubaid near Ur, which was inhabited at about 4000 B.C.

The Sumerians themselves are believed to have entered the region at around 3500 B.C., perhaps from Iran, whence their predecessors may also have come. Even if they did not invent some of the innovations formerly attributed to them, the Sumerians had the resourcefulness and intelligence to adopt and further develop Ubaid patterns of living. In the centuries that followed, their language replaced that of the Ubaid people as the dominant speech of southern Mesopotamia.

The Ubaid period was followed by a stage called Uruk (circa 3500–3000 B.C.) after the city of Uruk, the Erech of the Old Testament. During this period large ziggurats and imposing temples were built. Each Sumerian city-state had a temple dedicated to its main god, who was conceived to own and protect the land under his jurisdiction.

Part of the temple land, which may be called common, was worked by all the people for the welfare of their god, temple, and community. The temple provided seeds, tools, and draft animals for this labor. The stores of grain thus produced were kept at the temple for various uses: sacrifice to the god, food for his priests and other temple personnel, and rations for the workers, who were also subject to military service and corvée labor on irrigation ditches.

From this information we get the initial impression of a centralized ruling bureaucracy associated with a dominant religion exercising unchallenged control over a subject populace. But this picture needs to be modified; it does not tell the whole story. First of all, the temple did not own all the land. Some land was rented out to sharecroppers; the rest was the private property of individuals. Nor was private property a negligible institution. Kramer writes:

. . . there are quite a number of documents from Lagash as well as from other sites which indicate quite clearly that the citizens of the city-states could buy and sell their fields and houses, not to mention all kinds of movable property.[3]

Moreover, the temple was not the only source of political power, although it may have been so at first. The continual warfare of city-states led to the elevation of military leaders. The prototype of the king may have been elected at first or appointed by an assembly; but eventually a hereditary kingship developed, and the palace became a center of power equal to, or greater than, the temple. This may be seen by the mass burials in the Royal Tombs at Ur, clear evidence of the king's despotic power which developed during the Early Dynastic period (2900–2370 B.C.), fol-

---

[3] *Ibid.*, p. 75.

lowing the Uruk.[4] Yet this tyranny did not last. Both Kramer and Frankfort have described Sumerian society as being relatively democratic. If this was so, it may have been partly due to the fact that there was more than one power center. Perhaps palace and temple balanced one another, with neither side gaining complete control over the people for long. Moreover, the institution of private property made possible other channels of power and prestige than either temple or palace. It seems likely that a relatively free and open society existed much of the time in Sumer; otherwise it would be hard to explain the dynamic character of this most inventive, creative culture.[5]

Not only did Sumer produce the first writing but also the first schools of which we have evidence. Several "textbooks" have been uncovered at Shuruppak, dating from about 2500 B.C. Practice tablets with exercises have also been found, sometimes with corrections made by the teachers. At Mari an early schoolroom was excavated with rows of baked-brick benches. There are also texts which describe the boredom of school attendance and the severity of teachers' canings. Not everyone went to these schools, incidentally; there is good evidence that the students generally came from well-to-do or politically important families.

Since Sumer was the first civilization to develop city-states and a system of writing, it is not surprising that it was also the first to produce a set of codified laws, that of Ur-Nammu who ruled in Ur about 2100 B.C., 300 years before Hammurabi of Babylon, whose code of laws is better preserved, more complete, and better known to the modern reader. Sumerians developed the lost wax process of casting metals. Their contributions to military tactics have already been noted.

Sumer was also the first civilization to develop the principle of the true arch, dependent upon the keystone, while its neighbors were still making use of the less efficient corbel arch which lacked a keystone. The true arch was used in the Royal Tombs at Ur and also in private dwellings.

A charming invention of the Sumerians, which had its practical utility, was the decorated seal. Beginning in the Uruk period, carved stone seals were used to stamp the equivalent of a signature on moist clay tablets or to place a mark of ownership on merchandise. There would seem to be no need to make such things into objects of beauty, but that is what the Sumerians did, engraving mythical themes or scenes of everyday life with great precision and delicacy. The seals attest two things: the importance of private property in Sumer and the development of an aesthetic sense.

The Sumerians seem to have gone out of their way to excel. In an

---

[4] Late Uruk is also known as the Protoliterate period, since it contains the first evidence of writing.

[5] Some idea of this creativeness may be gained by scanning the table of contents of Kramer's book, *History Begins at Sumer*, which lists a long row of "firsts."

analysis of Sumerian texts, Kramer has argued that a competitive drive for success and superiority was a leitmotiv in their culture. This again suggests that Sumer was a relatively open society in which there was some mobility and freedom within its stratified order.

Egypt

The civilization which grew up along the banks of the Nile River was relatively isolated and protected by deserts to the east and west. Invaders would have had to spend about a week crossing desert country to reach the Nile. Although this journey could be made, it would have been difficult for large invading forces in the days before the Hyksos launched their attack with horses and chariots. Egypt was also protected to the south by difficult terrain beyond the First Cataract and by the Nubian deserts. Approaches could be made from the Mediterranean, but sea travel did not attain importance until large seaworthy craft were built. In the beginning, at least, Egypt was relatively safe from invasion, unlike the exposed city-states on the plains of Sumer.

In the Predynastic period, between around 4500 and 3200 B.C., there were farming communities strung along the valley of the Nile, some of which produced well-made pottery. The people lived in huts made of grass and reeds. These settlements seem to have been quite self-sufficient. There were no large population clusters.

Conditions changed around 3200 B.C., when the Two Lands, North and South Egypt, were unified by the semilegendary king, Menes, who may have been Narmer, a ruler from the South. Menes (Narmer), founder of the First Dynasty, became the first pharaoh of a united Egypt. His conquest of the North was memorialized in a carved palette, in which the king was depicted standing over and striking a fallen enemy. Corpses, bound prisoners, and severed heads are shown.

A notable aspect of the Narmer palette is the presence of a Mesopotamian art motif: two fabulous beasts ("serpo-pards") face one another with long intertwined necks. In the late Predynastic period, some other Mesopotamian culture traits had already appeared in Egypt. One of the most important of these was the use of bricks, similar in size and shape to Mesopotamian bricks and laid in the same fashion. Still more important was the use of writing. To be sure, early Egyptian hieroglyphs were quite different from cuneiform writing. This seems to have been a case of stimulus diffusion; probably the idea of writing, rather than the characters themselves, spread from the one society to the other.

More clear-cut evidence of Mesopotamian contact is supplied by three Sumerian cylinder seals found in Egypt. The custom of using cylinder seals was temporarily adopted. The first monumental architecture also began to appear. It is interesting that we find no evidence of a reverse current; there seems to have been no Mesopotamian borrowing from Egypt at this time.

The period following the unification of Egypt was one of rapid culture change, perhaps due partly to the new political organization and partly to the novel ideas coming in from abroad.

The pharaoh who ruled Egypt was believed to be a living god, not simply an agent of the gods. One cannot tell whether this idea was generally accepted at first or whether the notion was gradually instilled into the population. At any rate, it does not seem to have been effectively challenged for a period of about 2,500 years. During his lifetime the pharaoh was conceived to be the god Horus. When he died, he became the god Osiris and his son became Horus; so there was always a Horus on the throne.

The king was the head of both church and state. In both cases, he delegated his powers to lesser authorities, priests and government officials, who acted on his behalf throughout the kingdom. There was usually no independent counterpoise to the state; the influence of the merchant class was much weaker than at Sumer. The word *merchant* does not appear until the second millennium B.C., when it designates the official of a temple privileged to trade abroad.[6] Most foreign trade was under the direction of the king, who also dominated internal trade. Although merchants existed, they had little power and influence. There seem to have been no Egyptian laws regulating trade. For that matter, there were no publicly displayed legal codes corresponding to those of Mesopotamia, for justice ultimately lay in the hands of the god-king who did not need to make his legal system explicit to his subjects.

A god-king requires fitting monuments. Pyramids and colossal royal tombs were logical consequences of such a regime. The first giant pyramid-and-tomb complex was built around 2750 B.C. for King Djoser (or Zoser) by his vizier Imhotep, evidently a man of genius. At Sakkarah, Imhotep built a step pyramid and a funerary temple made of small stone bricks, laid as mud bricks were laid, with paneling in the style of brick tombs. The step pyramid was not faced to give a smooth slope from top to bottom, as was done later. This was the first stone structure of such imposing size. Nothing like it had ever existed before; it must have convinced at least some Egyptian peasants that their rulers were truly gods.

The Great Pyramid of Khufu (or Cheops) at Gizeh was built not much later, being completed around 2600 B.C. It is still the largest stone structure in the world. Inside the pyramid there was an intricate network of passageways leading to two burial chambers. All this was accomplished without the benefit of any wheels, pulleys, or cranes; only ramps, rollers, and levers were used.

The period of massive pyramid building lasted about 400 years, al-

---

[6] Henri Frankfort, *The Birth of Civilization in the Near East* (New York: Doubleday Anchor Books, 1956), p. 118.

though smaller pyramids continued to be raised during the next four centuries. Later, during the New Kingdom (1567–1085 B.C.), mortuary temples were constructed instead.

Two things are striking about Egyptian culture: one is the speed with which culture change took place after the unification of North and South; the other is the stability of culture after that first creative outburst gave way to a more conservative way of life. Both cultural stability and change pose problems for analysis. The stability of Egyptian culture is perhaps the most remarkable, since it extended over such immense periods of time. We can contrast it with our own history when we reflect that the Declaration of Independence was signed less than 200 years ago and that Columbus came to the New World less than 500 years ago. We reckon the years of our history in the hundreds. But ancient Egypt's runs to almost 3,000 years during most of which time (at least from our point of view) culture does not seem to have changed very much. This conservatism may be due partly to the country's relative isolation, partly to the restraining influence of a state in which political control, religion, and commerce were all centralized in the hands of a single ruling group.

This is not to say that there were no shifts in power, conflicts, or crises in all that time. During what has been called the First Intermediate Period, toward the end of the third millennium, the nobles became relatively independent of the pharaoh and decided to appropriate the Pyramid Texts which had originally been meant for the use of god-kings alone. They wanted to take advantage of the funeral rituals which insured deification in the afterworld. "Every man a king," at least after death, seems to have been their slogan.

There were other oscillations of power. Reference has been made (page 235) to the invasion of the Hyksos and the imperial expansion which followed their expulsion. There were times when the priesthood, enriched by the rulers' foreign conquests, seemed to pose a threat to the pharaoh's authority. There was the effort by Ahkenaton or Ikhnaton (1369–1353 B.C.) to bypass the priesthood, abolish the old religion, and establish an exclusive cult of the sun-god Aton. But traditional customs seem to have persisted most of the time. Strict conventions governed the arts, religious observances, and priestly prerogatives to the time of Cleopatra.

Egypt had some influence on other early Old World civilizations. Part of the splendor of ancient Crete may be attributed to Egypt, for there seems to have been considerable contact between Egypt and Crete during the 12th Dynasty (about 2000–1785 B.C.). Stone bowls of Early Dynastic style and an Egyptian statue of the 12th or 13th Dynasty have been found at Knossos. Scarab seal stones have also been discovered in Crete.

Apart from such legacies as the pyramids, the Sphinx, and the royal tombs, Egypt made some important practical contributions to the later culture of the world: paper made from papyrus, the making of glassware, and methods of tanning leather which are still in use today. But compared with Sumer's many innovations, this list is brief, despite Egyptian civilization's enormous span of time.

Not as much is known about the Indus Valley civilization, now commonly called the Harappa culture, as about the civilizations of Sumer and Egypt. This is partly because the very existence of this civilization was not known until the 1920's, by which time the cultures of Mesopotamia and Egypt had already been extensively investigated. Then, too, scholars have learned to read Mesopotamian cuneiform and Egyptian hieroglyphs, and abundant texts are available in clay, papyrus, and stone; but there are no Indus Valley texts. The only available writing is on seals and on pottery fragments, and the script has not yet been deciphered.

Harappa

The Harappa culture overlapped in time with the civilizations of Sumer and Egypt but was not quite as old. It was formerly dated back to around 3000 B.C., but recent radiocarbon dates suggest that 2500 B.C. would be more accurate. This civilization seems to have collapsed between around 1700 and 1500 B.C. Its span was thus shorter than those of either Sumer or Egypt. Although some attractive figurines have been found at its two principal cities, Harappa and Mohenjo-daro, its art was not as rich or abundant as those of the other two centers of civilization. But the territorial expanse of the Harappa culture was more farflung than that of either Sumer or Egypt, covering about 1,200 miles by 700 miles in extent. This whole area may not, however, have been occupied simultaneously. The Indus Valley civilization was not limited to the banks of the Indus and its tributaries but extended far south along the coast of the Arabian Sea to the present state of Gujarat and as far east as Delhi.

Harappa and Mohenjo-daro were nearly 400 miles apart. They had fairly large populations, one estimate for Mohenjo-daro being 40,000. About 80 settlements have been found so far. What is striking is the uniformity of their culture. These communities had standard sizes of bricks, uniform weights and measures, and very similar pottery throughout.

The cities were not just agglomerations of houses but gave evidence of careful city planning. The streets were straight and intersected at right angles like American city blocks. There were drains in the streets, showing an unusual attention, for that time, to the problems of sewage disposal. Drains led down from individual houses into the public sewers. Almost every house had its own well, but there were also public wells.

As in Sumer, the houses did not have windows in their outer walls; light and air came from a courtyard around which the rooms were grouped. The houses had two stories, with a steep staircase of masonry leading to the upper floor. Some homes had only two rooms; others were large and elaborate—an indication of class differences.

Many people in India at the present time are vegetarians, but the presence of burnt animal bones in Indus Valley sites show that beef, mutton, poultry, and fish were eaten in those days. Cows, humped zebu, buffaloes, sheep, elephants, cats, dogs, and other animals were known to the Indus Valley folk. They raised wheat, barley, and peas. Moreover, they seem to have been the first people to grow cotton, and it is likely that they traded it in Sumer. At any rate, there is evidence of trade with the contemporary cities of Mesopotamia, for seals of Indus Valley type have been found in Sumerian cities.

There are many similarities between the Indus Valley settlements and those of Sumer. The crops and domesticated animals were largely the same; so was the style of house building. Copper and bronze ornaments were found in both areas, although their workmanship was finer in Mesopotamia. Women's vanity cases found in Harappa are similar to those of Sumer, and similar eye shadow and face paint were used. Pottery was made on the potter's wheel in both areas. It is evident that these two centers of civilization developed from a basically similar Neolithic culture. The precursors of the Harappans may have lived in Baluchistan and had cultural ties with regions further to the west. Trade and communication between Mesopotamia and the Indus Valley also made it possible for new ideas to spread from one center to the other.

Nevertheless, there were some differences between Mesopotamian and Indus Valley cultures. Harappan bronze axes and similar tools were inferior in workmanship, lacking sockets for handles which had long been known in Sumer. The arch, first invented in Mesopotamia, did not appear in Indus Valley architecture; nor did round columns. On the other hand, town planning and sanitation were more highly developed in Harappa and Mohenjo-daro, where there was also much more use of fired brick than in Sumer. The writing systems of the two cultures were different. There are no stores of clay tablets in the Indus Valley, like those of Mesopotamia. The Indus Valley script appears in brief inscriptions on small steatite seals, on which there are also well-made figures of animals in bas relief. These seals have been found in abundance in the homes of both rich and poor—over 1,200 were found in Mohenjo-daro alone. Perhaps every citizen had one as a kind of identification. Or perhaps they were used in trade, to mark merchandise. Their exact purpose is still not known.

The Indus Valley cities differ from those of Egypt or Mesopotamia in having no identifiable temples or monumental sculpture. This does not mean that Indus Valley people had no places of worship. There is a large bath at Mohenjo-daro which may have had some religious functions. It looks rather like a modern rectangular swimming pool, with steps going down into the water. Perhaps it was only a place to bathe and nothing more, but bathing has religious connotations in India today—especially at traditionally sacred places such as the Ganges River at Banaras. Since this is such a widespread custom in India, it is evidently very old and may date back to Indus Valley times.

At both Harappa and Mohenjo-daro there was a fortified mound to the west of the city, made of piles of sundried brick, with a facing of fired brick about 50 feet high. On top of the mound at Mohenjo-daro, the bath and a large granary were built. Harappa had granaries with a total floor space of over 9,000 square feet, similar to that of Mohenjo-daro, with rows of small houses nearby where the workers may have lived.

The smaller communities of the Indus Valley had the same grid layout of the larger cities and the same kind of drain system and house type.

Statuettes give us some idea of the clothing worn. There was a shawl-like cloth, worn over the left shoulder and under the right arm, and a lower garment like the cotton *dhoti* which is now worn by men in India. Finger rings, bangles, bracelets, and anklets have been found and earrings of gold, silver, and copper. Bronze razors were used.

A metal saw with toothed edge has been found at Mohenjo-daro, the first true cutting saw in the archaeological record.

The artwork of the Indus Valley is on a small scale, consisting of the seal carvings and the small statuettes and figurines which include many realistic carvings of bulls and female clay figures which may represent mother goddesses. There is a bronze figure of a naked dancing girl with rows of bangles on her arm.

Small carts were modeled in clay, perhaps as children's toys. They closely resemble oxcarts used in southern Asia today. There were many animal figurines, some with movable parts pulled by strings—a bull with a nodding head, a monkey with movable arms, and pottery rams on wheels, with a hole through the neck for a drawstring.

Large numbers of dice have been found, some of which are like the cubic dice of the present day with dots from one to six on their respective sides. They differ from modern dice only in the ways in which the dots are arranged. Marbles were also used, as in Sumer and Egypt.

The Harappans had to import many materials from elsewhere: gold from southern India or Afghanistan, turquoise, silver, and lapis lazuli from Afghanistan or Iran, copper from Rajasthan or Afghanistan, and jadeite perhaps from Tibet. That they traded with Sumer is suggested by Harappan seals which have been found in Mesopotamia. They may have exported cotton, the earliest remains of which have been found in the Indus Valley. Timber and ivory were probably exported.

The Indus Valley civilization must have had a well-developed political system, judging from the city planning and the standardization of the size of bricks and of weights and measures. Both Wheeler and Piggott believe that it must have been an autocratic regime, but this is an inference derived from the archaeological remains; there are no texts to demonstrate it.

These communities seem to have had a relatively high standard of liv-

Indus Valley seals.

ing. Many of the homes were fairly large in size. But in spite of the appearance of comfort and the unusual attention given to sanitation, the life expectation seems to have been short. Judging from the skeletons found in Harappan cemeteries, few people lived much beyond 30 years of age; most were dead by the age of 40.

Harappan culture seems to have existed without much change for hundreds of years and then declined between 1700 and 1500 B.C., at least in the more northerly areas. Many explanations have been offered for this decline. One attributes it to the progressive dessication of the landscape due to deforestation, overgrazing, and perhaps changes in rainfall and climate.

Another theory is that the coastal area of the Arabian Sea is an active geological zone which has been gradually rising for thousands of years. Some areas which were formerly islands are now part of the mainland, and some former seaports are now located inland far from the coast.

It is also believed that Mohenjo-daro and other Indus Valley settlements suffered from flooding and deposits of silt and may have become engulfed in mud.

The period of decline is traditionally associated with the entry into the Indian subcontinent of the Aryans, the nomadic cattle-herding people who came down through the mountain passes in the northwest. In the Vedas, ancient hymns of the Aryans, there are references to their conquest of large walled cities. It may be that these were the cities of the Indus Valley. The Aryans cannot have wiped out the Indus Valley people, who must have been numerous, but they were evidently strong enough to establish themselves before long as the dominant power in northern India.

The civilization which subsequently developed in northern India must have represented a blend of the two cultures: the ancient civilization of the Indus Valley and the culture of the pastoral herders.

Civilization flowered in China during the Shang Dynasty, a little before 1500 B.C. Here again we find a riverine civilization. It developed in the northern part of Honan province north of the Huangho or Yellow River. Excavations made at Anyang, a Shang capital city, have thrown much light on this advanced Far Eastern culture.

Shang China

Here we find the traditional characteristics of a civilization: city life, a system of writing, a state organization, use of bronze, monumental constructions, class stratification, division of labor, widespread trade and communication, development of warfare, and increased knowledge of astronomy and calendrical calculations. Since these features all appeared rather suddenly, a good deal later than the development of civilization in the Near East, it seems likely that at least some aspects of Shang culture resulted from diffusion of ideas from the West. On the other hand, Shang culture seems to have developed naturally from the already complex Lungshan Neolithic described in Chapter 19. In that chapter it was noted that the use of barley and wheat probably diffused eastward along the southern edge of the steppes and that cattle were introduced in Neolithic times.

The writing system, ancestral to modern Chinese, was quite different from those of Sumer, Egypt, or the Indus Valley, although it followed similar principles. This may be another instance of stimulus diffusion, although in this case the distance from the Western centers of civilization is great.

Some of the new metal tools of the Shang period, such as socketed axes, resemble those of Europe. Shang ritual bronze vases and urns are famous for their craftsmanship. Their style seems to owe nothing to the West. Moreover, early Chinese bronze work had a local peculiarity: the regular practice of adding lead to the alloy.

Chariots were used in late Shang times, very similar to those of Sumer, Egypt, and Greece. The method of harnessing the horse was the same, the weight being borne by the horse's neck.

Some Shang art motifs are thought to be traceable to Sumer. Li Chi cites an intertwined serpent motif as one example. He also mentions an unusual jar cover shaped like a flower pot with a "phallic" handle similar to jar covers found in Jemdet Nasr and Mohenjo-daro.[7]

Early Chinese culture may thus have been influenced by new ideas

---

[7] Li Chi, *The Beginnings of Chinese Civilization: Three Lectures Illustrated with Finds at Anyang* (Seattle: University of Washington Press, 1957), pp. 26–29.

spreading from the West, but it seems to have been quite selective and to have developed in relative isolation with a characteristic style of its own. Some useful culture patterns were slow in reaching China or in being accepted, such as the use of bricks in architecture. Bricks were not introduced until the time of the Han dynasty (206 B.C.–A.D. 220). The Chinese did not make use of stone in building construction, although stone was available. Roof tiles, which we think of as characteristically Chinese, date from the Chou period (traditionally dated 1122–221 B.C.).

In Shang times, houses were built on raised platforms of pounded earth. The soil was held in on all sides by a broad frame; loose earth was then poured in and beaten. The walls of house compounds were made in the same manner.

Village walls were already characteristic of the Neolithic Lungshan period. In Shang times, large city walls were built. The one at the Shang capital of Ao is estimated to have required the work of 10,000 men for 18 years.[8] Wall building was the type of monumental construction favored by the Chinese. Some Shang cities had an inner wall within which lived the aristocracy. Later in the Ch'in dynasty (221–206 B.C.), the 1,400-mile Great Wall of China was built, to keep out the barbarians.

Shang bronze vessel.

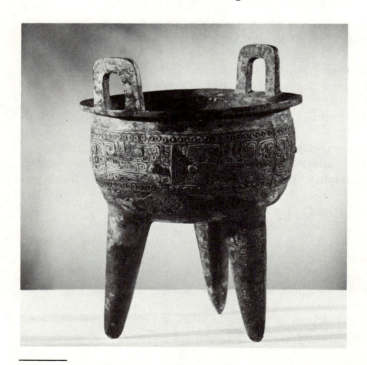

[8] Chester S. Chard, *Man in Prehistory* (New York: McGraw-Hill Book Co., 1969), p. 259.

The Shang capital at Anyang had special sections or quarters for bronze metallurgists, stoneworkers, and specialists who made bone tools such as arrowheads, hairpins, and ladles. Objects of jade were also made.

There is evidence of class stratification and political centralization. The population was divisible into three groups: aristocracy, craftsmen, and peasants. Shang "royal tombs" show patterns similar to those of Sumer and Egypt, servants of the king being killed and buried with their master. Horses and chariots were also interred with the dead ruler. Sacrificial victims were buried when buildings were constructed.

The use of bronze was limited to the upper class. Metal was not employed for agricultural tools. The peasants used stone reaping knives and still lived at a Neolithic technological level. Chariots driven by members of the ruling group were fitted with bronze ornamentation. Bronze ritual vessels were made for and buried with upper-class owners.

Much of our knowledge about Shang culture comes from oracle inscriptions. The early Chinese resorted to divination to get advice from the supernatural world. The Neolithic Lungshan people practiced scapulimancy, or shoulder blade divination. They exposed the shoulder blade of a cow to fire and then examined the cracks which appeared in the bone to find answers to their questions, just as a modern tea leaf reader interprets the arrangement of the tea leaves in a cup to foretell the future.

Scapulimancy was practiced in the Shang period with some innovations. Turtle shells were now used as well as animal bones, and the questions to be answered were first scratched onto the bone before it was heated. More than 100,000 pieces of oracle bones have been recovered. Most of their inscriptions are brief; the longest ones have little more than 60 words, and most have only 10 or 12. Nevertheless, these earliest Chinese writings are most informative because they tell us something about the concerns, hopes, and anxieties of the people. Certain themes recur. One concerns sacrifices. To what spirits should I offer sacrifice? What should I offer, and when? Another category deals with announcements to the spirits. Spirits were told about war raids, the numbers of captives, sicknesses, and other important matters. Evidently the spirits were expected to help in these matters in some way. Questions were also asked about impending journeys, what route to take, and where to spend the night.

Many questions concerned hunting, indicating that this activity occupied an important place in the life of the Shang aristocracy. Some bone inscriptions give the results of the hunt, perhaps to show that the oracle had been correct. One inscription records that 348 animals were killed on one occasion. Another lists a kill of 162 deer, 10 boars, 1 rabbit, and 114 animals of an unidentified species. Elephants are sometimes mentioned.

Li Chi holds that it is no coincidence that an animal style of art flourished at this time. It testifies to the hunting traditions of the ruling Shang group.[9]

The Shang dynasty came to a close when it was overthrown by a western tribe, the Chou, whose dynasty traditionally lasted from 1122 to 221 B.C.[10] Culture patterns established during the Shang period were perpetuated in the Chou dynasty. Indeed, in spite of the many upheavals China has experienced, Chinese culture has shown much continuity from Shang times down to the present.

Sumer

Suggestions for further reading

The best guide to Sumerian culture is Samuel Noah Kramer, who has written several books and articles about Sumer. One of these is a popular, well-illustrated introduction, *Cradle of Civilization* (New York: Time, Inc., 1967). Kramer's list of Sumerian "firsts" appears in *History Begins at Sumer* (New York: Doubleday-Anchor Books, 1959). See also *The Sumerians: Their History, Culture, and Character* (Chicago: University of Chicago Press, 1963). All are well written.

An early, absorbing account of archaeological discovery is C. Leonard Woolley, *Ur of the Chaldees: A Record of Seven Years of Excavation* (Harmondsworth, Middlesex; Penguin Books, 1940). A later, more up-to-date version appears in Leonard Woolley, *Excavations at Ur: A Record of Twelve Years' Work* (London: Ernest Benn, 1955). A learned work which deals more with the later Mesopotamian cultures (Babylonia, Assyria) than with Sumer is A. Leo Oppenheim, *Ancient Mesopotamia: Portrait of a Dead Civilization* (Chicago: University of Chicago Press, 1964). For an imaginative interpretation, contrasting the Egyptian and Mesopotamian civilizations, see Henri Frankfort, *The Birth of Civilization in the Near East* (New York: Doubleday-Anchor Books, 1956).

Egypt

For a brief, well-illustrated popular account, see Lionel Casson, *Ancient Egypt* (New York: Time, Inc., 1965).

A more advanced general survey is available in John A. Wilson, *The Culture of Ancient Egypt* (Chicago: University of Chicago Press, 1951).

A classic early study of Egyptian religion, which contains much textual material, is James Henry Breasted, *Development of Religion and Thought in Ancient Egypt* (New York: Harper & Bros., 1959 [1912]).

A thoughtful, more recent treatment of the same subject is Henri Frankfort, *Ancient Egyptian Religion: An Interpretation* (New York: Harper & Bros., 1961).

---

[9] Li Chi, *op. cit.*, p. 25.

[10] Goodrich gives the dates as circa 1027 to 256 B.C. (L. Carrington Goodrich, *A Short History of the Chinese People* [3d ed.; New York: Harper Torchbooks, 1963], p. 18). Linton, in *The Tree of Culture*, states that the temporal control of the Chou emperors came to an end about 770 B.C. (p. 538).

For interesting information on the Egyptian priesthood, see Serge Sauneron, *The Priests of Ancient Egypt,* trans. Ann Morrissett (New York: Grove Press, 1960).

Ralph Linton's chapter on Egypt in *The Tree of Culture* (New York: Alfred A. Knopf, 1955), pp. 400–424, is also recommended.

Harappa

A good general work on Indian prehistory is Stuart Piggott, *Prehistoric India to 1000 B.C.* (Harmondsworth, Middlesex: Penguin Books, 1950).

More recent surveys may be found in the following works by Mortimer Wheeler, *Early India and Pakistan, to Ashoka* (New York: Frederick A. Praeger, 1959), pp. 93–117. "Ancient India," in Stuart Piggott (ed.), *The Dawn of Civilization: The First World Survey of Human Cultures in Early Times* (New York: McGraw-Hill Book Co., 1961), pp. 229–52; and *Civilizations of the Indus Valley and Beyond* (New York: McGraw-Hill Book Co., 1966).

Shang China

For both the Chinese Neolithic and Shang China, see Kwang-chih Chang, *The Archaeology of Ancient China* (New Haven, Conn.: Yale University Press, 1963).

An early work which is still of value is Herrlee Glessner Creel, *The Birth of China: A Study of the Formative Period of Chinese Civilization* (New York: Frederick Ungar Publishing Co., 1937 [3d printing, 1954]). See also Li Chi, *The Beginnings of Chinese Civilization: Three Lectures Illustrated with Finds at Anyang* (Seattle, Wash.: University of Seattle Press, 1957).

Surveys are available in Ralph Linton, *The Tree of Culture* (New York: Alfred A. Knopf, 1955), pp. 520–37; Kwang-chich Chang, "China," in Robert J. Braidwood and Gordon R. Willey, *Courses toward Urban Life: Archaeological Considerations of Some Cultural Alternates* (Chicago: Aldine Publishing Co., 1962), pp. 193–210; Chester S. Chard, *Man in Prehistory* (New York: McGraw-Hill Book Co., 1969); and William Watson, "A Cycle of Cathay" in Stuart Piggott (ed.), *The Dawn of Civilization: The First World Survey of Human Cultures in Early Times* (New York: McGraw-Hill Book Co., 1961), pp. 253–76. The latter is well illustrated.

Other centers of Old World civilizaton

See Will Durant, *Our Oriental Heritage, The Story of Civilization* (New York: Simon & Schuster, 1954), Part I; Ralph Linton, *The Tree of Culture* (New York: Alfred A. Knopf, 1955); and Edward Bacon (ed.), *Vanished Civilizations of the Ancient World* (New York: McGraw-Hill Book Co., 1963).

Chapter 23

Diffusion and spread of
Old World cultures

Each of the four centers of Old World civilization reviewed in the last chapter—Sumer, Egypt, Harappa, and Shang China—continued to influence surrounding peoples, sending out feelers of trade and communication and engaging in war and diplomacy. For example, from before 3000 B.C. to around 1650 B.C., there was frequent trade between Egypt and Crete, where a wealthy, sophisticated mercantile civilization developed. The Minoan palace at Knossos had over 1,000 rooms, some decorated with lively frescoes. Here again we have the use of bronze tools, a state, class stratification, a writing system, and the other usual attributes of civilization.

Cretan influence was felt on the mainland of Greece, where the Mycenaean civilization developed between around 1700 and 1100 B.C. Impressive stone chambers and tombs were built by the Mycenaeans, in which modern excavators have found fine pottery, gold, and silverware.

Meanwhile, new centers of civilization developed in India and the Far East. Cities appeared in the Ganges Valley in India east of the Indus between 1000 and 500 B.C., and Hastinapura and Kaushambi became centers of power and influence.

The vast steppe regions between Europe and China, formerly something of a barrier between East and West, became more open with the introduction of horseback riding soon after the 14th century B.C. Covered wagons had also been invented by this time, which facilitated a nomadic way of life; pottery models of such wagons have been found in a few sites on the steppes. Archaeological information about some of the equestrian nomads of the steppes comes from mounds or barrows where princely chiefs were buried. The magnificence of the artwork in such burials shows that this was not a "primitive" society; it was clearly in touch with advanced urban centers. Indeed, this kind of pastoralism seems to require some contact with cities and towns, since pastoralists need metal tools, cloth, grain, and other goods which they cannot produce themselves and which they can acquire only through barter, trade, pillage, or domination.

Horseback riding gave the nomads remarkable mobility, enabling them to attack settled communities and, if need be, quickly withdraw. It happened that many pastoral tribes in the western steppes spoke Indo-European languages. Between 1900 and 1000 B.C., waves of Indo-European migrants and raiders moved down into Europe, the Near East, and southern Asia, dominating several areas of advanced civilization. The Aryans moved down across northern India. The Mitanni and Iranians occupied Iraq and Iran. The Hittites entered Anatolia. Later nomadic invasions occurred at the other end of the steppes toward the east, when the cities of China were overrun and temporarily ruled by four great invasions of nomadic tribes: the Ch'i-tan, the Jurchen, the Mongols, and the Manchus.

Bas relief from Angkor Wat, Cambodia.

Although they were tremendously disruptive, the nomadic tribes of the steppes also provided channels for the diffusion of culture traits between East and West.

China continued to be an important source of cultural diffusion. Bronze implements were imported into Japan in the third century B.C., while writing was brought to Japan from Korea in about A.D. 450. There was a sophisticated civilization in Japan by the seventh century A.D. This civilization owed much to China, not only in the realm of material culture but also in the spheres of philosophy and religion. The first Buddhist temples in Japan were built around A.D. 600. Despite much borrowing from China and later from the Western world, Japanese culture remained distinctively different in many ways.

In Southeast Asia there appeared societies which were also influenced by China but which owed still more to Indian civilization, as may be seen in the elaborate monuments of Borobudur in Central Java (late 8th century A.D.) and Angkor Wat in Cambodia (first half of the 12th century A.D.).

The development of ironworking

The development of iron metallurgy had many consequences for the civilizations of the Old World, in some ways quickening, in others destructive. Iron objects have been found in Bronze Age sites, so the metal was known in the period discussed in the preceding three chapters; but iron was not used much until around 1400 B.C., when some tribesmen in Armenia learned how to work the metal more effectively. About 200 years later the knowledge of ironworking began to diffuse rather quickly, so that iron tools finally came to be used not only by agriculturalists but also by many pastoral nomads and hunting-gathering peoples, who often acquired them through trade. The knowledge of ironworking was introduced to Egypt from Asia Minor in the first millennium B.C. and diffused south of the Sahara to tribes in both West and East Africa. But this knowledge never reached Australia, Polynesia, or the New World until the coming of Europeans.

Although the furnaces of early times were unable to liquefy iron, the ore could be reduced to a spongy mass filled with slag, which had to be pounded out while the metal was white hot. Early metallurgists also found that the hardness and flexibility of the metal could be increased by heating it with wood and by repeatedly hammering and bending it. Bellows were used to keep the fire at high temperature.

Once these techniques were mastered, the resulting iron tools proved to be tougher and more useful than those made of bronze. Moreover, iron was much more abundant and readily available. Its use is often said to have had a democratizing effect, for copper and bronze were for the upper classes, but iron was used by the common people. There were iron hoe blades, plowshares, sickles, and knives in Palestine before 1000 B.C. From around 700 B.C., iron axes were used to clear forests in Europe. Greek and

Roman farmers had iron shovels and spades, scythes, hooks, and other implements. Iron shears for shearing sheep, and iron saws, tongs, hammers, and chisels were known from around 500 B.C. Pulleys and lathes were also known in the early Iron Age.

All these useful inventions aided the common man and greatly raised his standard of living. Unfortunately, however, iron was also used for improved weaponry—swords, daggers, and spears. Barbarous tribes thus equipped were able to assault the centers of former Bronze Age civilizations. The Dorian invasion led to Greece's Dark Age (circa 1100–750 B.C.), during which communities reverted to a self-sufficient agrarian and pastoral economy, trade relations were broken, and traditions of literacy lost. During the centuries that followed, new states rose and fell in various parts of the Old World.

Between around 800 B.C. and 300 B.C., there was a distinctive civilization in central Italy, that of the Etruscans, whose craftsmanship in bronze was highly developed. The Etruscans lived in city-states similar to those of Greece and had class stratification, including slavery. They were defeated by the Romans in a final battle in 281 B.C., after which the Romans proceeded to spread their influence and to dominate the Mediterranean and its border regions, until Rome itself collapsed in the fifth century A.D.

During the 6th century B.C., the Persians under Cyrus conquered most of the Near East, so that by the time of Darius (521–485 B.C.) the Persian Empire stretched from the Nile to the Indus Valley, threatening both Greece and the cities of India. An impressive capital city was built at Persepolis. After the Persian Empire was broken up by the Greek invasion of Alexander the Great, a new civilization developed in India at Pataliputra (modern Patna), showing Persian influences in art, techniques of political control, and courtly life.

The Mauryan Empire came to dominate most of the Indian subcontinent by the third century B.C., but then collapsed. Expansion and contraction, with occasional inroads and conquest by barbarians was also the lot of the Chinese Empire. Although there were periods of peace and order, all the Old World empires, Roman, Persian, Indian, and Chinese, experienced much political instability and unrest.

Perhaps this widespread disorder helps to explain the appearance of new trends in Old World religions during the sixth century B.C. In many of these religions, there was a world-renouncing other worldly emphasis, a pessimistic view of life, and a stress on the need for personal salvation. In Buddhism and Jainism, monastic orders were founded to help persons withdraw from wordly concerns and focus on spiritual matters. These religions were often founded by a particular teacher who set forth a body of doctrine about the right way of life. Since these religions generally appeared in the more advanced civilizations, the movements were often

New trends in religion

literate, and the doctrines of the master and his disciples could be put in writing as sacred texts. Most of the sixth-century religions had a strong concern with ethics. This applies to movements in such disparate regions as China, India, the Near East, and Greece. Confucius, Lao-Tse, Gautama Buddha, Mahavira, Zoroaster, Jeremiah, Ezekial, Isaiah, and Pythagoras, seem to have been roughly contemporaneous. They often differed considerably from one another in their teachings, but all were concerned with ethical problems. New religions developed from the teachings of Gautama Buddha (563–483 B.C.); Mahavira (599–527 B.C.), founder of Jainism; Confucius (551–479 B.C.); Lao-Tse (604–531 B.C.), founder of Taoism; and Zoroaster (circa 660–583 B.C.), founder of Zoroastrianism. Some of these religions, such as Buddhism, were proselytizing cults which ultimately influenced millions of persons.

It is instructive that something similar to the Golden Rule appeared in many of these religious traditions. Diffusion may have been involved in some cases; in others it may have been a matter of independent invention. The concept is not always quite the same in different religious contexts; sometimes there are subtle differences. For example, the later Christian statement of the Golden Rule in Matthew 7:12 reads: "So whatever you wish that men would do to you, do so to them; for this is the law and the prophets."[1]

In the *Analects* of Confucius (15:23) we read: "Is there any one maxim which ought to be acted upon throughout one's whole life? Surely the maxim of loving-kindness is such—Do not unto others what you would not they should do unto you."

Here the difference is in the positive phrasing of the Christian text—to do unto others—as opposed to the negative phrasing in the Confucian advice: "Do not unto others what you would not they should do unto you."

Despite such differences in these and in the following texts, the basic idea seems to have been much the same.

A Taoist text: "Regard your neighbor's gain as your gain; and regard your neighbor's loss as your own loss" (*T'ai Shang Kon Ying P'ien*).

A Buddhist text: "Hurt not others with that which pains yourself" (*Udanavarga,* 5:18).

A Jain text: "In happiness and suffering, in joy and grief, we should regard all creatures as we regard our own self, and should therefore refrain from inflicting upon others such injury as would appear undesirable to us if inflicted upon ourselves" (*Yogashtra,* 2:20).

A Hindu text: "This is the sum of duty: do naught to others which if done to thee would cause thee pain" (*Mahabharata,* 5:1517).

A Zoroastrian text: "That nature only is good when it shall not do unto

---

[1] *The Holy Bible, Revised Standard Version* (New York: Thomas Nelson & Sons, 1952).

another whatever is not good for its own self" (*Dadistan-i-dinik*, 94:5).

A Hebrew text: "What is hurtful to yourself do not to your fellow man. That is the whole truth of the Torah and the remainder is but commentary. Go learn it" (*Talmud*).[2]

Six centuries later, similar views were expressed in the teachings of Jesus, and six centuries after that, in the doctrines of Mohammed.

Since Buddhism, Christianity, and Islam were all proselytizing religions, their influence was not confined within one country but swept across large portions of the world. Buddhism originated in India but was carried to Ceylon, Nepal, Tibet, the countries of Southeast Asia, China, and Japan. Christianity originated in the Near East and diffused through Greece, Rome, and the rest of Europe, and later, after the great period of exploration, to the New World and other portions of the globe. Islam spread westward from the Near East across North Africa, temporarily gaining a foothold in Spain, and finding converts among tribesmen of the African savannas. The religion of Mohammed moved northward and eastward to become established in Turkey, Iraq, Iran, large sections of the Indian subcontinent and the Eurasian steppes, and parts of China and most of Indonesia.

Until recently, it was not widely known that civilization had developed in Africa south of the Sahara before the period of European colonization. Most of these African societies had no writing systems, but they did possess other attributes of civilization, such as city life, metallurgy, class stratification, and the development of a state apparatus. Some of the societies had extensive road building; in Kenya there were roads extending for 500 or 600 miles. **Advanced cultures of Africa**

The diffusion of ironworking greatly facilitated the development of culture south of the Sahara. A center for this diffusion from around the third century B.C. was Meroë in the land of Kush on the southern edge of Egypt. Meroë had large iron-smelting works. Since it lay on caravan routes leading to the Abyssinian highlands and ports of the Indian ocean, iron goods were transported eastward, but they may also have moved westward to Nigeria across North Africa. People in the western Sudan, at any rate, were working iron in the last centuries before our era, having learned the process either from a northerly source or from Meroë.

Iron tools helped to open up the forests for settlements and cultivation. They also aided tribes which had them to defeat those which lacked iron weapons. This gave the peoples of Ghana an initial advantage over their

---

[2] For these quotations and others drawn from other religious traditions, see Selwyn Gurney Champion, *The Eleven Religions and Their Proverbial Lore: A Comparative Study* (New York: E. P. Dutton & Co., 1945), p. xviii. Copyright 1945 by E. P. Dutton & Co., Inc., publishers, and reprinted with their permission.

Ife bronze head.

neighbors. Ghana became a centralized state by A.D. 800. Mali, another western savanna state, existed from the 13th to the 17th century. These communities had trade links with North Africa and the Mediterranean by camel caravans. Mali imported silks, damascened blades, and horses from the Mediterranean and Egypt.

Evidence of high civilization comes from the beautiful bronze portrait heads of Ife and Benin, made between the 13th and 18th centuries A.D., in what is now southern Nigeria, by the lost wax process of casting.

While advanced cultures were developing in west Africa, a similar process was under way in east Africa. In the west, commerce was carried via camel caravans across the Sahara, while on the east coast, trade came from across the Indian Ocean from Arabia, India, and even China. In the excavations of one east African port, the archaeologist G. Mathew found some glazed stoneware which had probably come from Thailand, a mass of Chinese porcelain of the Sung to early Ming periods (circa A.D. 1127–1450), some coins from Mesopotamia and Persia, and beads from India.

There was a demand in India for the iron of east Africa, considered superior to Indian iron in the making of swords. Gold was exported to India from southeast Africa.

Most famous of the lost cities of Africa is Zimbabwe, a 60-acre stone-walled inland city in southern Rhodesia, which existed from around the

The conical tower
at the Zimbabwe
ruins.

6th to the 17th century A.D. Less than 200 miles away is the roughly contemporary site of Mapungubwe, which has yielded many objects of plate
gold.[3]

One of the most remarkable and dramatic phases of man's advance
across the globe was the peopling of the Pacific Islands. This was a relatively late migration, having to depend upon the development of adequate
means of navigation, the outrigger canoe, and other seaworthy craft.

**Occupation of
the Pacific
Islands**

---

[3] Evidence about these forgotten civilizations is set forth in Basil Davidson, *The
Lost Cities of Africa* (Boston: Little, Brown & Co., 1959), from which the foregoing
brief summary has been drawn.

(Some Polynesian canoes were over 100 feet long and 6 or more feet wide). The migration had to proceed in easy stages, since the ocean is vast and islands are often hundreds or thousands of miles apart. Some, like New Zealand or Easter Island, were from 1,000 to 1,800 miles away from the nearest other inhabited island.

Where did these people come from? How could they travel for hundreds of miles without sight of land and without knowing where they were going? These questions have been much debated ever since the 17th- and 18th-century discoveries of the Polynesian islands by Europeans. All sorts of explanations have been offered. One, for example, was that the Polynesians were the surviving inhabitants of a former continent which sank below the sea and left only scattered islands above the surface.

One authority, Andrew Sharp, believes that the long voyages of the Polynesians must have been largely accidental, made in canoes blown off course. Without instruments of navigation, the Polynesians had to steer by the sun by day and by the stars at night; but the heavenly bodies were often hidden by clouds. Sea currents were changeable. The early voyagers cannot have set out on deliberate expeditions to distant, unknown islands; they must have been blown there by unexpected storms and then been unable to find their way home again. Sharp gives an example of a late 17th-century canoe which was lost at sea for 70 days and traveled for 1,000 miles. The people in the canoe had no idea where they were.[4]

This seems to be a minority view among anthropologists. Those who disagree with Sharp concede that accidental storm-driven voyages must have often occurred, but they believe that deliberate expeditions also took place. This is suggested by the fact that dogs, pigs, and the various domesticated plants used for food by the Polynesians, were transported to distant islands. The men and women who made these trips had all the necessities for beginning life over again in a new setting. Some of these voyagers were exiles, either going voluntarily or else being driven off by a more powerful faction. While many such parties must have disappeared, some did land on distant islands such as Hawaii and Easter Island.

Also seen as a minority view is the variant of the accidental voyage theory set forth by Thor Heyerdahl. His notion is that some Peruvians were carried out to sea on a raft and drifted to the islands of Polynesia. Instead of coming from Asia, as most anthropologists hold, they came from the New World, according to Heyerdahl. He has presented some cultural and linguistic evidence for this view. For example, the sweet potato is found in both Polynesia and Peru. In the Quechua language of Peru, the sweet potato is called *kumar*, while in Polynesia is is called *umara, kumala,* or some variant. Heyerdahl believes that the sweet potato is an indigenous American plant which was transported to Polynesia by Peruvians. But it

---

[4] Andrew Sharp, *Ancient Voyages in the Pacific* (Harmondsworth, Middlesex: Penguin Books, 1957), p. 15.

could have been the other way around. Several botanists have claimed an Old World origin for the sweet potato, as for most other Polynesian plants. The breadfruit, pandanus, yam, and sugarcane all came from Southeast Asia, while the taro may have originated in southern Asia.[5] The few domesticated animals of Polynesia, the dog, pig, and jungle fowl, also have an Old World origin.

The Malayo-Polynesian language has ties with the Old World, not with the New. It is spoken as far west as the large island of Madagascar near the southeastern coast of Africa and as far east as Easter Island, 2,000 miles from the coast of Peru. The Malayo-Polynesian language stock includes the languages of Polynesia, Micronesia, Melanesia, Indonesia, and the Philippines; and it is related to some languages spoken in Thailand and Taiwan. Thus the evidence of botany, biology and linguistics seems to point to Southeast Asia as a point of origin for the Polynesians. There is similar evidence in material culture. For example, a type of adze used in southern China in Neolithic times, and not found elsewhere in Asia, is very similar to the Polynesian adze.

Robert C. Suggs believes that the expansion of the Shang state in northern China some time before 1600 B.C. was a catalyst which resulted in emigration among coastal peoples in southern China who had a Neolithic horticultural and maritime culture. These emigrants are believed to have settled first in the Philippines, later moving through Melanesia and Papua. The Marianas Islands are thought to have been settled by migrations from the Philippines.

According to radiocarbon dating, New Caledonia and Fiji were inhabited by around 800 B.C. or earlier. The Society Islands and the Marquesas were occupied around the second or third centuries B.C. The Society Islands in the heart of Polynesia may have been the point from which Hawaii, New Zealand, and other islands were settled. Hawaii became inhabited around the second century A.D.; Easter Island in the fourth century, and New Zealand not until around A.D. 1000.[6]

The culture carried through these islands was a Neolithic one based on root crop horticulture, breadfruit, and fishing. Bark cloth clothing was made from the paper mulberry. Evidently this culture was well adapted to its tropical island environment, since population generally built up in the islands. But this led to warfare and sometimes emigration. There was much fighting in Polynesia; the natives of Tonga built forts with moats, walls, and lookout towers, while the Samoans had fortified villages. Chiefs

---

[5] Robert C. Suggs, *The Island Civilizations of Polynesia* (New York: Mentor Books, 1960), p. 23.

[6] The foregoing reconstruction is based on Suggs, *op. cit.* Some quite different radiocarbon dates are given in Edwin N. Ferndon, "Polynesian Origins," in Andrew P. Vayda (ed.), *Peoples and Cultures of the Pacific. An Anthropological Reader* (New York: Natural History Press, 1968), p. 100. According to Ferndon, an early occupation date for Fiji comes as late as 46 B.C.

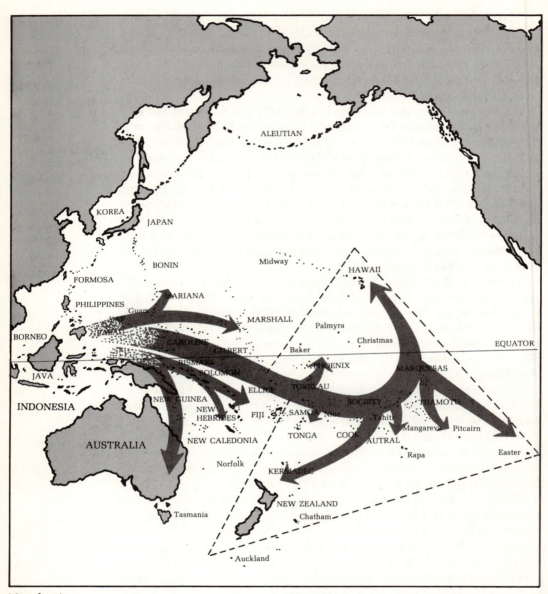

**Map showing
routes in the
peopling of the
Pacific.**

Samoan woman.

acquired high status. Rules of primogeniture determined relative rank. Some chiefs gave expression to their status by directing the building of large ceremonial structures. Megalithic architecture appeared in Tahiti, the Marquesas, Hawaii, and Easter Island.

Ideas of sacredness became attached to chiefs, expressed in the concepts of mana—impersonal supernatural power—and taboo. A chief was believed to be too sacred to be touched by an ordinary person; even his belongings, charged with mana, were taboo to others. This resulted in a certain degree of awe-inspiring isolation from the common people. These are some aspects of the culture encountered by Europeans in the 17th and 18th centuries.

Having advanced so far eastward across the Pacific, did the Polynesians ever go further and reach the New World? It is possible; some scattered Polynesian objects have been found in South America, but their archaeological context has usually been uncertain.[7]

As a general source for information on the diffusion and spread of Old World cultures, see Ralph Linton, *The Tree of Culture* (New York: Alfred A. Knopf, 1955). For Africa, see Basil Davidson, *The Lost Cities of Africa* (Boston: **Suggestions for further reading**

---

[7] See Suggs, *op. cit.*, pp. 206–11.

Little, Brown & Co., 1959). For Polynesia, see Robert C. Suggs, *The Island Civilizations of Polynesia* (New York: Mentor Books, 1960), and Andrew P. Vayda (ed.), *Peoples and Cultures of the Pacific: An Anthropological Reader* (New York: Natural History Press, 1968).

On the sixth century B.C., "new trends in religion," see under Historic Religion in Robert N. Bellah, "Religious Evolution," in William A. Lessa and Evon Z. Vogt (eds.), *Reader in Comparative Religion: An Anthropological Approach* (2d ed.; New York: Harper & Row, Publishers, 1965), pp. 73–87.

Cultural evolution in
the New World

Chapter 24

The development of culture in the New World

This chapter concerns the evolution from a hunting-gathering to a food-producing level in the New World, a development which in many ways was parallel to that of the Old World. It culminated in sedentary village life characterized by agriculture, weaving, and pottery making. The following chapter deals with the advanced civilizations of Mesoamerica and Peru, which shared many features similar to those of the Bronze Age civilizations of the Old World.

Man entered the New World with a Palaeolithic culture. His discoveries of agriculture, weaving and pottery were probably independent inventions for the most part, although there are some anthropologists who would attribute New World pottery to diffusion from the Old World.

Man was certainly in the New World by 10,000 B.C.; he may have come much earlier—between 40,000 and 20,000 B.C. Most anthropologists are in agreement that the probable route of entry was via a former land bridge in the Bering Straits region.

The Bering Straits land bridge

Siberia and Alaska are not far apart. On a clear day one may see the Siberian shore from the heights of Cape Prince of Wales, Alaska. St. Lawrence Island, Big Diomede Island (Russian), and Little Diomede Island (American) form stepping stones in between. During a large part of the Pleistocene, this area was dry land. With water being locked up in glaciers, there came a lowering of sea levels. When the Wisconsin glacier reached its maximum, 40,000 years ago, the sea level is estimated to have dropped by as much as 460 feet, leaving a corridor 1,300 miles wide, wider than present-day Alaska.[1]

This was not a temporary land bridge; it lasted for several thousand years, during which time many animals and plants moved from Siberia to Alaska, while others passed in the reverse direction. Among the first animals to move from Asia to America were various kinds of rodents, followed later by larger mammals, such as mastodon, mammoth, bison, moose, elk, mountain sheep and goats, camels, bears, and horses. The human beings who unwittingly entered a new continent must have been hunting these animals. There were probably many bands of such migrants. It seems likely that their movements into the interior of the continent were sometimes held up by ice sheets; if so, they still had about 200,000 square miles of hunting land in Alaska in which to roam about. Some ice-free corridors to the south appeared during the latter part of the last period of glaciation. Thus the newcomers were able to make their way southward, some probably following the eastern flanks of the Rocky Mountains, while others traveled between the Rocky and Cascade Mountains to the Pacific Coast, to California and Mexico. Some groups moved eastward, fanning out across North America. Others continued to head south through Mexico, the Isthmus of Panama, and into South America. There were hunting people living at Tierra del Fuego, the bottommost tip of South America, in the eighth millennium B.C.

The new migrants were all of the *Homo sapiens sapiens* stage; no remains of a *Homo erectus* or of Neandertaloid types have been found in the Americas. We know that man did not evolve in the New World from simpler forms. There are no apes in the Americas, and all the finds of australopithecines and *Homo erectus* have been made in the Old World.

The first migrants

The first migrants from Asia must have brought with them a rather simple Palaeolithic material culture, perhaps including scrapers and chopping tools like those used in eastern Asia. They probably knew how to make fire and may have woven mats and made baskets.

One possible clue to the content of the early American cultures lies in the fact that there are many "biperipheral" traits found to be largely restricted to the most northerly groups of North America on the one hand and to the more southerly tribes of South America on the other. They are missing in the central areas from Mesoamerica to Peru, where the higher civilizations developed and where the early biperipheral traits were apparently displaced by later patterns. Among the biperipheral traits are folklore motifs, such as tales of a rolling-head monster, and various games,

---

[1] William G. Haag, "The Bering Strait Land Bridge," *Scientific American*, Vol. 206, No. 1 (1962), pp. 112–23.

including lacrosse, hoop and pole, ring and pin, and multiple two-sided dice. Other items include fire making with pyrites and flint, use of fish glue, sewed bark vessels, smoke signaling, and the taking of scalps. There are also various similarities in puberty rites, religious concepts, and musical styles. Some of these parallels in extreme northern North America and far southern South America may be due to later independent inventions, but it seems likely that many of them are survivals from very early times.[2]

We gather, then, that the early migrants in the New World were hunting-gathering peoples with simple technologies but having many nonmaterial culture patterns which have left no permanent traces in the archaeological record. These early Americans spoke many different languages, or else their languages eventually became very differentiated through isolation, for it has been estimated that by 1492 there were about 2,000 mutually unintelligible languages spoken in the Americas. There seem to be no clear-cut relationships between any of these languages and the languages spoken in the Old World. This linguistic differentiation suggests a very long time span for the occupation of the New World.

The Big-Game Hunters

The first clearly distinguishable culture in the New World is what Willey has called the Big-Game Hunting Tradition. This is not necessarily the first culture to have appeared on the scene; it was probably preceded by what Krieger has called the Pre-Projectile Point stage.[3]

In his review of the archaeological evidence Willey acknowledges that such a stage probably existed, but he finds that the evidence is not adequate to support it, "beyond reasonable doubt."[4] This account will follow Willey's presentation.

The Big-Game Hunting Tradition was organized around the hunting of herding animals, particularly in the western plains. The characteristic tools were projectile points of the Clovis, Sandia, Folsom, and Plano types. Clovis, Sandia, and Folsom are sites in New Mexico where the characteristic projectile points were discovered. These points have usually been found at kill sites, sometimes imbedded in the bones of extinct animals. The time of origin of this tradition is uncertain, but it may date back to

---

[2] See A. L. Kroeber, *Anthropology* (New York: Harcourt, Brace, & Co., 1948), p. 781; and Betty J. Meggers, "North and South American Cultural Connections and Convergences," in Jesse D. Jennings and Edward Norbeck (eds.), *Prehistoric Man in the New World* (Chicago: University of Chicago Press, 1964), p. 514.

[3] Alex D. Krieger, "Early Man in the New World," in Jennings and Norbeck (eds.), *op. cit.*, pp. 23–81.

[4] Gordon R. Willey, *An Introduction to American Archaeology;* Vol. 1: *North and Middle America* (Englewood Cliffs, N.J.: Prentice-Hall, 1966), p. 37.

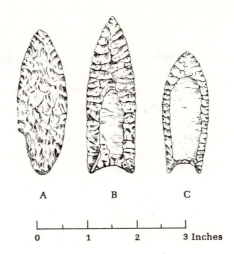

Projectile points.
A) Sandia point.
B) Clovis fluted point.
C) Folsom fluted point.

A   B   C

0   1   2   3 Inches

about 14,000 B.C. Most radiocarbon tests for such sites give a date of around 10,000 or 9,000 B.C. The tradition seems to have declined after 8,000 B.C. with the advent of warmer, drier weather.

Clovis points were used to tip spears, not arrows. They are associated with mammoth, while the later and smaller Folsom fluted points have been found in association with extinct forms of bison. Other extinct animals hunted by the Big-Game Hunters included mastodon, camel, and horse. Although most of the sites have been found in the Great Plains and Southwest areas, fluted points have also turned up in many parts of eastern North America. Fluted points are characteristic New World artifacts; they are not found in Eurasia and must have been developed here.

The Big-Game Hunting Tradition was a specialized one, depending on the presence of large mammals. When these animals began to disappear, either through their extermination by hunters, through climatic changes, or other causes, new bases of subsistence had to be found.

Contemporaneous with the Big-Game Hunting Tradition was what Willey has called the Old Cordilleran Tradition of the Pacific Northwest. This was based on a more diversified way of life involving hunting, fishing, and plant collecting. Overlapping in time with the two preceding traditions was a Desert Tradition, which dated from around 8000 B.C. and persisted in some groups down to historic times. It was adapted to arid regions in the Great Basin, the Southwest, and Mesoamerica.

Social units in these areas were small, consisting of extended families including men, their wives, and children. A pattern of cyclic wandering was common, depending on the ripening of plants or the availability of

Other New World traditions before 2000 B.C.

animals in different valleys and uplands. Material possessions were scanty, the most important being the basket and the flat milling stone.

In the eastern Woodlands, the Big-Game Hunting Tradition gave way around 8000 B.C. to the Archaic, in which subsistence was based on small-game hunting, fishing, and the collection of wild plants. Polished stone tools such as grooved axes and adzes were used for working wood. Carved and polished bone ornaments were made and stone vessels used. The Archaic culture shows a greater variety of tools and more sophistication than that of the Big-Game Hunters.

The foregoing traditions covered most parts of aboriginal North America in the period before 2000 B.C. This was before the development of horticulture and settled village life; the people were hunters and collectors, nomadic or seminomadic.

Village life without horticulture did develop in the Northwest Coast, although it is not certain when this began. Around 5000 B.C. some Old Cordilleran groups which had specialized in river salmon fishing moved to the coast and took up maritime hunting as well. Between 5000 and 1000 B.C., they acquired a series of traditional Northwest Coast traits, including polished stone tools, ground slate weapons, and stone sculpture.

The beginnings of horticulture

Village life based on horticulture originated in Mesoamerica about 2000 B.C. Very loosely, Mesoamerica may be said to include the territory from northern Mexico to northwestern Costa Rica. In this area, between around 7000 and 2000 B.C., there were many groups with variants of the Desert Tradition, who hunted small game and collected wild plants. Very gradually plant collection was transformed into cultivation. Two archaeological sites involving cave deposits best document this transition: one in the mountains of Tamaulipas on the northeastern fringe of Mesoamerica, and the other in the Tehuacán Valley of southern Puebla in the heart of Mesoamerica. The two regions are about 400 miles apart. Metates and manos for grinding seeds were found at both sites. These became standard equipment used in grinding corn for tortillas.

It is interesting that the same plants do not appear to have been domesticated in the same periods at these two sites. There was wild maize (Indian corn) at Puebla in 5000 B.C.; but there was no maize in Tamaulipas until around 2500 B.C. Pumpkins were cultivated at Tamaulipas between 7000 and 5000 B.C., but do not appear at Puebla until 3000 B.C. Squash was known in Puebla in 6000 B.C. but not until 2000 B.C. at Tamaulipas. It seems likely that different plants began to be cultivated by different groups. Later, with the development of Mesoamerican culture and increased interaction between communities, there was an interchange of cultivated plant species. Finally, a complex of plants became widely diffused, particularly maize, pumpkins, squashes, beans, chili pepper, tobacco, and the bottle gourd. Cotton appeared at both Puebla and Tamaulipas around 1700 B.C.[5]

The principal plants developed in Neolithic times in the Old World—barley, wheat, millet, and rice—did not appear in the New World, where the main crops, instead, were maize, beans, and squash. These plants and the techniques of their cultivation were quite different from the plants and methods of cultivation in the Old World.

This shows that plant domestication was discovered by the American Indians, not taught to them by some superior invaders from abroad.

It is true that three New World plants are found also in the Old World: cotton, sweet potato, and the gourd. Some proponents of trans-Pacific diffusion have argued that cotton must have been brought across the sea to the Americas in pre-Columbian times. This cannot be ruled out as a possibility, but it has not been proven.

Sweet potatoes were grown in Polynesia and Melanesia as well as in the New World. Some authorities believe that the plant originated in the New World and spread to the Pacific Islands; others claim that the diffusion worked the other way around.

The early date of the gourd at Tamaulipas would seem to rule out the possibility of trans-Pacific diffusion. Gourds may have drifted across the ocean in pre-Columbian times.

Mesoamerica was not the only center of New World domestication. Bitter manioc was cultivated in tropical Venezuela and adjacent regions. Its consumption depended upon techniques for squeezing poisonous prussic acid from the roots—another original American Indian invention. In the Andean highlands potatoes were grown. But Mesoamerica was the center from which the important maize-beans-squash complex diffused to both North and South America. Maize had spread to the North American Southwest by around 2500 B.C. and to Peru by around 1500 B.C. Within 2000 years, maize was being cultivated from Canada to Florida in the eastern half of North America, as well as in the Southwest, and along the western coast of South America as far south as northwestern Argentina.

An important difference between Old World and New World agriculture is that it was not accompanied in the New World by much domestication of animals. A few animals were domesticated in the Americas: guinea pigs and muscovy duck in Peru, turkeys and bees in Mexico. Llamas were employed as pack animals in Peru; their wool and that of the vicuña and alpaca were used for textiles. Dogs had probably been brought over by emigrants from Asia.

There were no indigenous wild horses or cows to be domesticated in the

---

[5] The main research concerning the food plants at these sites has been done by Richard S. MacNeish.

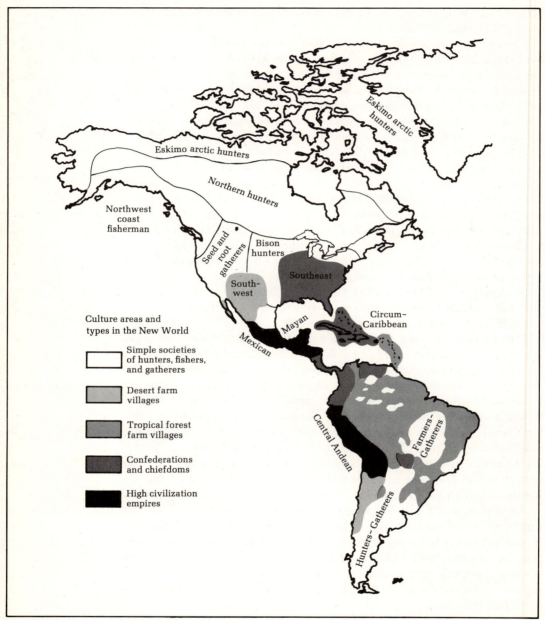

Culture areas and
types in the New World

Simple societies
of hunters, fishers,
and gatherers

Desert farm
villages

Tropical forest
farm villages

Confederations
and chiefdoms

High civilization
empires

Eskimo arctic hunters

Eskimo arctic
hunters

Northern hunters

Northwest
coast
fisherman

Seed and
root
gatherers

Bison
hunters

Southeast

South-
west

Circum-
Caribbean

Mayan

Mexican

Central Andean

Farmers–
Gatherers

Hunters–Gatherers

Map showing
culture areas and
types of society in
pre-Columbian
North and South
America.

New World. The horses of Pleistocene times had become extinct; these animals were not known to American Indians until their introduction by Europeans. American buffalos do not seem to be amenable to domestication. As a result, the Indians had no animals to serve for traction, and they developed no wheeled vehicles or plows. We have seen earlier that animal-drawn plows were important in increasing food productivity in the Old World. Fortunately, the American crops were of a sort that did not require plow cultivation; digging sticks were usually sufficient.

Housing

Thanks to the development of plant cultivation, permanent housing became possible, and we find some understandable parallels to Old World architecture, based on the limitation of possibilities. Only certain kinds of materials are useful in building construction, and there is a limited number of functionally effective ways in which they can be put together. Such features as doors and lintels in stone and adobe houses are understandable features from this point of view. Inca houses were generally rectangular, thatched, and gable roofed. They usually had no windows, but some late Inca buildings had them. The Pueblo Indians of the North American Southwest built closely massed apartment-house-like structures of adobe, stone, and wood which resembled the houses of Çatal Hüyük, while the Iroquois Indians of the eastern Woodlands of North America constructed longhouses which bore some similarities to those of the Neolithic Danubian peasants of eastern Europe. As in the Old World, the builders in each area were limited by the materials at hand. Rectangular adobe bricks were units of building construction in coastal Peru. The only people to use lime mortar were the Maya of Mesoamerica.

In the next chapter, we shall see that still more parallels to Old World architecture appeared in the higher centers of civilization in Mesoamerica and Peru, where city life developed.

Weaving

Domesticated cotton was used for textiles in Peru by 2000 B.C. The preceramic site of Huaca Prieta, dated at around that time, gives evidence of finger weaving; the loom was not yet known. By about a thousand years later, mantles uncovered at Paracas show that the loom had been invented. Looms and spindle whorls for spinning were also used throughout Mesoamerica. The most widespread form of New World loom was a belt or backstrap loom, in which the horizontal or slightly tilted loom was attached to the weaver by a belt around her back, while the other end was tied to a post or a tree.

The textiles of the Aztecs and Maya have not remained down to the present, but judging from paintings on pottery and murals and from contemporary descriptions by Spanish conquistadores, they must have been beautiful.

Because of the dryness of the climate, much Peruvian weaving has been preserved and may be seen in museums throughout the world. Peruvian textiles show impressive workmanship of great variety. The Peruvians had one advantage over all other American Indians: the use of wool obtained from llamas, alpacas, and vicuñas. The highlanders in the Andes, where the weather can be very cold, had a practical motivation to prepare warm clothing. As already noted, cotton was also known from early times. Both men and women wove in Peru, but the finest weaving was made by "Chosen Women" who were specialists in this art (see page 293). Among the Aztecs and Maya, spinning, dyeing, and weaving were all women's work.

The use of the loom spread through the areas of higher civilization in the New World—to Bolivia and Ecuador and even to some of the tropical forest peoples, such as the Jivaro. Weaving also diffused to the Pueblo area in the North American Southwest. Apparently as an independent invention, weaving developed among the tribes of the Northwest Coast of North America, who devised a suspended-warp upright loom. Textiles were made from spruce roots, wild hemp, and cedar bark. So-called "Chilkat blankets" were made of mountain goat wool spun and twined over a core of cedar bark string.

Belt loom, Mexico.

(Above) Caddoan style jars from Arkansas.

(Right) plate from Cocle, Panama.

(Below, left) Nazca B pottery, Peru; (right) coast Tiahuanaco pottery, Peru.

Pottery

What may be the oldest known pottery in the New World comes from Valdivia, Ecuador. Willey gives it a radiocarbon date of 3000 to 2500 B.C. Pottery from Puerto Hormigas on the Caribbean coast of Colombia is dated at around 2900 B.C. The earliest pottery in Mesoamerica is from 2300–1500 B.C., while in Peru pottery appears at some sites at around 1200 B.C.

It is interesting that the pottery from Valdivia, Ecuador, has been claimed to resemble Jomon pottery from Japan. Estrada and Meggers include this item in a complex of traits suggesting trans-Pacific diffusion.[6] However, Estrada and Meggers give a later radiocarbon date for this site than does Willey: 2500–1800 B.C. If they are right about the similarities to Jomon pottery, and if Willey's early radiocarbon date is also correct, this might mean that the idea of pottery making was an importation from abroad and not an American Indian independent invention. This is a minority view, one not shared by most anthropologists. Gordon F. Ekholm, who supports the trans-Pacific hypothesis, has argued that pottery making is a complex technical process which is not likely to have been invented more than once.[7] As against this view, which implies a lack of inventiveness on the part of the American Indians, there may be cited the list of inventions which appeared only in the New World before the coming of Columbus. Nordenskiöld and others have drawn up a lengthy inventory of such items, which include the following, among others: the hammock, the method of removing poisonous prussic acid from manioc and thus producing edible tapioca, the Peruvian whistling jar, the cigar, the cigarette, the tobacco pipe, the enema syringe, the rubber ball, and the toboggan.[8] If the Indians could invent these things which were not invented anywhere else, they could probably have invented the items in dispute, such as pottery. We have already seen that they domesticated uniquely New World plants, such as maize, potatoes, and pumpkins. To these may be added tomatoes, peanuts, lima beans, kidney beans, cacao (for chocolate), agave (for pulque), and avocado. American Indians discovered the properties of coca (for cocaine) and rubber. So they were not uninventive.

Pottery making does, however, seem to have diffused from Siberia to North America between 3000 and 1000 B.C. By the latter date Woodland peoples in eastern North America were using conoidal-based, cord-marked unpainted pots just like those used in Siberia. Other items, such as the

[6] Emilio Estrada and Betty J. Meggers, "A Complex of Traits of Probable Transpacific Origin on the Coast of Ecuador," *American Anthropologist,* Vol. 63, No. 5 (1961), pp. 913–39.

[7] Gordon F. Ekholm "Transpacific Contacts," in Jennings and Norbeck (eds.), *op. cit.,* p. 495.

[8] Erland Nordenskiöld, *Modifications in Indian Customs Through Inventions and Loans,* Comparative Ethnological Studies, No. 8 (1930), pp. 23–24.

adze and harpoon, are believed to have diffused from Siberia at around the same time. Thus we have at least two areas of pottery diffusion in the New World, one in the peripheral northern and eastern zone, and one in the centers of high civilization and their surrounding fringes. None of this pottery was shaped on the potter's wheel, an invention not made by the American Indians. But much American pottery is very beautiful, particularly the strikingly painted Nazca ware of Peru and the sophisticated ceramics of the Maya and the North American Southwest.

Suggestions for further reading

The best and most up-to-date general treatment of New World archaeology is Gordon R. Willey, *An Introduction to American Archaeology;* Vol. 1: *North and Middle America* (Englewood Cliffs, N.J.: Prentice-Hall, 1966). Vol. II of this well-written and finely illustrated book will deal with South America.

Two other works dealing with some of the same material, both consisting of articles by various specialists, are also recommended: Jesse D. Jennings and Edward Norbeck (eds.), *Prehistoric Man in the New World* (Chicago: University of Chicago Press, 1964); and Robert F. Spencer, Jesse D. Jennings *et al., The Native Americans* (New York: Harper & Row, Publishers, 1965). The latter work combines ethnographic description with archaeological summaries. See also William T. Sanders and Joseph Marino, *New World Prehistory: Archaeology of the American Indian* (Englewood Cliffs, N.J.: Prentice-Hall, 1970).

For a good work of popularization, directed to the general reader and well illustrated, see Jonathan Norton Leonard and the Editors of Time-Life Books, *Ancient America* (New York: Time, Inc., 1967).

The present chapter has followed Willey in many particulars, but other viewpoints should also be taken into account. See particularly Alex D. Krieger, "Early Man in the New World," and Gordon R. Ekholm, "Transpacific Contacts," both in Jennings and Norbeck (eds.), *op. cit.,* pp. 23–84 and 489–510.

Chapter 25

Characteristics of the higher centers
of civilization: Mesoamerica and Peru

This chapter will focus on the higher centers of civilization in Meso-america and Peru, particularly those of the Aztecs, Maya, and Incas. These three civilizations were quite different from one another in certain respects, just as were the civilizations of Sumer, Egypt, and Harappa. Nevertheless, like their Old World Bronze Age counterparts, the New World civilizations shared some common features. Some of these have already been discussed: permanent settlements based on agriculture, certain developments in architecture, highly skilled weaving, and finely made pottery.

Each of these centers saw the establishment of city life characterized by various features which were remarkably similar to those of the Old World: division of labor and class stratification, increased trade and communication, the appearance of a dominant priesthood-intelligentsia, emergence of a state, enlargement of the scale of warfare, and advances in certain spheres of knowledge, particularly systems for recording information, mathematics, and astronomical and calendrical calculations.

Advances in agriculture

Most early cultivation was of the slash-and-burn variety, depending upon adequate rainfall. But irrigation systems were developed in coastal Peru about 2,000 years ago, making it possible for farmers to raise two or more crops a year. Peruvian farmers also made use of guano—bird droppings—for fertilizer. In the highlands, terraces with strong retaining walls were built to provide level fields and to prevent erosion. This more productive kind of cultivation can be called agriculture rather than horticulture.

Irrigation was also practiced in the Valley of Mexico and in the North American Southwest in pre-Columbian times. A device used by the Aztecs to increase food productivity was the *chinampa*, a man-made islet composed of reeds, mud, and rotting vegetation which supported beds of topsoil. Although *chinampas* have been called "floating gardens," they were anchored by willow trees planted at their edges. *Chinampas* provided excellent soil, allowing for three harvests a year.

Through such devices as irrigation, terracing, and *chinampas*, agricultural productivity increased, allowing for greater concentrations of population.

Metallurgy

As far back as around 3000 B.C., there were Indians in northern Wisconsin making spearpoints, knives, and other objects from cold-hammered copper; but this was not metallurgy, for the metal was not smelted.

The first true metallurgy in the New World was developed in Peru by around 700 B.C. In the Chavín period various gold ornaments were made, including pendants, tweezers, crowns, pins, and spoons. The Peruvians learned how to make bronze, something not attained by the Aztecs, although knowledge of metallurgy diffused from South America to Mesoamerica. Platinum, which was not worked in Europe until A.D. 1730, was made into ornaments by the Indians of Colombia and Ecuador. The American Indians did not have an Iron Age.

The lost wax process of casting, which was known in both Mesopotamia and Shang China, was practiced in Peru, Central America, and Mexico. This is a relatively complex invention, since it depends upon a prior knowledge of the properties of wax, fired clay, and molten metal. Let us say that you wish to make a dagger; first you make a dagger of wax and then coat it with clay, leaving a hole to the outside. The clay is then fired and turned into pottery; the wax melts and pours out through the hole, leaving a dagger-shaped hollow in the interior. Molten metal is then poured in through the aperture. It fills up all the available space and takes on the dagger shape. After the metal has cooled and hardened, the pottery mold is broken; the dagger may then be filed and polished.

The Incas were able to make remarkable objects of gold and silver, including life-size gold statues of their rulers and replicas of local plants and animals in gold. Unfortunately, the Spaniards melted most of this artwork down into gold bullion.

Trade and communications

Generally, trade increased as culture advanced. But compared with Mesoamerica, there was relatively little trade in Peru, despite the Incas' excellent system of roads. The roads were built for military purposes, so that the army could strike quickly. The main road from north to south served no economic purpose; most of the trade was between coast and highland. Cotton and fish from the coast were exchanged for llama wool and potatoes from the highlands. But private travel and trade were restricted under the Incas. There was no standard medium of exchange, and most of the barter that took place was in regional markets.

Although movement and trade were limited, some systems of communication were highly developed in Peru. Relay runners were stationed at intervals along the highways, so that the rulers at Cuzco could be quickly informed of any disturbance in the provinces. Watch-fire signals were also used.

Mesoamerica did not have as good road systems as Peru, but there was more trade, partly because of the great ecological diversity of the region. Different valleys, mountains, and lowlands produced different kinds of products.

Much Mesoamerican trade took place in connection with temples. Wolf writes:

The temple centers became veritable storehouses of the gods, where costly produce accumulated in the service of the supernatural. Thus at Teotihuacán, we find shells imported from the two coasts, precious stones from Guerrero, rubber balls from the southern Gulf, mica from Oaxaca, feathers from the southern lands of the quetzal bird, and cotton from Morelos or from Veracruz.[1]

Temple centers were also marketplaces. Some, like the market at Tenochtitlán, the Aztec capital, were very large; the latter was judged by Cortés to serve 60,000 buyers and sellers daily. Since produce sold at the market was taxed, one was not allowed to buy and sell apart from the marketplace. The market had judges to decide disputes. There were separate sections or streets for different wares: pottery, herbs, game birds, textiles, and jewelry. Slaves were also sold. As in Peru, there was no money, and most exchange was by barter. But cacao (chocolate) beans were used to some extent as a medium of exchange, as were lengths of cloth. In the Maya area a slave was worth 100 cacao beans.

Among the Aztecs, merchants known as *pochteca* formed a special favored class. They lived in a separate quarter of the city and worshipped a god of their own. The Maya had a similar merchant class, not subject to taxation and having other special privileges. They were not concerned with the trade of the marketplace but with long-distance trade in luxury goods, slaves, and valued raw materials such as animal skins, precious stones, and the feathers of wild birds.

The Maya seem to have done more trading by sea than did the Aztecs or Peruvians. In 1502 Columbus saw a Maya trading canoe that was 40 feet long; its merchants were engaged in exchanging obsidian blades, copper hatchets, and textiles for parrot feathers and crystals at an island 20 miles from Honduras.

---

[1] Eric R. Wolf, *Sons of the Shaking Earth* (Chicago: University of Chicago Press, 1959), p. 81.

The Aztecs at Tenochtitlán made much use of dugout canoes for transportation, since the capital city was a kind of Venice, built out on the lake, with canals taking the place of streets. "Not a wheel turned or a pack animal neighed; transport was on the backs of men or in the bottoms of boats."[2]

The Aztecs had no use for boats larger than dugouts, for they were not seafaring people. Like the Incas, the Aztecs had a courier system. Through their reports, Moctezuma was able to receive a steady stream of information about the Spaniards who landed on the coast, long before Cortés' men arrived at Tenochtitlán.

Most hunting-gathering societies in North and South America had shamans or medicine men rather than priests. The shaman is generally concerned with individual crises, such as sickness; he attempts to make contact with the supernatural world through trance, magic, divination, or other means. The priest, who is engaged in ritual of a more collective, organized variety, is an official of a cult or church from which his authority derives. Priesthood is associated with higher centers of civilization. **Priesthood**

Julian H. Steward has made this contrast for the societies of South America. On the one hand, there were the hunting-gathering tribes of Brazil, the Gran Chaco, Patagonia, and Chile, and the farming tribes of the Amazonian forests. On the other hand, there were the more advanced civilizations of the Andes and of the Circum-Caribbean area which included Central America, Colombia, Venezuela, and the Greater Antilles; these societies had large settlements characterized by irrigation agriculture, public works, and religious centers.

Of the religion of the former group, Steward writes:

Its principal manifestations came in crisis situations—birth, puberty, death, sickness, and at other times when malevolent influences threatened the individual. These primitive tribes had little group worship, or cult religion, because economic and social activities provided few occasions for communal or collective projects that were of concern to the group.[3]

In the more advanced societies a priesthood emerged as an integrating factor, and patterns of group worship appeared. A similar development occurred in Mesoamerica, where the emergence of the priest has been dated at 900 B.C., when the first large-scale religious structures were built.[4] The pioneers in this development seem to have been the Olmecs, creators of a curious, distinctive art style that was widespread and influential in Mesoamerica. The main center of the Olmecs was at La Venta, an island

---

[2] George C. Vaillant, *The Aztecs of Mexico: Origin, Rise and Fall of the Aztec Nation* (Baltimore, Md.: Penguin Books, 1950), p. 218.

[3] Julian H. Steward, "South American Indian Religions," in Vergilius Ferm (ed.), *Ancient Religions* (New York: Philosophical Library, 1950), p. 287.

[4] Wolf, *op. cit.*, p. 70.

Olmec head.

in a marshy area near the Gulf of Mexico. Here, in 1939, archaeologists found four huge heads carved out of stone and a clay pyramid 110 feet high. There is no native stone on the island; the nearest source is 80 miles away. Since some of the stone heads weighed 40 tons, it is evident that some dominant leadership was in charge of this ambitious feat of engineering and sculpture. The island was too small to have supported many people; it was evidently mainly a ceremonial center. This was one of the first such centers in the archaeological record.

Ultimately, ceremonial centers of similar type appeared throughout Mesoamerica, all under the supervision of priest-intellectuals who were set apart from the rest of the people by distinctive dress and special knowledge. Part of this special knowledge was a system of writing first developed by the Olmecs or Zapotecs, ancestral to the Maya script. As mentioned above, ceremonial centers were associated with trade; they were also market centers. Priests were involved in economic affairs in another respect; as specialists in calendrical knowledge they could advise farmers when to plant or harvest crops. And, of course, they led the rituals and sacrifices which persuaded the gods to bring rainfall, fertility, and success in war. The priests were thus high-ranking specialists whose services became indispensable and who were able to maintain a dominant position in the societies of Mesoamerica for many hundreds of years.

The pattern of human sacrifice was particularly developed in the Aztec area. The Aztecs believed that their gods had to be offered human hearts in order to keep the universe going. This provided motivation for wars and raids on neighboring tribes; warriors captured were sacrificed. Sometimes thousands of victims were killed at a time. This practice understandably made the Aztecs unpopular with their neighbors, who were quite willing to ally themselves with Cortés, when the Spaniards appeared on the scene.

The Inca religion in Peru was state supported. The priests were fed by the labor of the common people; special storehouses were set apart to supply the religious order. The priesthood formed a hierarchy, at the top of which was a High Priest who was always a brother, uncle, or other close relative of the emperor. As in Mesoamerica, church and state were closely interlinked.

There were priestesses, as well as priests. Government officials visited each village from time to time to select some of the more attractive girls of about 10 years of age for special training and government service. Known as "Chosen Women," these girls filled various roles. Some became concubines of the Emperor or were given by him to members of the nobility as secondary wives. Some became priestesses of the sun cult and weavers attached to temples, and some were killed in sacrifice. The Incas did not, however, indulge in large-scale human sacrifice as the Aztecs did. They took it out on the llamas instead. A white llama was offered every morning at the Temple of the Sun in Cuzco. On special ceremonial occasions hundreds or thousands of llamas were killed. One form of Inca divination was based on the examination of entrails of sacrificed llamas.

A curious parallel with Christian practices was the Inca custom of confession of sins to priests, who exacted penance, usually a period of fasting or prayer. After penance was completed, the sinner washed in a stream to purify himself.

Cities

A ceremonial center which developed into a city flourished between A.D. 300 and 700 at Teotihuacán, 30 miles northeast of present-day Mexico City. It seems to have been a planned city, with long, straight avenues paved with hard cement; it covered nearly 7 square miles. At its heart was the huge Pyramid of the Sun, flanked by two smaller pyramids. There were also palaces decorated with frescoes, some of which still survive. It has been estimated that Teotihuacán could have had a population of 50,000 or more.

Teotihuacán collapsed and was looted and burned at around A.D. 700. But cities continued to be built in Mexico. One of them was Casas Grandes in the present-day north Mexican state of Chihuahua. Casas Grandes is of interest to archaeologists because it has been precisely dated by tree ring dating techniques at between A.D. 850 and 1336. This city is believed to have been a frontier outpost against invading tribes like those that destroyed Teotihuacán. It was also a trading center handling imports

Pyramid of the Sun,
Teotihuacán

Bas relief at
Teotihuacán.

such as turquoise from New Mexico and Arizona. Casas Grandes suffered the same fate as Teotihuacán; between A.D. 1310 and 1340 it was sacked and burned by unknown enemies.

Tenochtitlán, capital of the Aztecs, was built later and was still flourishing when Cortés and his men reached it. Several descriptions by the conquistadores attest to the city's magnificence. It had a population of about 300,000. Aztec cities tended to have a rectangular form, with a central plaza containing a temple and marketplace.

Pyramid of the
Moon, Teotihuacán.

Pyramid at
Xochicalco.

Most Maya ceremonial centers were not heavily populated. Since the farmers practiced slash-and-burn horticulture, they could not usually congregate in dense settlements. But some cities seem to have developed in relatively late times. One was Mayapán, founded in the 10th century A.D. and abandoned before the Spanish conquest, about A.D. 1450. An early Spanish report said it had been a walled city, like those of Spain, containing 60,000 dwellings, but a more recent estimate places the number of dwellings at about 2,000 or more. The walls were of dry-laid stone about 12 feet high, 9 to 12 feet thick, and 5½ miles long. The area within the city covered about 2½ square miles. According to Morley, the population must have totaled over 15,000. There were other walled cities in the Maya area, Tulum and Xelha being examples. One of the largest and oldest cities was Tikal, which contained enormous pyramids; another important center was Chichén Itzá in Yucatán, which showed much Mexican ("Toltec") influence.

Cities were also built in pre-Columbian Peru. At around A.D. 1000, there was an immense city on the coast, the Chimú capital of Chanchan. It covered over 8 square miles. Even more than the other cities mentioned, it shows evidence of planning; the long, straight streets intersect at right angles. Chanchan was divided into 10 subunits or wards, surrounded by high walls. There were reservoirs, pyramids, and other impressive structures. Chanchan was built before the rise of the Incas to power and was contemporaneous with the Incas after they became established. It is now a deserted ruin. The Incas built their own capital in the highlands at Cuzco, a city which is still thriving.

There seem to be many parallels between New World architecture and the architecture of the Old World Bronze Age centers of civilization. Pyramids appeared in Mesoamerica and Peru, temple mounds in the Mississippi Valley and the Southeast. The massive Inca fortifications at Sacsahuamán are reminiscent of Old World defense works.

The Peruvians specialized in the building of roads and suspension bridges. A mile-long aqueduct was built on the Peruvian coast at Ascope, and a 3-mile aqueduct was constructed by the Aztecs at Tenochtitlán.

Ball courts, where rubber-ball games were played, were a feature of the advanced Mesoamerican centers.

Emergence of the state

The early priest-dominated ceremonial centers of the Olmecs and of Teotihuacán seem to have been relatively peaceful settlements. At least, themes of death and warfare are not prominent in their early art, as in that of the Aztecs. Appearing around A.D. 1200, the Aztecs were latecomers in the Valley of Mexico, the last in a series of Chichimec tribes that came down from the north to attack the centers of advanced civilization. In 1325 the Aztecs settled in Tenochtitlán, where they engaged in trade, warfare, and the making of alliances. In regions where they held the upper hand, the Aztecs demanded tribute in food, clothing, and other produce. Class stratification developed at Tenochtitlán, with a class of nobles at the top and one of slaves at the bottom.

Although Tenochtitlán impressed the Spaniards as a well-organized capital, the Aztecs do not seem to have established an enduring political order. Eric R. Wolf has written that they ". . . remained little more than a band of pirates, sallying forth from their great city to loot and plunder and to submit vast areas to tribute payment, without altering the essential social constitution of their victims."[5]

Within the Aztec zone of influence there were areas which succeeded in maintaining independence. It was not a consolidated empire.

The Maya, similarly, were not organized into a single empire. Sylvanus Griswold Morley has drawn attention to the homogeneity of Maya culture—in writing, calendrics, religion, and architecture—over a very wide area. There must have been a great deal of trade, travel, and contact to bring about such relative uniformity.[6] In spite of this, the Maya area seems to have been broken up into different political spheres, a number of city-states, each ruled by a man who was believed to be divine, supported by councilors and various other officials. These men were of the upper class, not subject to taxation. The common people provided tribute of such items as vegetable produce, cotton cloth, game fowls, fish, cacao, copal for incense, honey and wax, and strings of jade, coral beads, and shells.[7]

It was the Incas of Peru who developed the most highly organized and widely extended political system in the New World. In their case, the Incas did not simply exploit the people whom they dominated; they provided some benefits and services which contributed to the stability of the empire. This empire was a sizable one, affecting an estimated 10 million persons in a territory extending 2,500 miles from north to south, including not only the present-day state of Peru but also large sections of the adjoining states of Ecuador, Bolivia, Chile, and Argentina. Great in length, the Inca realm had an average width of only 300 miles. The regime was tied together by the long north-south military highways built up by the Incas and by the roads which connected coast and highland.

Like the Aztecs, the Incas were a tribe which had overrun and dominated its neighbors. Their leader, the Emperor, called the Inca, was regarded as the son of the Sun, a divine being. His tribesmen, especially his closest relatives, made up the nobility, just below which came the *curaca,* or provincial nobles, who provided the lesser officials of the government.

The common people were distinguished from the nobles by dress. They were not allowed to wear the finer wool of alpaca and vicuña, but only llama wool. They could not wear gold and silver ornaments. In matters of food and drink they were also restricted, and they were not allowed to hunt. The commoners tilled the soil for the upper classes and for the state religion as well as for themselves, providing grain and other produce; they were liable to military and corvée service, working on roads, irriga-

---

[5] Wolf, *op. cit.,* p. 149.

[6] Sylvanus Griswold Morley, *The Ancient Maya,* revised by George W. Brainerd (3d ed.; Stanford, Calif.: Stanford University Press, 1956), p. 46.

[7] *Ibid.,* p. 158.

Nazca double cloth
mantle.

Machu Picchu,
Peru.

tion ditches, terraces, fortifications, and other public works projects. The nobles, who generally lived in the capital at Cuzco, were exempt from such work and service. The nobles were allowed to hold landed estates, to receive formal education, and to marry more than one wife—privileges not granted the common people.

The grain and produce provided by the commoners were placed in government storehouses, from which the state could withdraw goods as needed. In times of famine, grain could be transported from areas having a surplus. Very strict punishments were applied to criminal offenses, particularly those against the state.

The state even controlled marriage, making it obligatory for girls to marry by 18 and men by 25 years of age. Those who passed the deadline were paired off by a government official. Once a year there was a mass marriage at Cuzco for betrothed Inca couples. The Emperor performed the wedding ceremony; representatives of his did the same in provincial towns of the realm. The state provided each bride and groom with two sets of clothing; the community gave them a house. Marriages were endogamous within the community. Divorce was not allowed.

We see here a very authoritarian regime with some redistributive economic functions which helped to make up for the exactions imposed upon the commoners. More concern was shown for the well-being of the people than among the Aztecs; law and order were maintained over a great extent of territory. The Inca regime has been both praised and blamed as "communistic," "socialistic," or as a "welfare state," but it is probably mistaken to apply these terms to a preliterate preindustrial society whose way of life was very different from that of the modern world.

Advances in knowledge

In Mesoamerica the Olmecs, Mixtecs, Zapotecs, Aztecs, Totonacs, and Maya had writing systems. That of the Maya, which may have developed from the Olmec system of writing, was the most advanced. It was an ideographic script. Only about one fourth of the Maya glyphs have been deciphered.

Zapotecs, Totonacs, Aztecs, Mixtecs, and Maya made a kind of paper from beaten bark, strips of which, covered with writing, could be fashioned into a book folded in accordianlike fashion. The Spaniards found many such books, or codices, and burned all they could lay their hands on, for they believed that they dealt with the devil-inspired religion of the Indians. Nevertheless, some codices have been preserved down to the present. Only three remain from the Maya region, of which one, the Dresden Codex, concerns mathematics, astronomy, and calendrical matters, among other things.

The Dresden Codex shows that the Maya had developed much astronomical knowledge and a remarkable mathematical system. The latter was a vigesimal system, based on the number 20. The number 1 was indicated by a single dot, 2 by two dots, 3 by three, and 4 by four. The number 5 was indicated by a bar, 6 by a bar with a dot above it, 7 by a bar with two dots, and so on. Ten was indicated by two bars, one above the other, 11 by two bars with a dot above them. Fifteen was indicated by three bars. Twenty was symbolized by a shell (the symbol for zero) with a dot above it.

The invention of zero and position numbering was an independent invention of the Maya, paralleling the invention of the zero in India, but being dated even earlier in time. This, of course, weakens the possible significance of diffusion from the Old World as a source of higher civilization in Mesoamerica.

The Maya had an accurate calendrical system, but one involving elaborate astrological concepts of the relationships between gods and divisions of time. There were auspicious and inauspicious periods, just as in the astrological systems of the Old World. Both the Maya and the Aztecs distinguished a 52-year cycle. The Aztecs believed that the world might come to an end after such a cycle was finished. When this proved not to be the case, there was much celebration.

The priests had to keep track of the calendrical round and its astrological concomitants in order to perform the correct rituals and to offer appropriate sacrifices to the right god at the right time. It seems likely that this calendrical knowledge, together with the knowledge of writing and mathematics, was largely limited to the priesthood.

It is curious that the Incas did not develop a system of writing, since in some respects, such as metallurgy and political organization, their civilization was more advanced than those of Mesoamerica. So complex a society with such tight political control demanded some system of record keeping. In the case of the Inca, this need was met by strings of knotted cords, called *quipus*. A *quipu* had a main cord, from a few inches to over a yard in length, to which were attached smaller colored strings, knotted at intervals. Knots and colors had particular ascribed meanings. The knots could stand for numbers counted in a decimal system. The color may have indicated the category of items to be counted. In this way, a census was kept. At Cuzco, where the *quipus* were stored, it could be known how many families or how many men of fighting age lived in such-and-such community. The number of llamas, sandals, and other items could be quickly ascertained for particular regions.

A group of specialists memorized these *quipu* records, including historical accounts. Unfortunately, the system by which they worked has not been preserved.

One more achievement of the Peruvians may be mentioned: their accomplishments in surgery. This includes the early coastal peoples, perhaps more than the Incas. At any rate, the Peruvians performed such operations as amputations and the trepanning of skulls. They used forceps and tourniquets and bandaged with gauze and cotton. The purpose of the trepanning, whether medical or magical, is not known, but over 10,000 trepanned skulls have been found in Peru, and their appearance shows that this difficult operation was often successful.

Other cultures: South America

While the high cultures of Mesoamerica and Peru were flourishing, there were many other less advanced cultures in both North and South America, some of which had some contact with the centers of high civilization, while others were beyond the reach of their influence. Steward has divided the Indian peoples of South America who lived outside the Central Andean area of high civilization into Marginal tribes, Tropical Forest and Southern Andean peoples, and Sub-Andean and Circum-Caribbean peoples.[8]

The *Marginal* tribes were mainly hunting-gathering peoples with relatively small bands, living in areas with limited resources, such as plains or savannas. They did not have loom weaving, usually had no pottery making or basketry, and wore little clothing. The Ona and Yahgan of Tierra del Fuego, at the southern tip of South America, belong in this category, as do some of the tribes of the pampas and tropical forests.

Like the Marginal peoples, the *Tropical Forest* and *Southern Andean* peoples had sociopolitical groups based on kinship and lacked class systems such as were found among the Circum-Caribbean and Central Andean societies. Unlike the Marginal peoples, they lived in large semi-permanent villages with horticulture or agriculture, had large houses, loom-woven textiles, pottery, basketry, dugout canoes or balsa rafts, and a generally more advanced technology than those of Marginal peoples. The Tropical Forest peoples raised tropical root crops and other plants, while those of the southern Andes had potatoes and cereal crops, with some technological and other influences derived from Peru and Bolivia. There was much warfare and some cannibalism among Tropical Forest tribes, which may account for their strongly nucleated settlements, sometimes surrounded by palisades and pitfalls. Tropical Forest cultures were found throughout the Amazon Basin and adjacent regions, including such tribes as the Caribs of Guiana, Venezuela, and the Antilles Islands, the Tupinambá of coastal Brazil, the Guaraní of Paraguay, and the Mundurucú of the Amazon valley. Peoples of the southern Andes included the Atacameño, Diaguita, and Araucanians.

The *Sub-Andean* and *Circum-Caribbean* peoples had a material culture

---

[8] Julian H. Steward, "South American Cultures: An Interpretative Summary," in *Handbook of South American Indians* (Smithsonian Institution, Bureau of American Ethnology, Bulletin 143 [Washington, D.C., 1949], Vol. V, pp. 669–772. For a modified treatment of the same material, see Julian H. Steward and Louis C. Faron, *Native Peoples of South America* (New York: McGraw-Hill Book Co., 1959).

similar to that of the Tropical Forest tribes but a more effective subsistence base supporting larger populations in more permanent villages which had class stratification and chiefs with political authority. The Sub-Andean tribes included the Mojo, Bauré, Paressí, Manasí, and Xaray of eastern Bolivia.

The Circum-Caribbean tribes had well-developed agriculture, much seafood, and good transportation on land and by canoe. They had metallurgy, weaving, ceramics, and stone sculpture, and often built mounds and temples. Many of these peoples lived in large villages which were administrative and ceremonial centers, having hereditary social classes with chiefs exercising strong authority. There was much warfare and sometimes patterns of human sacrifice and temple-idol cults with a priesthood, reminiscent of Aztec practices. Circum-Caribbean tribes were found in coastal regions of Central America, Colombia, Venezuela, and islands of the Caribbean, such as the Greater Antilles.

Other cultures: North America The southeastern part of North America had cultures similar to those of the foregoing Circum-Caribbean peoples. The Natchez, for example, lived in large villages based on maize agriculture. They had mounds topped by temples, with a cult of the sun and an attendant priesthood. Natchez society was marked by class stratification, at the top of which was a deified chief known as the Great Sun, who was carried about in a litter.

Complex cultures were also found in the North American Southwest, centered in Arizona and New Mexico, but here there does not seem to have been any marked development of class stratification. Four subareas with different prehistoric cultures have been distinguished in the early Southwest: the *Mogollon,* in the mountains and valleys of north-central Arizona, moving southeastward into New Mexico; the *Anasazi* of the high plateaus of northern Arizona, southern Utah, southwestern Colorado, and northern New Mexico; the *Hohokam,* in the deserts of central and southern Arizona and Mexican Sonora; and the *Patayan,* centered in the Colorado River valley.

This whole area was influenced by the spread of ideas from Mexico, involving the cultivation of maize, beans, and squash, and also the use of pottery, which appeared first in the Mogollon region at about 100 B.C. Sedentary village life based on agriculture developed among the Mogollon people, who lived in relatively small pit houses which were randomly scattered. Later, houses were built above ground.

A later wave of Mesoamerican diffusion, in the Hohokam region between A.D. 500 and 1300, brought about the building of temple mounds and ball courts and the use of cast copper bells and the spinning of cotton. Architectural features of possible Mexican origin were colonnades, round towers, and rubble-core masonry in the Anasazi area. The Pueblo societies of historic times, such as the Hopi and Zuni, developed from this cultural background. The Navaho were later interlopers from the north (only a few centuries before Europeans came to America) whose culture soon became influenced in many ways by Pueblo culture.

North of the Southwest was the Rocky Mountain Plateau area, where hunting-gathering tribes such as the Shoshone roamed, while in California there was a relatively dense population of many different tribes which collected nuts and seeds and hunted small game; they lacked pottery, weaving, and agriculture, but made very beautiful basketry. Further north were the societies of the Northwest Coast, which also lacked agriculture and pottery, but which nevertheless had sedentary village life and an elaborate culture. Still further north were the Eskimos spread along the Arctic coastal regions, and the inland hunting-gathering nomads of the Barren Grounds and the Canadian forests.

Before the coming of the whites, who brought horses and guns which the Indians ultimately acquired, the great plains of North America east of the Rockies were relatively empty, but there were farming people such as the Mandan and Hidatsa, who lived in villages of large earth lodges.

In most of the large area between the Mississippi River and the Atlantic coast, and parts of Canada north of the Great Lakes and St. Lawrence River, there were tribes known as Woodland, which raised corn, beans, and squash, although the more northerly Indians, in areas where the growing season was short, depended mainly on hunting and gathering for subsistence. The cultures and social organization of these tribes were heterogeneous. The Iroquois, for example, lived in villages made up of longhouses, while the Canadian Ojibwa lived in smaller, more scattered units. The Iroquois had matrilineal descent, traced in the female line, while the Ojibwa had patrilineal descent, traced in the male line. Political organization was highly developed among the Iroquois, whose tribes were loosely united in a confederacy, but political organization was rudimentary among the Ojibwa. These two tribal groups had quite different languages of different linguistic stocks.

An advanced prehistoric culture which developed in the Woodland zone from around A.D. 700–1000 is known as the Mississippian, since it first developed in the Mississippi valley between St. Louis and Vicksburg and later spread up the valley as far north as Aztalan, Wisconsin. This culture seems to have been influenced by ceremonial concepts and practices from Mexico; it involved the building of large, flat-topped platform mounds with temples and the clearing of plazas where ceremonies were performed. Large fortified towns were built, and a great variety of ceramic ware was used. Cahokia, near East St. Louis, Illinois, is the site of the largest man-made structure in aboriginal North America north of Mexico: a pyramidal mound which covers 14 acres of ground and is accompanied by about 120 smaller mounds. This was one of several centers of Mississippian culture.

This brief review of pre-Columbian and historic cultures has been sufficient to show that in both North and South America there was a great variety of cultures at different levels of development, ranging from marginal nomadic hunting-gathering tribes to much more sophisticated and powerful societies which were influenced directly or indirectly by the centers of high civilization in Mesoamerica or Peru.

The higher civilizations of the New World, such as those of the Aztecs, Maya, and Incas, differed from one another in various respects, just as did those of Sumer, Egypt, and Harappa. At the same time, the New World civilizations shared some common features both among themselves and with the Bronze Age centers of civilization in the Old World. In each we see the development of city life, accompanied by division of labor and class stratification, increased trade and communication, the appearance of a dominant priesthood, emergence of a state, enlargement of the scale of warfare, and advances in knowledge in such spheres as mathematics, astronomy, and calendrical calculations.

There was some unevenness in the development of culture in these areas. Writing developed in Mesoamerica but not in Peru. Political organization, road building, and metallurgy were more advanced in Peru than in Mesoamerica. The Peruvians had llamas, alpacas, and vicuñas and were thus able to make woolen textiles, while other Indians were not. But there seems to have been more trade in Mesoamerica than in Peru. Special privileged classes of traders appeared among the Aztecs and the Maya. The Aztecs and Maya had slaves, but the institution of slavery does not appear among the Incas, although it might be argued that many of the commoners were virtually slaves.

The many parallels in the development of Old World and New World civilizations give an impression of orderly sequences in cultural evolution, of cross-cultural regularities. Julian H. Steward has presented a scheme for conceptualizing the development of complex societies, subdivided into certain stages: Pre-Agricultural Era, Incipient Agriculture, Formative Era, Era of Regional Development and Florescence, and Period of Cyclical Conquests. Thus the *Formative Era* is one in which basketry, pottery, weaving, metallurgy, and construction are developed and in which there is a growth of population, relative peace and wide diffusion of culture between centers of civilization. In the *Era of Regional Development and Florescence* there are theocratic states with a priestly intelligentsia and class stratification. The *Period of Cyclical Conquests* is marked by increasing militarism, urbanization, and building of fortifications.[9]

[9] Julian H. Steward, "Development of Complex Societies: Cultural Causality and Law: A Trial Formulation of the Development of Early Civilizations," in Julian H. Steward, *Theory of Culture Change: The Methodology of Multilinear Evolution* (Urbana: University of Illinois Press, 1955), pp. 178–209.

Some writers have attempted to apply this scheme or similar ones cross-culturally to different societies, sometimes with changes in the terminology for eras or stages.[10]

It is sometimes difficult to apply the same yardsticks or criteria to different sequences of culture change; but the efforts that have been made to do this and to discover significant cross-cultural regularities are based on the many striking similarities that do appear in the development of civilized societies in the Old World and the New.

Suggestions for further reading

For Mesoamerica, see Eric R. Wolf, *Sons of the Shaking Earth* (Chicago: University of Chicago Press, 1959).

For the Maya: Sylvanus Griswold Morley, *The Ancient Maya*, revised by George W. Brainerd (3d ed.; Stanford, Calif.: Stanford University Press, 1956), and Michael D. Coe, *The Maya* (New York: Frederick A. Praeger, 1966).

For the Aztecs: George C. Vaillant, *The Aztecs of Mexico* (Baltimore, Md.: Penguin Books, 1956). See also Michael D. Coe, *Mexico* (New York: Frederick A. Praeger, 1962).

For the Inca: J. Alden Mason, *The Ancient Civilizations of the Andes* (Baltimore, Md.: Penguin Books, 1957), and John H. Rowe, "Inca Culture at the Time of the Conquest," in Julian H. Steward (ed.), *Handbook of South American Indians* (Smithsonian Institution, Bureau of American Ethnology, Bulletin 143, [Washington, D.C., 1946]), Vol. II, pp. 183–330.

Two early sources for our knowledge about the Aztecs and the Incas, respectively, which are well worth reading, are: *The Bernal Díaz Chronicles: The True Story of the Conquest of Mexico*, trans. and ed., Albert Idell (New York: Doubleday & Co., Dolphin Books, 1956); and *The Incas: The Royal Commentaries of the Inca, Garcilaso de la Vega*, trans. by Maria Jolas from the critical annotated French edition of Alain Gheerbrant (New York: Orion Press, 1962).

A popularized account of the Aztecs, Maya, and Incas is available in Victor Wolfgang Von Hagen, *The Ancient Sun Kingdoms of the Americas* (Cleveland and New York: World Publishing Co., 1961). There are brief descriptions of Aztec and Inca culture in George P. Murdock, *Our Primitive Contemporaries* (New York: Macmillan Co., 1934), pp. 359–450, and of Maya and Inca culture in Elman R. Service, *A Profile of Primitive Culture* (New York: Harper & Bros., 1958), pp. 287–337.

---

[10] Julian H. Steward, Robert M. Adams, Donald Collier, Angel Palerm, Karl A. Wittfogel, Ralph L. Beals, *Irrigation Civilizations: A Comparative Study. A Symposium of Method and Result in Cross-Cultural Regularities* (Washington, D.C.: Pan American Union, 1955); and Robert J. Braidwood and Gordon R. Willey, *Courses toward Urban Life: Archaeological Considerations of Some Cultural Alternates* (Chicago: Aldine Publishing Co., 1962).

Illustrations

Illustrations

Section IV

Section V

Index

Index

Miocene epoch, 75, 77, 96
Mississippian culture, 303
Mitosis, 36–37
Mogollon, 302
Mohenjo-daro, 224n, 225, 253, 254, 255
Mongoloid, 122, 124, 126, 136, 144
Mongoloid spot, 127
Montagna, William, 82n, 84
Montagu, M. F. Ashley, 26, 42, 94–97, 110, 123, 129, 134, 140, 141, 147n, 148
Monumental constructions, 225–26, 251–52
Moore, Ruth, 42
Morley, Sylvanus Griswold, 296, 297, 305
Morris, Desmond, 72, 82n
Morton, Samuel George, 25
Mother goddess cult, 204, 212
Mounds
early speculations about American, 156
Indus Valley, 225, 255
Mt. Carmel, Palestine, 115
Mousterian, 114, 180
Murdock, George P., 305
Mutation, 39–40, 195
Mycenae, 158, 262
Myrdal, Gunnar, 149, 150

N

Napier, John R., 94
Natchez Indians, 302
Natufian, 205
Natural selection, 31–34
Navaho Indians, 303
Nazca
pottery, 287
weaving, 298
Neandertal Man, 23, 96, 111–17, 180–81
"Classic," 113, 114
"generalized," 113, 114
relation to modern man, 114–15
Negrito; see Negroid
Negroid, 122, 125, 127, 128, 144, 145
African, 126, 127, 128, 131, 134, 139, 146, 211
American, 129, 147–49
Negrito, 126, 127, 128
Nilotic, 126, 127, 128
Oceanic, 126, 127, 128, 129
Pygmies of Congo, 127, 128, 133

Neolithic, 158–59, 169–70, 176, 194–222
in China, 216–17, 271
diffusion of, 210–19
in India, 215
in Southeast Asia, 217–18
in Southwest Asia, 218–19
in steppes, 219
New Grange, 211–12
New Zealand, 270, 271
Nile River, 232, 250
Nomadism, 194, 198, 215, 219, 262–64
Norbeck, Edward, 287
Nordenskiöld, Erland, 286
Nordic; see Caucasoid

O

Oakley, Kenneth, 118–19, 171, 177n, 179, 182
Oceanic Negro; see Negroid
Ojibwa Indians, 303; see also Chippewa Indians
Old Cordilleran Tradition, 279–80
Oldowan choppers, 107, 108, 177
Olduvai Gorge, Tanzania, 89, 92, 94, 95, 108–9, 116, 177
Oligocene epoch, 75, 77, 96
Oligopithecus, 75
Olmec Indians, 291–92, 296
Omo River, Ethiopia, 88
Ona Indians, 134, 301
Oppenheim, A. Leo, 233n, 240, 241n, 260
Orangutan, 56, 62
Oreopithecus bambolii, 78, 79
Orthogenesis, 31
Ovesey, Lionel, 150
Ox, 223–24, 232

P

Pacific Islands, occupation of, 174, 269–73
Palaeolithic, 158, 159, 174–92; see also Lower Palaeolithic; Middle Palaeolithic; and Upper Palaeolithic
Paleocene epoch, 74, 77, 96
Palerm, Angel, 305n
Pan-p'o-ts'un, 216–17
Paranthropus, 92–97, 110
Passage grave, 204, 211–12, 213
Pastoralism, 210–11, 214–15, 263
Pataliputra, 265
Patayan, 302

Peasantry, 231–32
Pehrson, Robert N., 215
Pei, W. C., 98, 99
Peking Man, 82, 96, 102, 103–4, 105–7, 122
Pelvis
in apes, 80
in man, 80
Penis bone absent in man, 81
Peppercorn hair, 126
Persepolis, 265
Persian empire, 265
Personality, definition of, 7–8
Petrie, William Flinders, 157, 170–71
Pettigrew, Thomas F., 150
Pfeiffer, John E., 47, 89
Pharaoh of Egypt, 232, 233, 235, 237, 241, 250–52
Phenotype, 35, 37, 129
Philippine Islands, 271
Phillips, E. D., 219
Phillips, Philip, 171
Philtrum, 80
Physical anthropology, 52–150
areas of research, 2–3, 26
historical background of, 18–26
Pig, 196, 197, 209, 216, 218, 271
Piggott, Stuart, 182, 190n, 193, 209, 219, 235, 255, 261
Pigmentation, 130–32
Piltdown find, 117–19
Pithecanthropus erectus, 82, 98, 101–2, 107, 122
Pithecanthropus robustus, 98
Plano point, 278–79
Plants
collecting of, 196, 199, 205, 280
domesticated in the New World, 280–81, 286
domesticated in the Old World, 195–96, 205, 206, 207, 216, 218, 254, 271
domesticated in Polynesia, 271
Platyrrhini, 59–60, 74
Pleistocene epoch, 77, 79, 88–89, 96, 101, 167
Pliocene epoch, 76, 77, 78–79, 96, 174
Pliopithecus, 75
Plow, 223–24, 283
Polanyi, Karl, 233
Pollen analysis, 165, 169–70
Polygenesis, concept of, 25
Polynesians, 125, 126, 269–73
Polyploidy, 38
Pompeii, 155

This book has been set in 10 and 9 point Caledonia, leaded 2 points. Chapter numbers and titles, section numbers and titles, and part numbers and titles are in Melior and Melior Semibold. The size of the type page is 33½ by 46½ picas.